W9-CCY-012

CROSS STITCH
Threads of Time™
the Needlecraft Shop™

Publisher: Donna Robertson

Design Director: Fran Rohus

Production & Photography Director: Ange Van Arman

Editorial

Senior Editor: Janet Tipton

Editor: Nancy Harris

Associate Editor: Marylee Klinkhammer

Copy Editor: Diana Kordsmeier

Production

Book Design & Production: Glenda Chamberlain

Production: Cathy Drennan

Color Specialist: Betty Radla

Photography

Photography Coordinator/Stylist: Ruth Whitaker

Assistant Photo Stylist: Jan Jaynes

Photographers: Russell Chaffin, Keith Godfrey

Cover Photograph: Russell Chaffin

Cover Photograph Stylist: Ruth Whitaker

Product Design

Design Coordinator: Pam Prather

Business

C.E.O: John Robinson

Vice President/Marketing: Greg Deily

Credits

Sincerest thanks to all the designers, manufacturers and other professionals whose dedication has made this book possible. Special thanks to Quebecor Printing Book Group, Kingsport, TN.

Library of Congress Cataloging-in-Publication Data

ISBN: 1-57367-094-4
First Printing: 1998
Library of Congress Catalog Card Number: 97-68264
Published and Distributed by
The Needlecraft Shop, LLC, Big Sandy, Texas 75755
Printed in the United States of America.

Dear Friend,

All my life I have appreciated fine needlework and the creative joy that is experienced working needle and thread over a fabric canvas. As a young girl I can remember watching in awe while my grandmother and mother spent endless hours with thread and needle in hand and seeing the unforgettable works they created. I was eager to learn, and my mother guided me through the basic stitches and endured my endless questions. Through the years my love of stitching has developed many special bonds with other devoted needleworkers.

Everlasting memories can be made with one simple stitch, and this book was created to pay tribute to these special moments and the people we share them with. Needleart is often the thread that ties, and is the labor of love that fills our lives with moments of joy. Needleart can also celebrate special events in our lives — such as a birth or a marriage or the milestones of achievement.

The designs in this book have rekindled my own special moments of joy, happiness and times shared with family and friends that had been tucked away in my heart. Now I can only anticipate the new stitching experiences — prompted by the treasures of these pages — that will be wonderful memories in years to come.

Nancy

Table of Contents

Romantic Gardens

Sentimental Stroll

Exclusively Samplers

Christmas Festivities

Zachary

SINGER

Collective Comforts

General Instructions

Romantic Gardens

An enchantment that is all your own awaits your first stitch as you slip into the pages of these delightful designs. The vivid colors of nature caress your senses as you meander through the projects that only await your loving touch to spring to life.

Designed by Jacquelyn Fox

MATERIALS FOR ONE

11" x 12" piece of antique white 28-count Monaco; 3/4 yd. fabric #1; 2/3 yd. fabric #2; 1/4 yd. fabric #3; 14" square pillow form

INSTRUCTIONS

1: Center and stitch design of choice, stitching over two threads and using two strands floss for Cross-Stitch and Straight Stitch. Use three strands floss for Lazy Daisy Stitch. Use four strands floss for Backstitch of stamens on "Poppy" design. Use one strand floss for remaining Backstitch and French Knot.

NOTES: Trim design to 6½" x 7½". From fabric #1, cut two 4¾" x 15" pieces for top and bottom, two 5¼" x 7½" pieces for sides and four 4" x 21½" pieces for bands. From fabric #2, cut two 13½" x 21" pieces for back. From fabric #3, cut one 1½" x 70" strip (piecing is necessary) for trim. Use ½" seam allowance.

2: With right sides facing, sew design, top, bottom and side pieces together according to Assembly Diagram, forming center. With right sides facing, sew band pieces to center, mitering corners, forming front.

3: Hem one long edge of each back piece. Place one hemmed edge over the other, overlapping approximately 3", creating a 21" x 21" back with opening. Baste across ends. With right sides facing, sew front and back together. Trim seams; turn right sides out. For pillow pocket, sew around front close to inside edge of band pieces.

4: With right sides facing, sew long edges of trim together. Turn right sides out; press. Beginning in one corner, tack trim around outside edge of pillow pocket and knot corners as shown in photo. Insert pillow form.❦

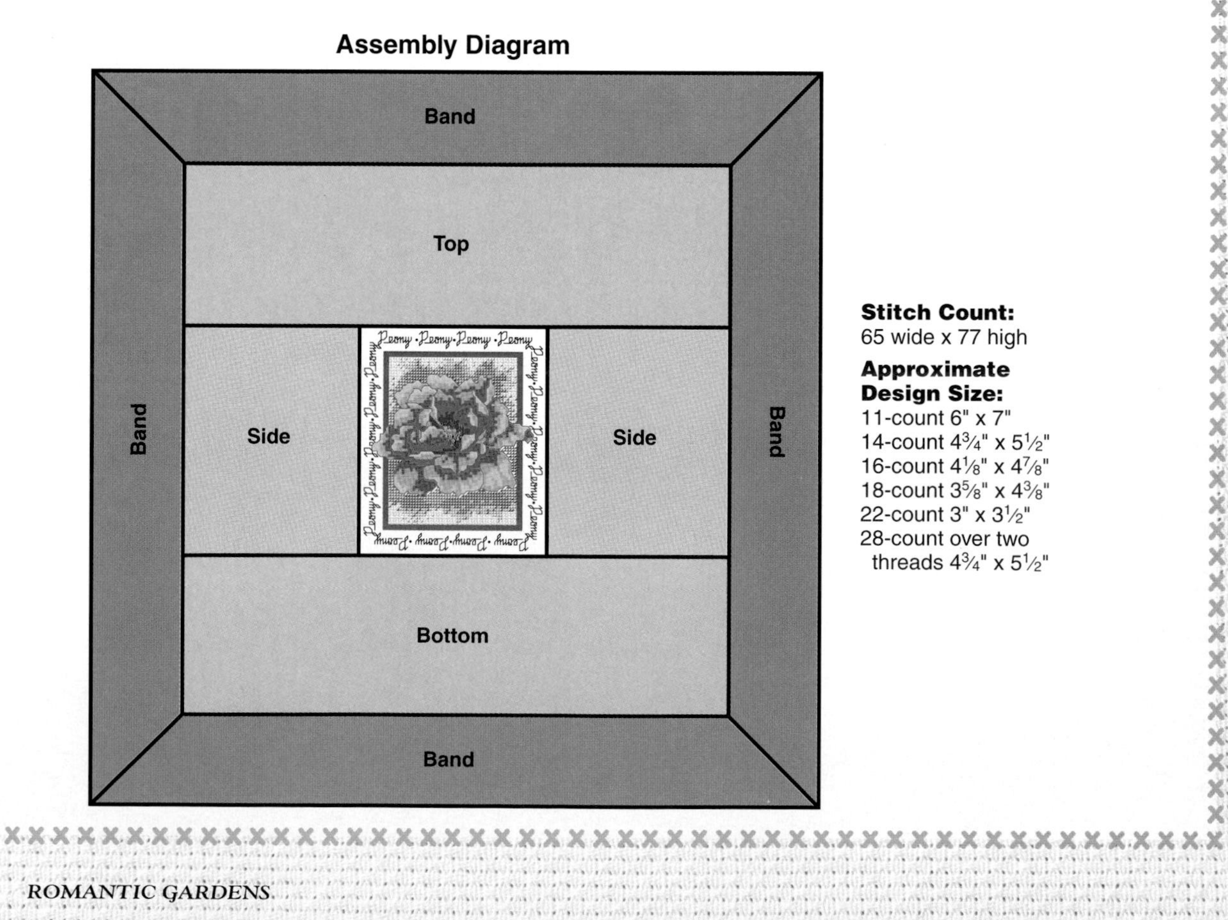

Stitch Count:
65 wide x 77 high

Approximate Design Size:
11-count 6" x 7"
14-count 4¾" x 5½"
16-count 4⅛" x 4⅞"
18-count 3⅝" x 4⅜"
22-count 3" x 3½"
28-count over two threads 4¾" x 5½"

Cushion your life with beautiful, vivid flowers stitched on inviting pillows.

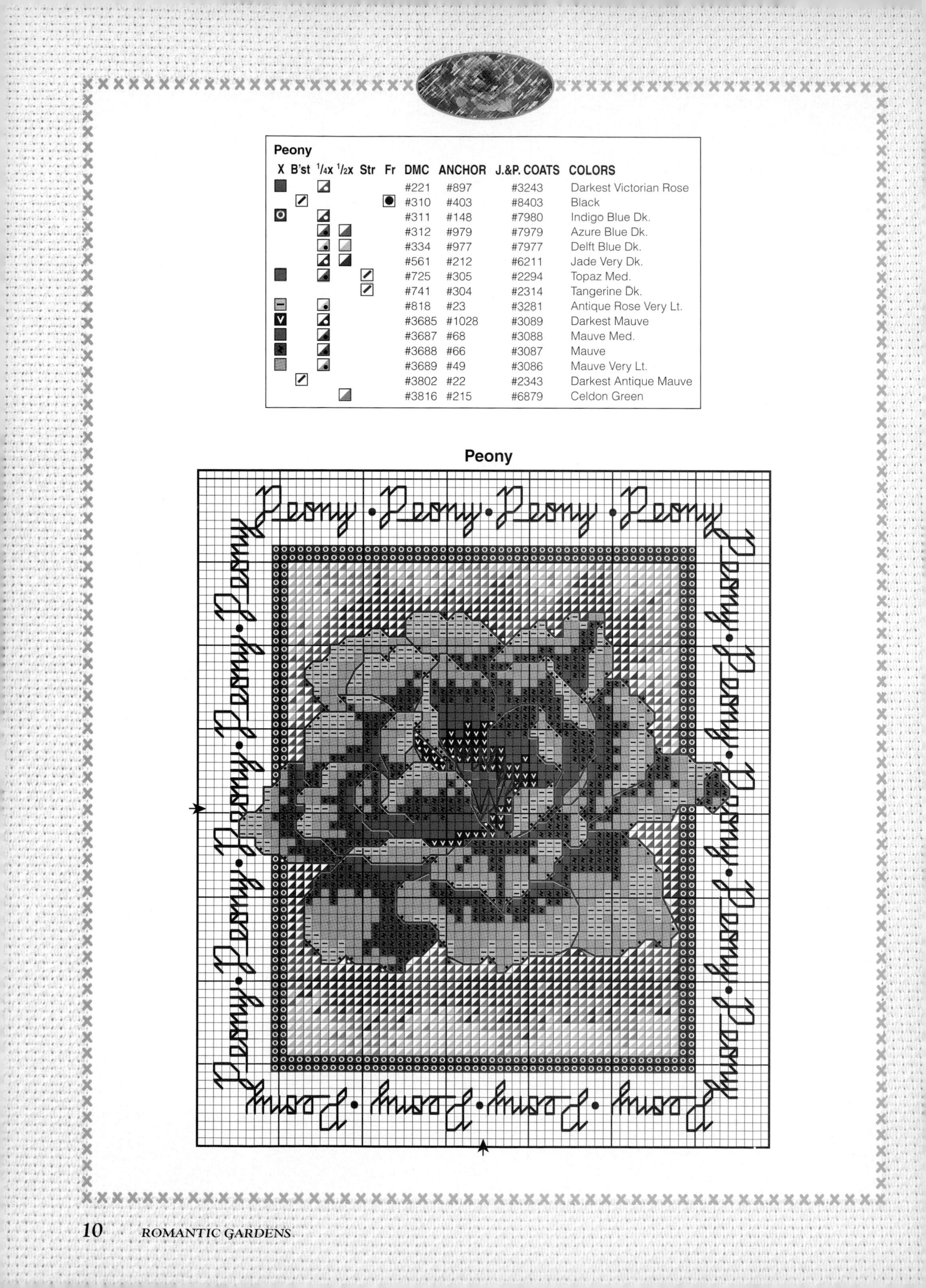

Peony

X	B'st	1/4x	1/2x	Str	Fr	DMC	ANCHOR	J.&P. COATS	COLORS
■		◩				#221	#897	#3243	Darkest Victorian Rose
	/				●	#310	#403	#8403	Black
O		◩				#311	#148	#7980	Indigo Blue Dk.
		◩	◩			#312	#979	#7979	Azure Blue Dk.
		◩	◩			#334	#977	#7977	Delft Blue Dk.
		◩	◩			#561	#212	#6211	Jade Very Dk.
■		◩		/		#725	#305	#2294	Topaz Med.
				/		#741	#304	#2314	Tangerine Dk.
–		◩				#818	#23	#3281	Antique Rose Very Lt.
V		◩				#3685	#1028	#3089	Darkest Mauve
■		◩				#3687	#68	#3088	Mauve Med.
■		◩				#3688	#66	#3087	Mauve
■		◩				#3689	#49	#3086	Mauve Very Lt.
	/					#3802	#22	#2343	Darkest Antique Mauve
			◩			#3816	#215	#6879	Celdon Green

Peony

Poppy									
X	B'st	1/4x	1/2x	LzD	Fr	DMC	ANCHOR	J.&P. COATS	COLORS
	■				●	#310	#403	#8403	Black
■		■				#311	#148	#7980	Indigo Blue Dk.
		■	■			#312	#979	#7979	Azure Blue Dk.
■	■	■				#315	#972	#3082	Antique Mauve Very Dk.
				■		#316	#1017	#3081	Antique Mauve Med.
			■			#334	#977	#7977	Delft Blue Dk.
		■	■			#561	#212	#6211	Jade Very Dk.
■		■				#754	#1012	#2331	Peach Flesh Lt.
■		■				#760	#1022	#3069	Salmon
■		■				#761	#1021	#3068	Salmon Lt.
	■					#815	#43	#3000	Garnet Dk.
V		■				#902	#897	#3083	Darkest Garnet
	■					#938	#381	#5381	Darkest Mahogany
■		■				#3328	#1024	#3071	Salmon Dk.
			■			#3816	#215	#6879	Celdon Green

Poppy

Create this lovely afghan stitched with a romantic medley of pastel hearts and flowers.

Designed by Nancy Marshall

MATERIALS

50" x 50" piece of white/pastel threads 14-count Angelica afghan fabric

INSTRUCTIONS

1: Center and stitch designs onto afghan fabric following Stitching Diagram, stitching over two threads and using three strands floss for Cross-Stitch and Backstitch.

2: Stay stitch 3" from edges; fray edges.❦

Stitching Diagram

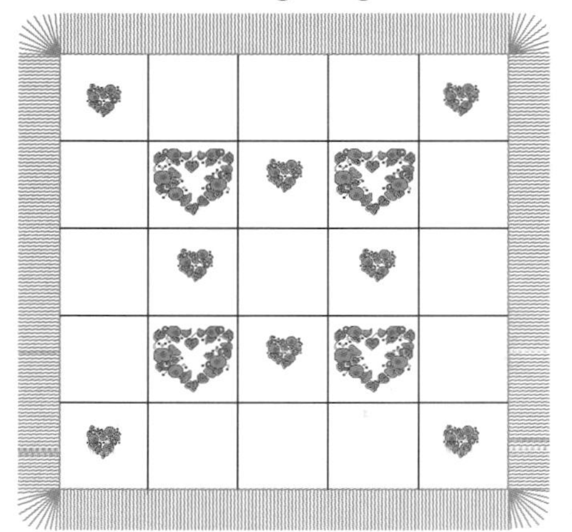

Large Heart

Small Heart

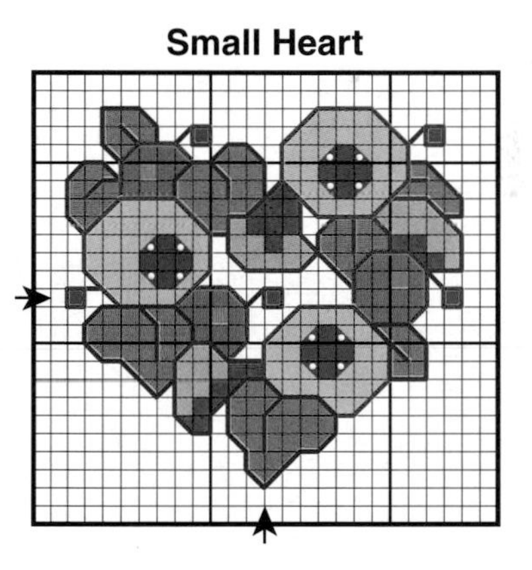

Large Heart
Stitch Count:
38 wide x 36 high
Approximate Design Size:
11-count 3½" x 3⅜"
14-count 2¾" x 2⅝"
16-count 2⅜" x 2¼"
18-count 2⅛" x 2"
22-count 1⅞" x 1⅝"
14-count over two threads 5½" x 5¼"

X	B'st	¼x	¾x	DMC	ANCHOR	J.&P. COATS	COLORS
	⧄			#320	#215	#6017	Pistachio Green Med.
■	⧄	◩		#334	#977	#7977	Delft Blue Dk.
■	⧄		◩	#335	#38	#3283	Rose Pink Dk.
■		◩		#369	#1043	#6015	Pistachio Green Pale
■		◩		#727	#293	#2289	Topaz Lt.
■		◩		#776	#24	#3281	Rose Pink Lt.
■		◩		#3325	#129	#7976	Delft Blue
■	⧄	◩		#3746	#1030	#7150	Blue Violet Med.

Small Heart
Stitch Count:
22 wide x 21 high
Approximate Design Size:
11-count 2" x 2"
14-count 1⅝" x 1½"
16-count 1⅜" x 1⅜"
18-count 1¼" x 1¼"
22-count 1" x 1"
14-count over two threads 3¼" x 3"

SEEDS
HEAVENLY BLUE
MORNING GLORY
E.J. SWEET AND CO.
E.J. SWEET AND CO.
MINIATURE PUMPKIN
JACK-BE-LITTLE
SEEDS
E.J. SWEET AND CO.
JUICY-SWEET DELICIOUS
SUGAR BABY WATERMELON
SEEDS

Harvest a garden of nature's blessings with these tempting designs.

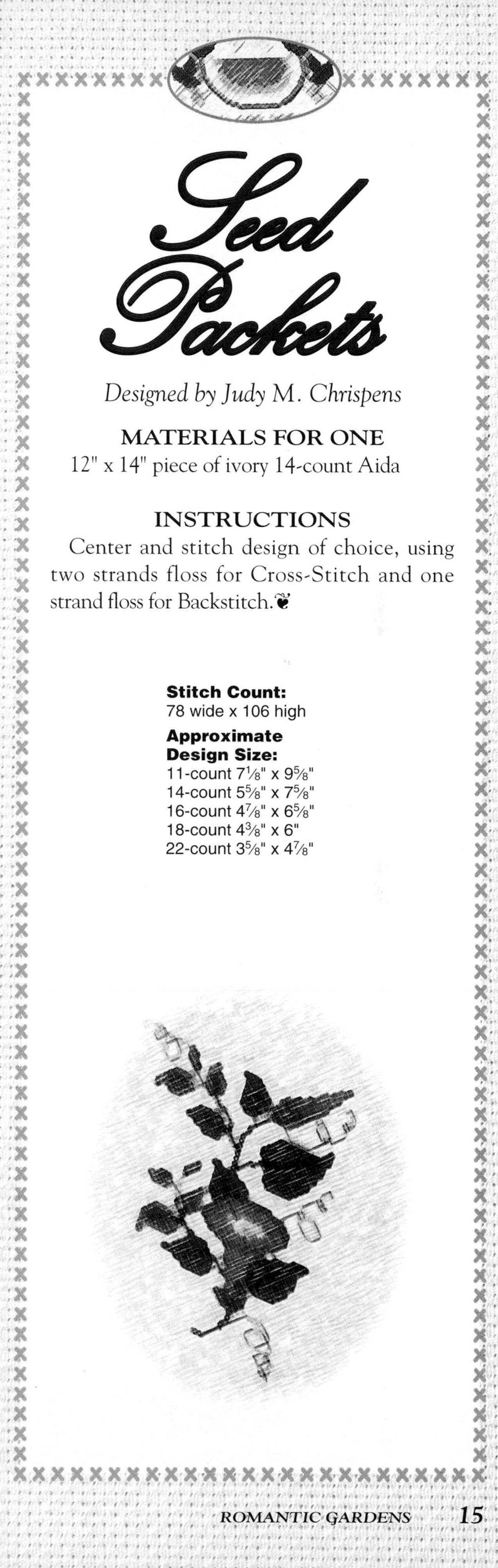

Seed Packets

Designed by Judy M. Chrispens

MATERIALS FOR ONE

12" x 14" piece of ivory 14-count Aida

INSTRUCTIONS

Center and stitch design of choice, using two strands floss for Cross-Stitch and one strand floss for Backstitch.❦

Stitch Count:
78 wide x 106 high

Approximate Design Size:
11-count $7\frac{1}{8}$" x $9\frac{5}{8}$"
14-count $5\frac{5}{8}$" x $7\frac{5}{8}$"
16-count $4\frac{7}{8}$" x $6\frac{5}{8}$"
18-count $4\frac{3}{8}$" x 6"
22-count $3\frac{5}{8}$" x $4\frac{7}{8}$"

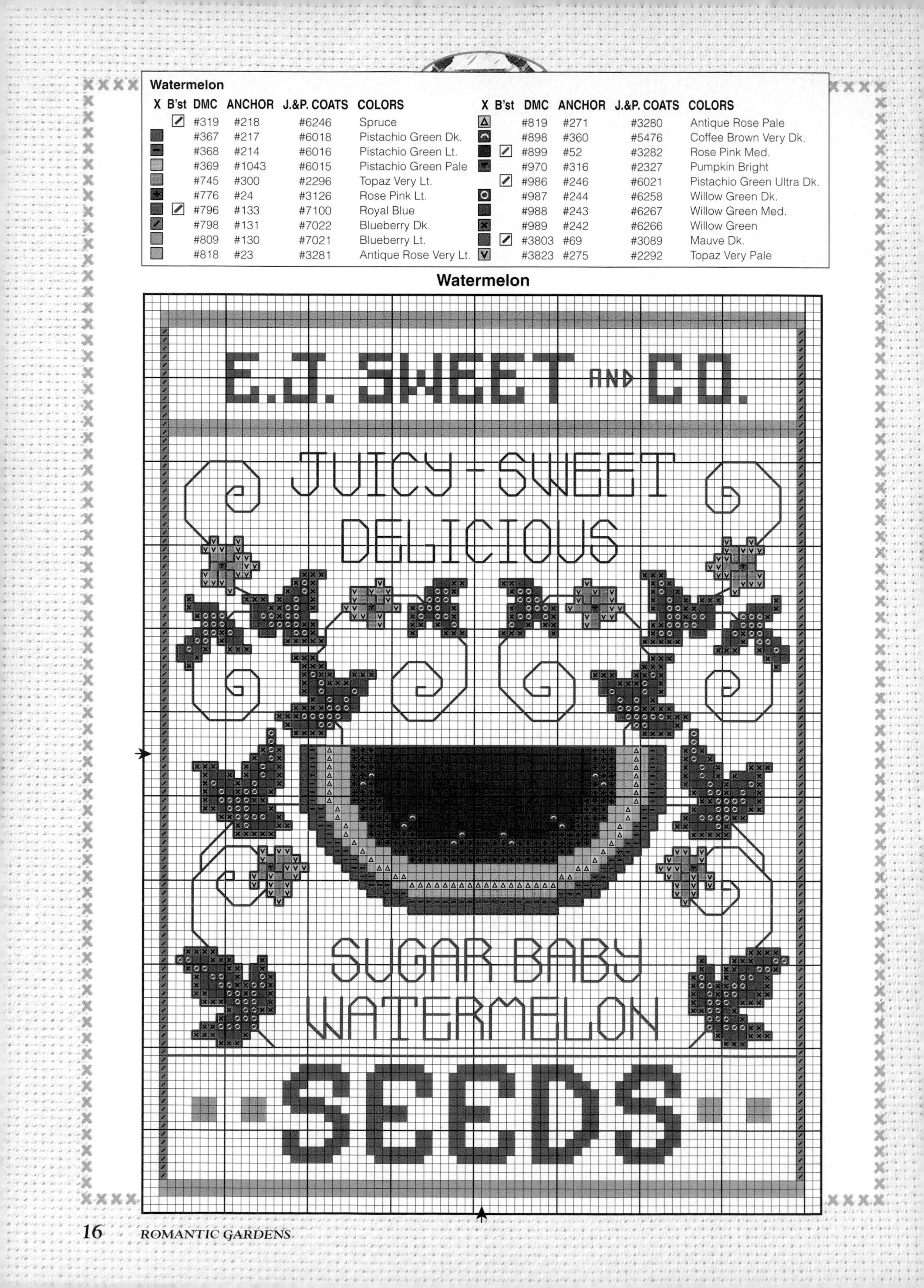

Watermelon

X	B'st	DMC	ANCHOR	J.&P. COATS	COLORS
	/	#319	#218	#6246	Spruce
■		#367	#217	#6018	Pistachio Green Dk.
−		#368	#214	#6016	Pistachio Green Lt.
■		#369	#1043	#6015	Pistachio Green Pale
■		#745	#300	#2296	Topaz Very Lt.
+		#776	#24	#3126	Rose Pink Lt.
■	/	#796	#133	#7100	Royal Blue
/		#798	#131	#7022	Blueberry Dk.
■		#809	#130	#7021	Blueberry Lt.
■		#818	#23	#3281	Antique Rose Very Lt.
Δ		#819	#271	#3280	Antique Rose Pale
⌒		#898	#360	#5476	Coffee Brown Very Dk.
■	/	#899	#52	#3282	Rose Pink Med.
⊤		#970	#316	#2327	Pumpkin Bright
	/	#986	#246	#6021	Pistachio Green Ultra Dk.
o		#987	#244	#6258	Willow Green Dk.
■		#988	#243	#6267	Willow Green Med.
x		#989	#242	#6266	Willow Green
■	/	#3803	#69	#3089	Mauve Dk.
V		#3823	#275	#2292	Topaz Very Pale

Watermelon

Morning Glory

X	B'st	DMC	ANCHOR	J.&P. COATS	COLORS
		#718	#88	#4089	Plum Med.
		#744	#301	#2293	Tangerine Pale
		#746	#275	#2275	Honey Pale
		#793	#176	#7110	Cornflower Blue Lt.
		#794	#175	#7977	Cornflower Blue Very Lt.
		#797	#132	#7143	Deep Blueberry
		#800	#144	#7020	Blueberry Pale
		#915	#1029	#3065	Plum Very Dk.
		#917	#89	#4087	Plum Dk.
		#3345	#268	#6258	Ivy Green Dk.
		#3346	#267	#6261	Ivy Green Med.
		#3347	#266	#6010	Ivy Green
		#3348	#264	#6266	Apple Green

Morning Glory

Pumpkin

X	B'st	DMC	ANCHOR	J.&P. COATS	COLORS
■		#319	#218	#6246	Spruce
■		#434	#310	#5000	Darkest Toast
■		#435	#1046	#5371	Toast Dk.
■		#470	#267	#6010	Avocado Green Lt.
■		#471	#266	#6266	Avocado Green Very Lt.
■		#472	#253	#6253	Avocado Green Pale
■		#606	#334	#2334	Bright Orange Red
	/	#796	#133	#7100	Royal Blue
	/	#798	#131	#7022	Blueberry Dk.
■	/	#801	#359	#5472	Coffee Brown Dk.
■		#814	#45	#3044	Garnet Very Dk.
■	/	#902	#897	#3083	Darkest Garnet
■		#947	#330	#2330	Burnt Orange
■		#970	#316	#2327	Pumpkin Bright
	/	#3346	#268	#6261	Ivy Green Med.
■		#3803	#69	#3089	Mauve Dk.

Pumpkin

Ring of Flowers

Complement a decorative footstool with an artistic arrangement of stitched florals.

Ring of Flowers

Designed by Judy M. Chrispens

MATERIALS

16" x 16" piece of wood violet 28-count Jobelan®; 13" x 10" high footstool

INSTRUCTIONS

1: Center and stitch design, stitching over two threads and using two strands floss for Cross-Stitch and one strand floss for Backstitch.

2: Cover footstool following manufacturer's instructions.

X	B'st	DMC	ANCHOR	J.&P. COATS	COLORS
		#208	#110	#4301	Lavender Dk.
		#209	#109	#4302	Lavender Med.
		#210	#108	#4104	Lavender Lt.
		#211	#342	#4303	Lavender Pale
		#319	#218	#6246	Spruce
		#320	#215	#6017	Pistachio Green Med.
		#335	#38	#3283	Rose Pink Dk.
		#341	#117	#7005	Blue Violet Lt.
		#367	#217	#6018	Pistachio Green Dk.
		#433	#358	#5471	Coffee Brown
		#434	#310	#5000	Darkest Toast
		#744	#301	#2293	Tangerine Pale
		#745	#300	#2296	Topaz Very Lt.
		#793	#176	#7110	Cornflower Blue Lt.
		#794	#175	#7977	Cornflower Blue Very Lt.
		#819	#271	#3280	Antique Rose Pale
		#838	#380	#5478	Darkest Pecan
		#961	#76	#3176	Antique Rose Dk.
		#962	#75	#3153	Antique Rose Med.
		#987	#244	#6258	Willow Green Dk.
		#988	#243	#6267	Willow Green Med.
		#3051	#681	#6318	Pine Green Dk.
		#3052	#262	#6316	Pine Green
		#3053	#261	#6315	Pine Green Lt.
		#3348	#264	#6266	Apple Green
		#3350	#59	#3004	Dusty Rose Very Dk.
		#3363	#263	#6317	Celery Green Med.
		#3607	#87	#4087	Plum
		#3608	#86	#4086	Plum Lt.
		#3609	#85	#4085	Plum Very Lt.
		#3687	#68	#3088	Mauve Med.
		#3688	#66	#3087	Mauve
		#3713	#1020	#3068	Salmon Very Lt.
		#3716	#25	#3125	Antique Rose
		#3731	#52	#3282	Dusty Rose
		#3733	#36	#3126	Dusty Rose Lt.
		#3803	#69	#3089	Mauve Dk.

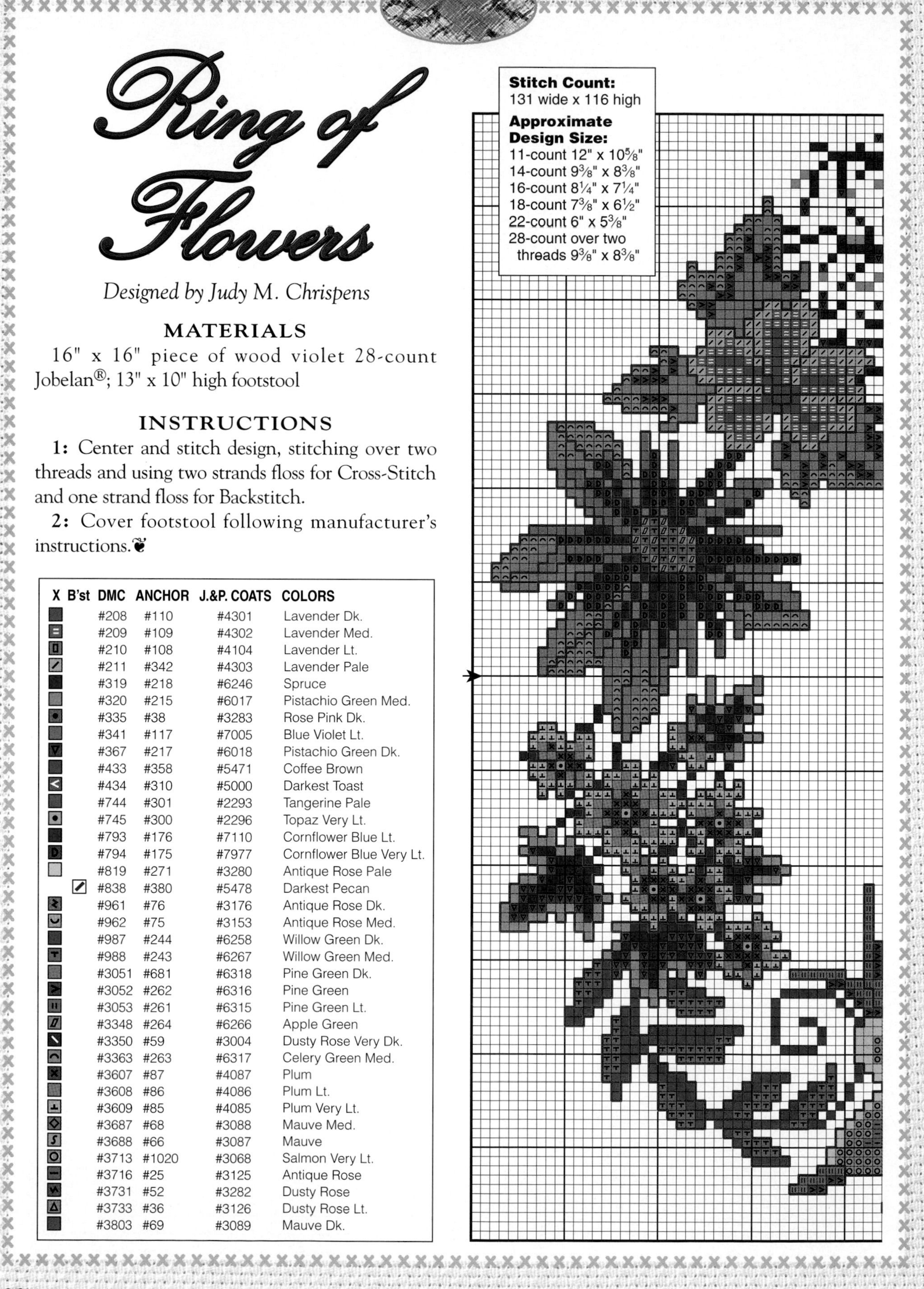

GARDENING WITH COLOR MARY
RANDOM HOUSE
Better Homes and Gardens
NATURE'S GARDENS
Meredith
Country Living
COUNTRY GARDENS
HEARST BOOKS

Spring Flowers

Designed by Jacquelyn Fox

MATERIALS FOR ONE

8" x desired length of antique white 28-count Monaco; Towel of choice; Piping; Bias tape

INSTRUCTIONS

1: Center and stitch design of choice, stitching over two threads and using two strands floss for Cross-Stitch and one strand floss for Backstitch, French Knot and Bullion Stitch.

NOTE: Trim design to fit towel as desired.

2: With right sides facing, sew piping along long edges of design; finish short edges. Position on towel and sew along outside edges as shown in photo. Encase bottom edge of towel with bias tape as shown.

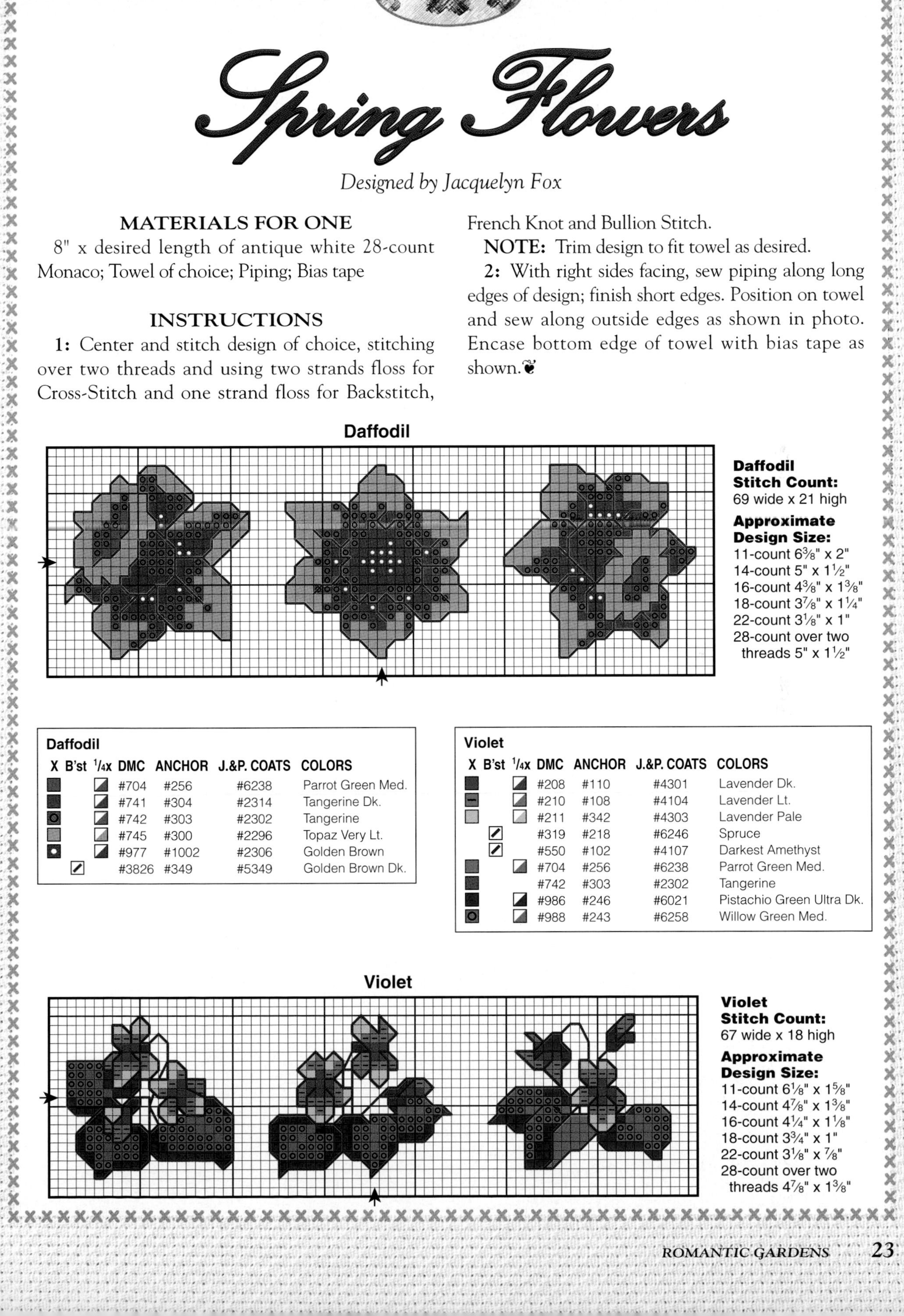

Daffodil

Daffodil Stitch Count: 69 wide x 21 high

Approximate Design Size:
11-count 6 3/8" x 2"
14-count 5" x 1 1/2"
16-count 4 3/8" x 1 3/8"
18-count 3 7/8" x 1 1/4"
22-count 3 1/8" x 1"
28-count over two threads 5" x 1 1/2"

Daffodil

X	B'st	1/4x	DMC	ANCHOR	J.&P. COATS	COLORS
■		◪	#704	#256	#6238	Parrot Green Med.
■		◪	#741	#304	#2314	Tangerine Dk.
■		◪	#742	#303	#2302	Tangerine
■		◪	#745	#300	#2296	Topaz Very Lt.
■		◪	#977	#1002	#2306	Golden Brown
	/		#3826	#349	#5349	Golden Brown Dk.

Violet

X	B'st	1/4x	DMC	ANCHOR	J.&P. COATS	COLORS
■		◪	#208	#110	#4301	Lavender Dk.
■		◪	#210	#108	#4104	Lavender Lt.
■		◪	#211	#342	#4303	Lavender Pale
	/		#319	#218	#6246	Spruce
	/		#550	#102	#4107	Darkest Amethyst
■		◪	#704	#256	#6238	Parrot Green Med.
■			#742	#303	#2302	Tangerine
■		◪	#986	#246	#6021	Pistachio Green Ultra Dk.
■		◪	#988	#243	#6258	Willow Green Med.

Violet

Violet Stitch Count: 67 wide x 18 high

Approximate Design Size:
11-count 6 1/8" x 1 5/8"
14-count 4 7/8" x 1 3/8"
16-count 4 1/4" x 1 1/8"
18-count 3 3/4" x 1"
22-count 3 1/8" x 7/8"
28-count over two threads 4 7/8" x 1 3/8"

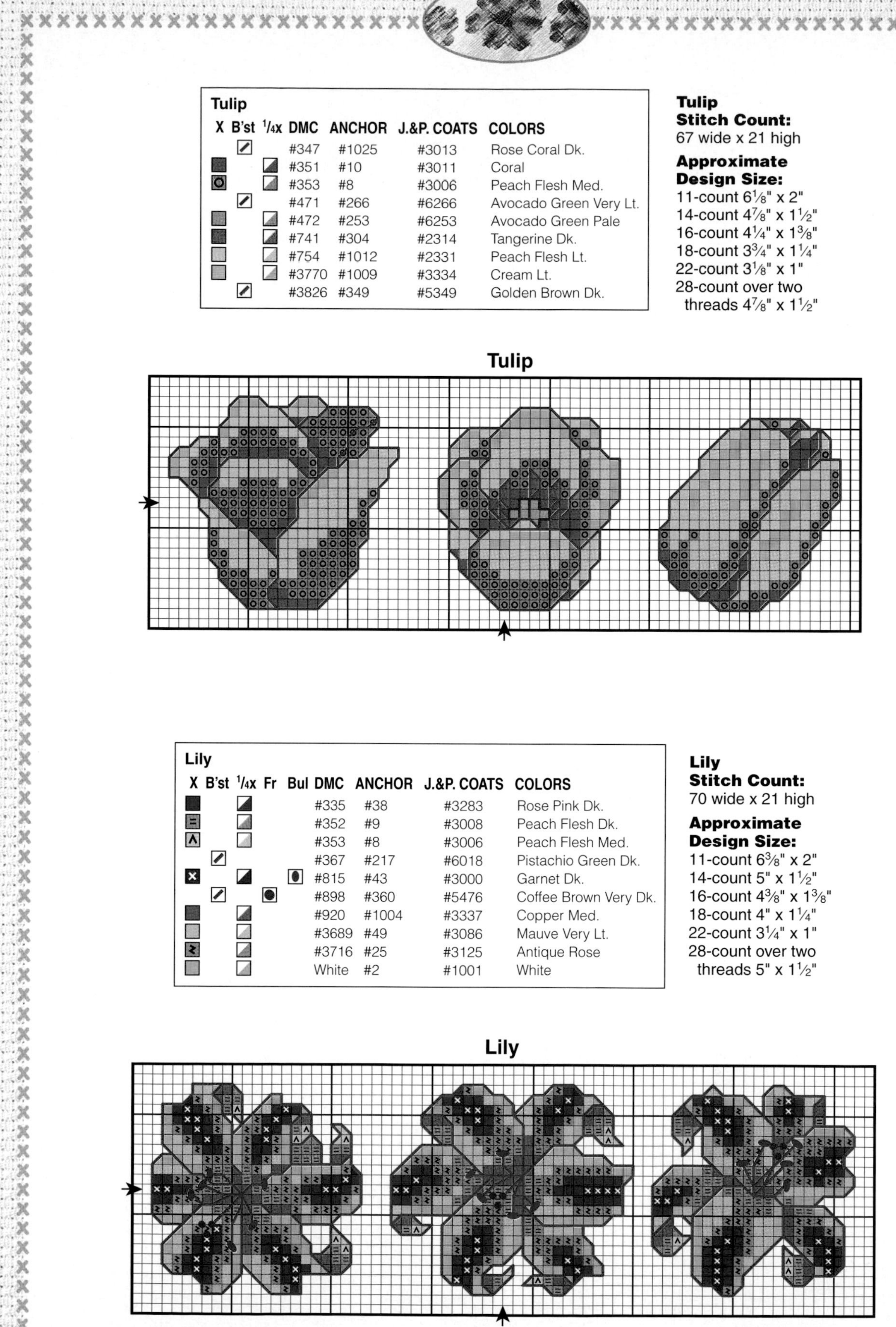

Tulip

DMC	ANCHOR	J.&P. COATS	COLORS
#347	#1025	#3013	Rose Coral Dk.
#351	#10	#3011	Coral
#353	#8	#3006	Peach Flesh Med.
#471	#266	#6266	Avocado Green Very Lt.
#472	#253	#6253	Avocado Green Pale
#741	#304	#2314	Tangerine Dk.
#754	#1012	#2331	Peach Flesh Lt.
#3770	#1009	#3334	Cream Lt.
#3826	#349	#5349	Golden Brown Dk.

Tulip
Stitch Count:
67 wide x 21 high

Approximate Design Size:
11-count 6 1/8" x 2"
14-count 4 7/8" x 1 1/2"
16-count 4 1/4" x 1 3/8"
18-count 3 3/4" x 1 1/4"
22-count 3 1/8" x 1"
28-count over two threads 4 7/8" x 1 1/2"

Tulip

Lily

DMC	ANCHOR	J.&P. COATS	COLORS
#335	#38	#3283	Rose Pink Dk.
#352	#9	#3008	Peach Flesh Dk.
#353	#8	#3006	Peach Flesh Med.
#367	#217	#6018	Pistachio Green Dk.
#815	#43	#3000	Garnet Dk.
#898	#360	#5476	Coffee Brown Very Dk.
#920	#1004	#3337	Copper Med.
#3689	#49	#3086	Mauve Very Lt.
#3716	#25	#3125	Antique Rose
White	#2	#1001	White

Lily
Stitch Count:
70 wide x 21 high

Approximate Design Size:
11-count 6 3/8" x 2"
14-count 5" x 1 1/2"
16-count 4 3/8" x 1 3/8"
18-count 4" x 1 1/4"
22-count 3 1/4" x 1"
28-count over two threads 5" x 1 1/2"

Lily

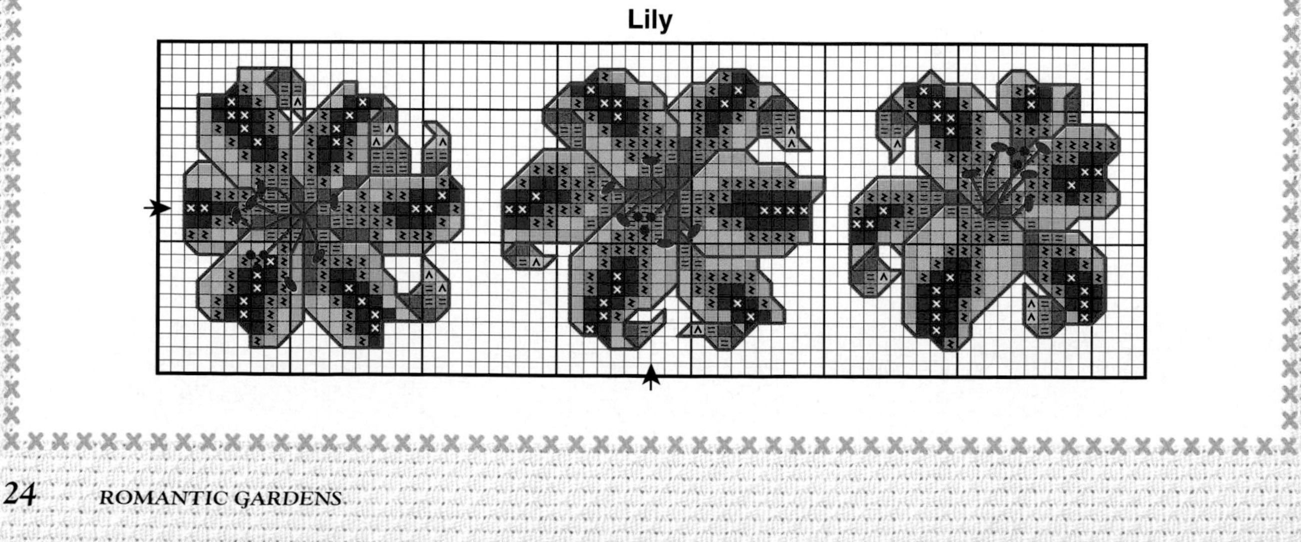

Countryside Nursery

Countryside Nursery

Designed by Dayna Stedry

MATERIALS

16" x 17" piece of antique white 16-count Aida; 1 yd. fabric; 11½" x 13" piece of batting

INSTRUCTIONS

NOTE: Graph Diagram shows complete design.

1: Center and stitch design, using two strands floss for Cross-Stitch and Backstitch of lettering. Use one strand floss for remaining Backstitch.

NOTES: Trim design to 13" wide by 11½" tall. From fabric, cut one 11½" x 13" for back, one 1½" x 55" bias strip (piecing is necessary) for binding and one 3" x 12" piece for hanger.

2: With wrong sides facing and batting between, baste design and back together, forming banner. Press under ¼" on each long edge of binding. With right sides facing, sew binding to front outside edges of banner, folding corners as you sew. Fold binding to back and slip stitch in place.

3: Sew ¼" hem on short edges of hanger. With right sides facing, sew long edges of hanger together. Turn right sides out; press. Slip stitch hanger to top back of Banner.❦

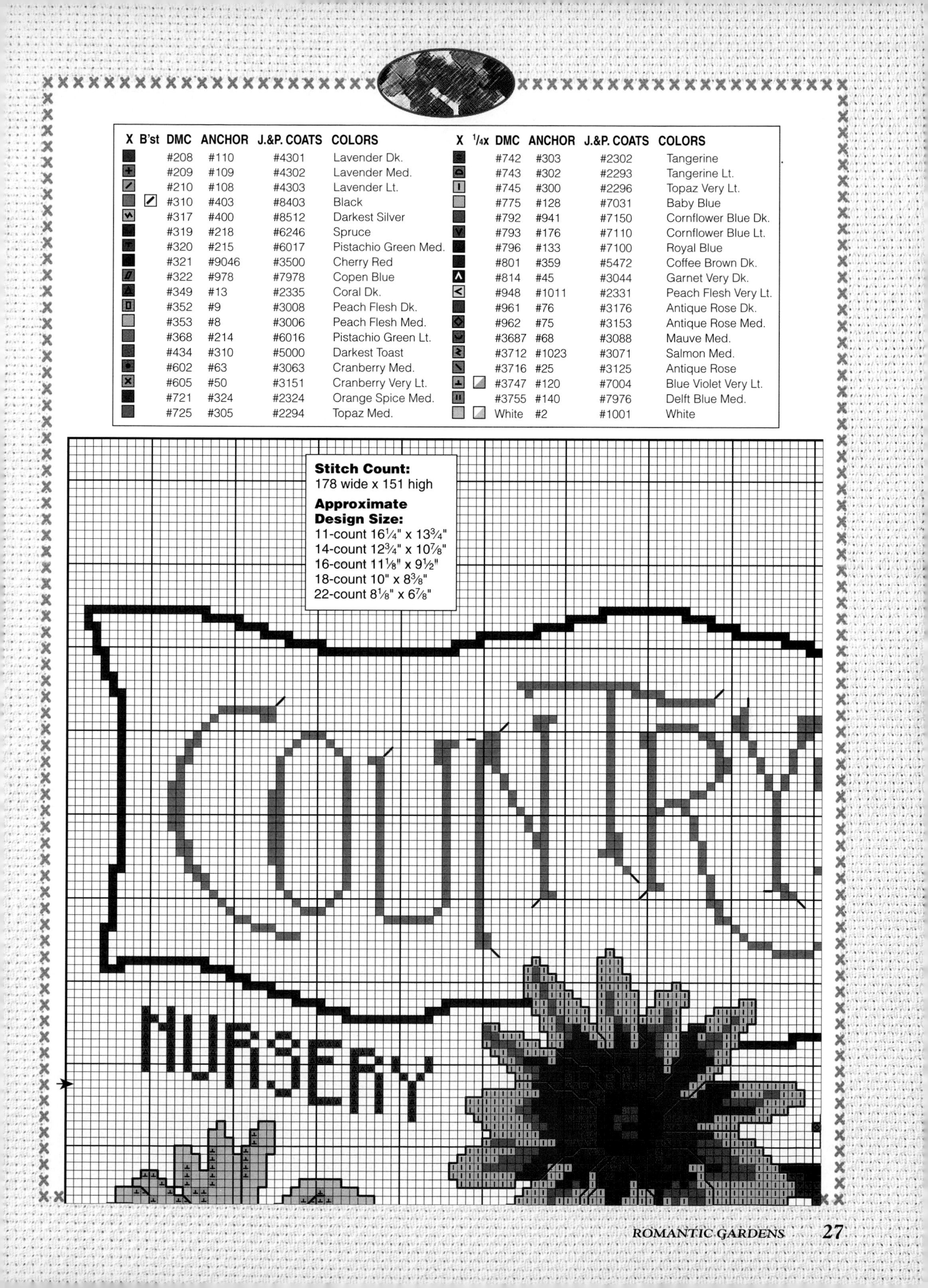

X	B'st	DMC	ANCHOR	J.&P. COATS	COLORS
		#208	#110	#4301	Lavender Dk.
		#209	#109	#4302	Lavender Med.
		#210	#108	#4303	Lavender Lt.
	/	#310	#403	#8403	Black
		#317	#400	#8512	Darkest Silver
		#319	#218	#6246	Spruce
		#320	#215	#6017	Pistachio Green Med.
		#321	#9046	#3500	Cherry Red
		#322	#978	#7978	Copen Blue
		#349	#13	#2335	Coral Dk.
		#352	#9	#3008	Peach Flesh Dk.
		#353	#8	#3006	Peach Flesh Med.
		#368	#214	#6016	Pistachio Green Lt.
		#434	#310	#5000	Darkest Toast
		#602	#63	#3063	Cranberry Med.
		#605	#50	#3151	Cranberry Very Lt.
		#721	#324	#2324	Orange Spice Med.
		#725	#305	#2294	Topaz Med.

X	¼x	DMC	ANCHOR	J.&P. COATS	COLORS
		#742	#303	#2302	Tangerine
		#743	#302	#2293	Tangerine Lt.
		#745	#300	#2296	Topaz Very Lt.
		#775	#128	#7031	Baby Blue
		#792	#941	#7150	Cornflower Blue Dk.
		#793	#176	#7110	Cornflower Blue Lt.
		#796	#133	#7100	Royal Blue
		#801	#359	#5472	Coffee Brown Dk.
		#814	#45	#3044	Garnet Very Dk.
		#948	#1011	#2331	Peach Flesh Very Lt.
		#961	#76	#3176	Antique Rose Dk.
		#962	#75	#3153	Antique Rose Med.
		#3687	#68	#3088	Mauve Med.
		#3712	#1023	#3071	Salmon Med.
		#3716	#25	#3125	Antique Rose
	/	#3747	#120	#7004	Blue Violet Very Lt.
		#3755	#140	#7976	Delft Blue Med.
	/	White	#2	#1001	White

Stitch Count:
178 wide x 151 high

Approximate Design Size:
11-count 16¼" x 13¾"
14-count 12¾" x 10⅞"
16-count 11⅛" x 9½"
18-count 10" x 8⅜"
22-count 8⅛" x 6⅞"

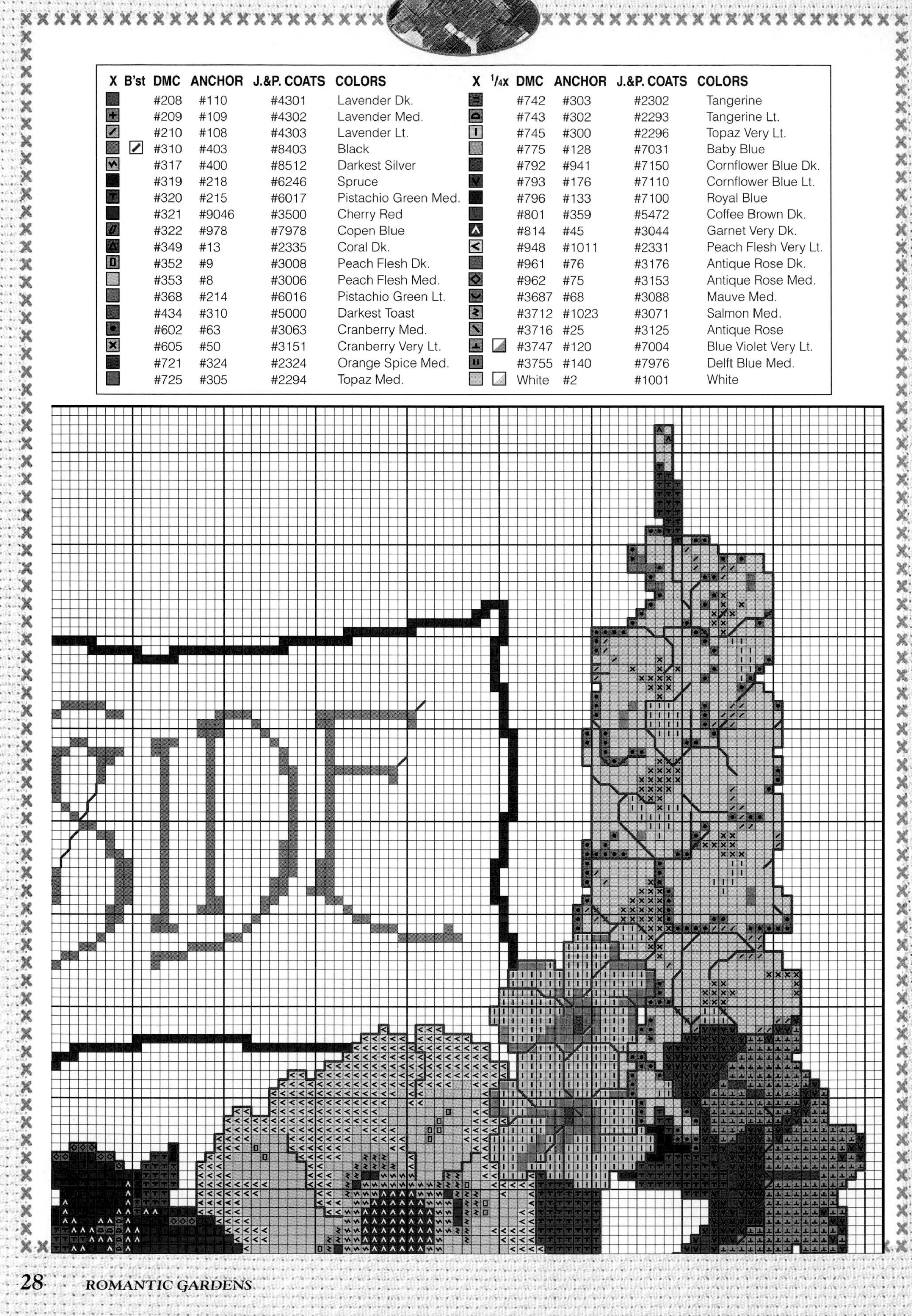

X	B'st	DMC	ANCHOR	J.&P. COATS	COLORS
		#208	#110	#4301	Lavender Dk.
		#209	#109	#4302	Lavender Med.
		#210	#108	#4303	Lavender Lt.
		#310	#403	#8403	Black
		#317	#400	#8512	Darkest Silver
		#319	#218	#6246	Spruce
		#320	#215	#6017	Pistachio Green Med.
		#321	#9046	#3500	Cherry Red
		#322	#978	#7978	Copen Blue
		#349	#13	#2335	Coral Dk.
		#352	#9	#3008	Peach Flesh Dk.
		#353	#8	#3006	Peach Flesh Med.
		#368	#214	#6016	Pistachio Green Lt.
		#434	#310	#5000	Darkest Toast
		#602	#63	#3063	Cranberry Med.
		#605	#50	#3151	Cranberry Very Lt.
		#721	#324	#2324	Orange Spice Med.
		#725	#305	#2294	Topaz Med.

X	1/4x	DMC	ANCHOR	J.&P. COATS	COLORS
		#742	#303	#2302	Tangerine
		#743	#302	#2293	Tangerine Lt.
		#745	#300	#2296	Topaz Very Lt.
		#775	#128	#7031	Baby Blue
		#792	#941	#7150	Cornflower Blue Dk.
		#793	#176	#7110	Cornflower Blue Lt.
		#796	#133	#7100	Royal Blue
		#801	#359	#5472	Coffee Brown Dk.
		#814	#45	#3044	Garnet Very Dk.
		#948	#1011	#2331	Peach Flesh Very Lt.
		#961	#76	#3176	Antique Rose Dk.
		#962	#75	#3153	Antique Rose Med.
		#3687	#68	#3088	Mauve Med.
		#3712	#1023	#3071	Salmon Med.
		#3716	#25	#3125	Antique Rose
		#3747	#120	#7004	Blue Violet Very Lt.
		#3755	#140	#7976	Delft Blue Med.
		White	#2	#1001	White

Victorian Squares

Designed by Mike Vickery

MATERIALS

One 13" x 13" piece of water lily 32-count Danish linen; One 13" x 13" piece of china white 28-count Danish linen; One 13" x 13" piece of cherub pink 28-count Danish linen; 1 yd. fabric; 2¾ yds. twisted cord; Two tassels; 8" dowel rod; Batting; Craft glue or glue gun

INSTRUCTIONS

1: Center and stitch "Shoes" design onto china white, "Teapot" design onto water lily and "Violin" design onto cherub pink linen, stitching over two threads and using two strands floss for Cross-Stitch and one strand floss for Backstitch.

NOTES: Trim each design to 8¼" x 8¼". From fabric, cut four 2" x 8¼" A pieces, two 2" x 26¾" B pieces and one 10¼" x 26¾" for back. Use ½" seam allowance. From batting, cut one 10¼" x 26¾".

2: Sew A and B pieces to designs according to Assembly Diagram for front. Sew cord to right side of front. Baste batting to wrong side of front. With right sides facing, sew front and back together, leaving an opening. Turn right sides out; slip stitch opening closed.

3: Glue rod and remaining cord for hanger and attach tassels according to Assembly Diagram.❦

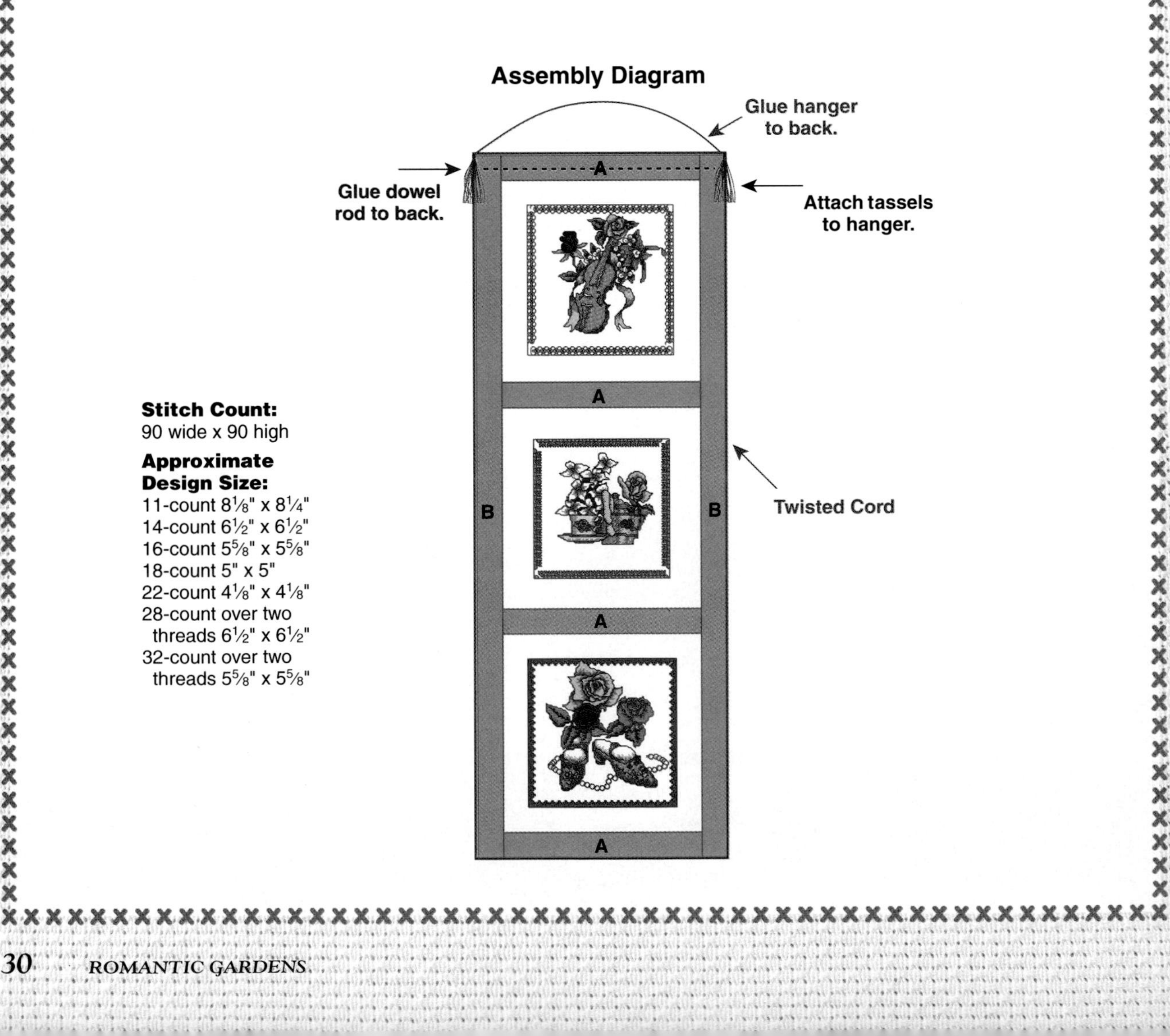

Show your admiration for treasured keepsakes representative of an enchanting era with this elegant wall display.

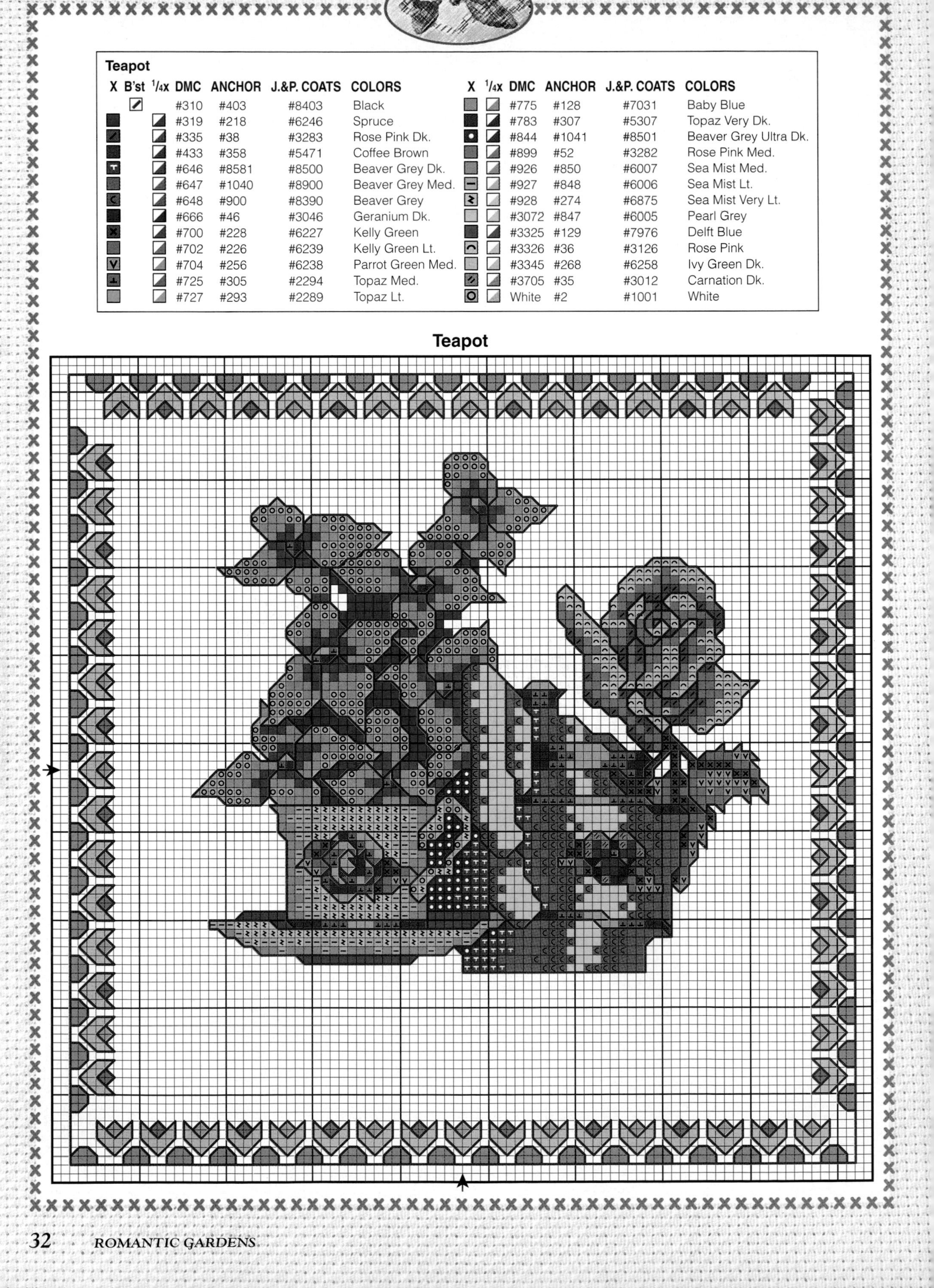

Teapot

X	B'st	¼x	DMC	ANCHOR	J.&P. COATS	COLORS
			#310	#403	#8403	Black
			#319	#218	#6246	Spruce
			#335	#38	#3283	Rose Pink Dk.
			#433	#358	#5471	Coffee Brown
			#646	#8581	#8500	Beaver Grey Dk.
			#647	#1040	#8900	Beaver Grey Med.
			#648	#900	#8390	Beaver Grey
			#666	#46	#3046	Geranium Dk.
			#700	#228	#6227	Kelly Green
			#702	#226	#6239	Kelly Green Lt.
			#704	#256	#6238	Parrot Green Med.
			#725	#305	#2294	Topaz Med.
			#727	#293	#2289	Topaz Lt.
			#775	#128	#7031	Baby Blue
			#783	#307	#5307	Topaz Very Dk.
			#844	#1041	#8501	Beaver Grey Ultra Dk.
			#899	#52	#3282	Rose Pink Med.
			#926	#850	#6007	Sea Mist Med.
			#927	#848	#6006	Sea Mist Lt.
			#928	#274	#6875	Sea Mist Very Lt.
			#3072	#847	#6005	Pearl Grey
			#3325	#129	#7976	Delft Blue
			#3326	#36	#3126	Rose Pink
			#3345	#268	#6258	Ivy Green Dk.
			#3705	#35	#3012	Carnation Dk.
			White	#2	#1001	White

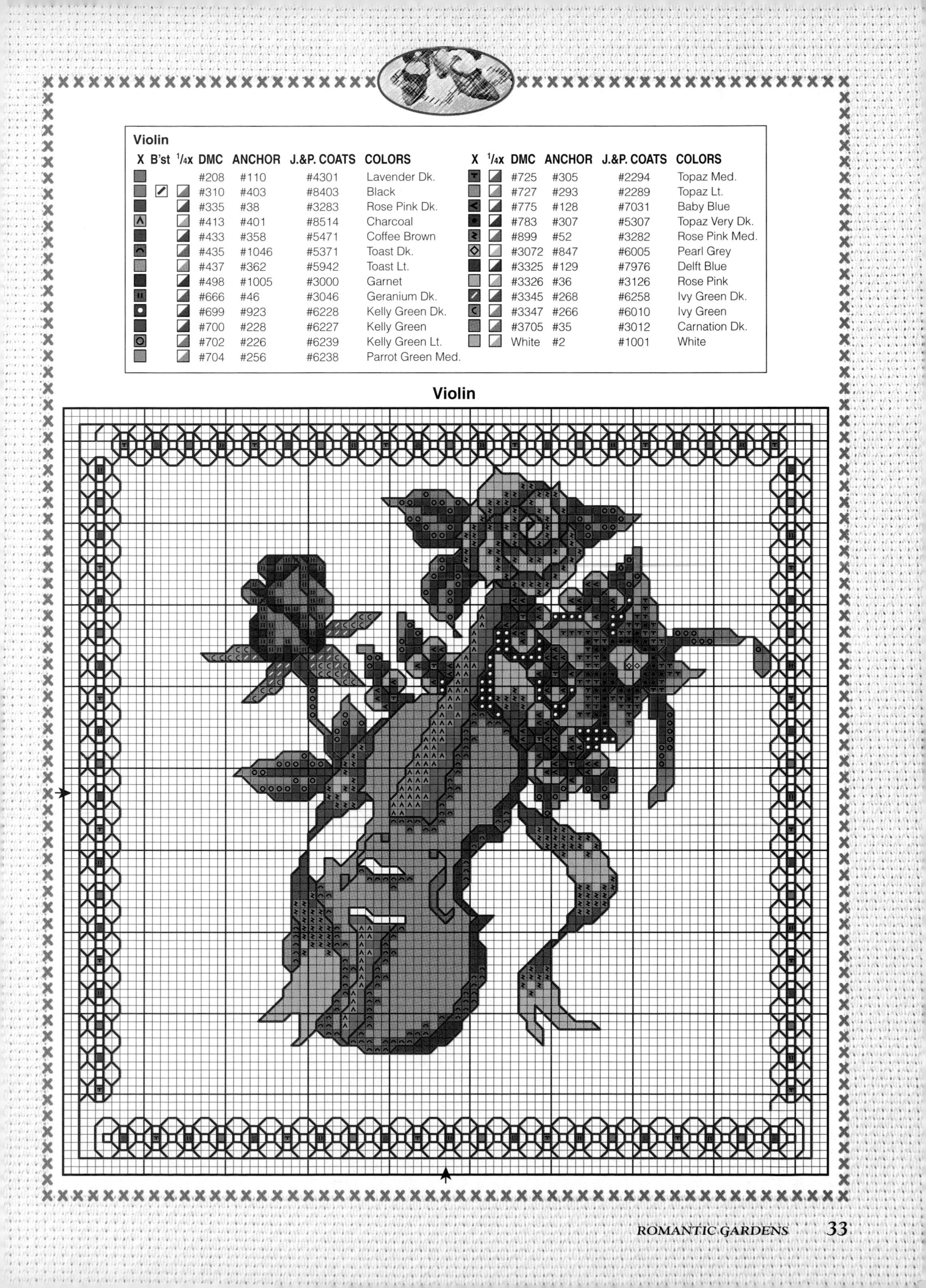

Violin

DMC	ANCHOR	J.&P. COATS	COLORS
#208	#110	#4301	Lavender Dk.
#310	#403	#8403	Black
#335	#38	#3283	Rose Pink Dk.
#413	#401	#8514	Charcoal
#433	#358	#5471	Coffee Brown
#435	#1046	#5371	Toast Dk.
#437	#362	#5942	Toast Lt.
#498	#1005	#3000	Garnet
#666	#46	#3046	Geranium Dk.
#699	#923	#6228	Kelly Green Dk.
#700	#228	#6227	Kelly Green
#702	#226	#6239	Kelly Green Lt.
#704	#256	#6238	Parrot Green Med.
#725	#305	#2294	Topaz Med.
#727	#293	#2289	Topaz Lt.
#775	#128	#7031	Baby Blue
#783	#307	#5307	Topaz Very Dk.
#899	#52	#3282	Rose Pink Med.
#3072	#847	#6005	Pearl Grey
#3325	#129	#7976	Delft Blue
#3326	#36	#3126	Rose Pink
#3345	#268	#6258	Ivy Green Dk.
#3347	#266	#6010	Ivy Green
#3705	#35	#3012	Carnation Dk.
White	#2	#1001	White

Violin

Shoes

X	B'st	¹/₄x	DMC	ANCHOR	J.&P. COATS	COLORS
			#208	#110	#4301	Lavender Dk.
			#310	#403	#8403	Black
			#335	#38	#3283	Rose Pink Dk.
			#498	#1005	#3000	Garnet
			#648	#900	#8390	Beaver Grey
			#666	#46	#3046	Geranium Dk.
			#676	#891	#2305	Honey
			#677	#886	#5372	Honey Lt.
			#700	#228	#6227	Kelly Green
			#702	#226	#6239	Kelly Green Lt.
			#704	#256	#6238	Parrot Green Med.
			#725	#305	#2294	Topaz Med.
			#727	#293	#2289	Topaz Lt.

X	¹/₄x	DMC	ANCHOR	J.&P. COATS	COLORS
		#729	#890	#2875	Old Gold
		#783	#307	#5307	Topaz Very Dk.
		#899	#52	#3282	Rose Pink Med.
		#928	#274	#6006	Sea Mist Very Lt.
		#3072	#847	#6005	Pearl Grey
		#3326	#36	#3126	Rose Pink
		#3345	#268	#6258	Ivy Green Dk.
		#3347	#266	#6010	Ivy Green
		#3705	#35	#3012	Carnation Dk.
		#3777	#1015	#2326	Darkest Terra Cotta
		#3778	#1013	#2338	Terra Cotta
		#3830	#341	#2339	Terra Cotta Dk.
		White	#2	#1001	White

Shoes

Love is Eternal
Love
springs
Eternal
Barbara Donald
6-3-97

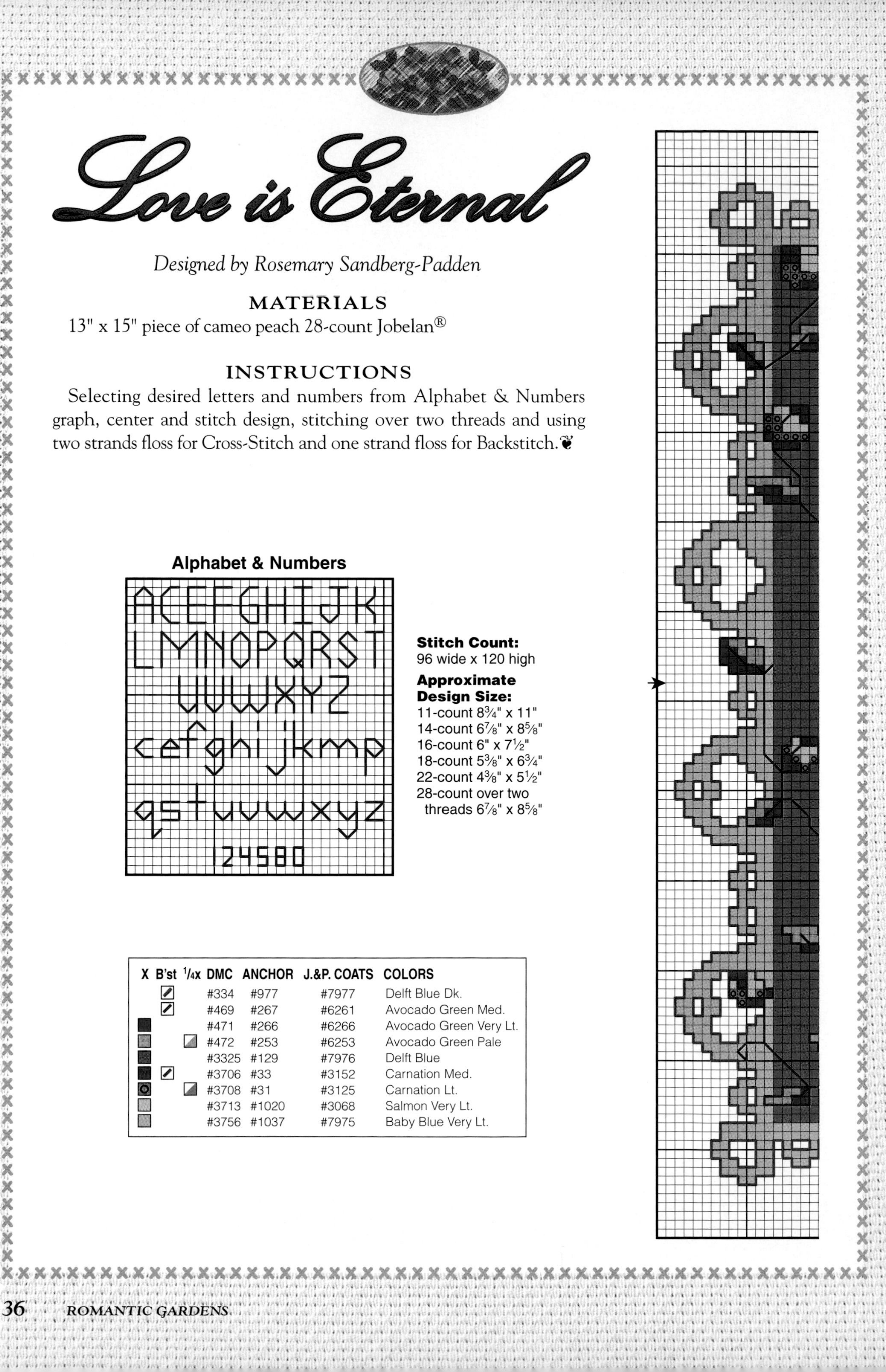

Love is Eternal

Designed by Rosemary Sandberg-Padden

MATERIALS

13" x 15" piece of cameo peach 28-count Jobelan®

INSTRUCTIONS

Selecting desired letters and numbers from Alphabet & Numbers graph, center and stitch design, stitching over two threads and using two strands floss for Cross-Stitch and one strand floss for Backstitch.❦

Alphabet & Numbers

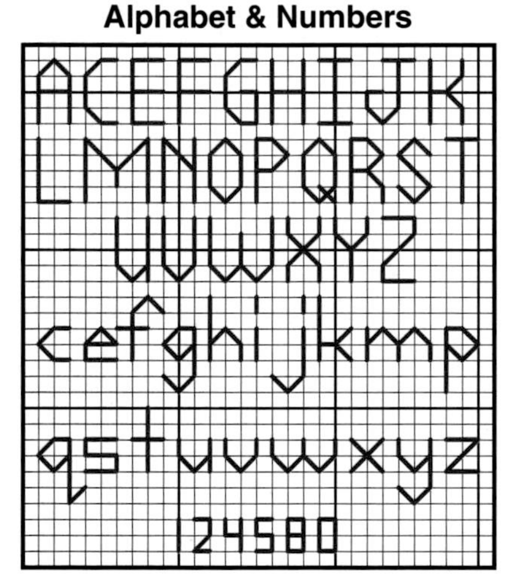

Stitch Count:
96 wide x 120 high

Approximate Design Size:
11-count 8¾" x 11"
14-count 6⅞" x 8⅝"
16-count 6" x 7½"
18-count 5⅜" x 6¾"
22-count 4⅜" x 5½"
28-count over two threads 6⅞" x 8⅝"

X	B'st	¼x	DMC	ANCHOR	J.&P. COATS	COLORS
	■		#334	#977	#7977	Delft Blue Dk.
	■		#469	#267	#6261	Avocado Green Med.
■			#471	#266	#6266	Avocado Green Very Lt.
■		■	#472	#253	#6253	Avocado Green Pale
■			#3325	#129	#7976	Delft Blue
■	■		#3706	#33	#3152	Carnation Med.
■		■	#3708	#31	#3125	Carnation Lt.
■			#3713	#1020	#3068	Salmon Very Lt.
■			#3756	#1037	#7975	Baby Blue Very Lt.

Love
Springs
Eternal
Barbara Donald
6-3-97

Sentimental Stroll

Create beautiful memories to share with those you love as you spend your present moments stitching gifts from you heart. Then, step lightly into the future as you present these masterpieces infused by your loving thoughts.

Fairy Footprints
'Tis not freckles
that I see
Sprinkled on your
precious cheeks.
Tiny footprints
mark the place
Where fairies dance
Upon your face.

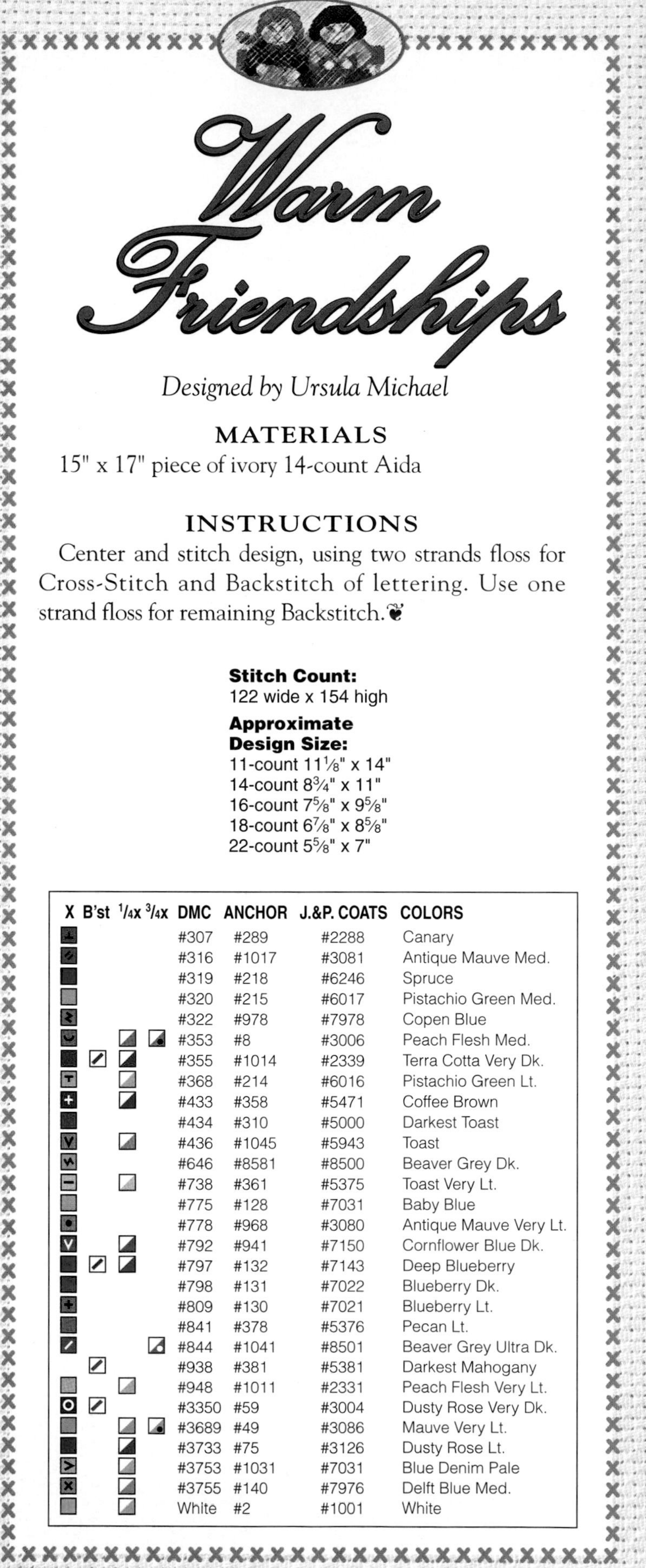

Warm Friendships

Designed by Ursula Michael

MATERIALS

15" x 17" piece of ivory 14-count Aida

INSTRUCTIONS

Center and stitch design, using two strands floss for Cross-Stitch and Backstitch of lettering. Use one strand floss for remaining Backstitch.❦

Stitch Count:
122 wide x 154 high

Approximate Design Size:
11-count 11⅛" x 14"
14-count 8¾" x 11"
16-count 7⅝" x 9⅝"
18-count 6⅞" x 8⅝"
22-count 5⅝" x 7"

X	B'st	¼x	¾x	DMC	ANCHOR	J.&P. COATS	COLORS
■				#307	#289	#2288	Canary
■				#316	#1017	#3081	Antique Mauve Med.
■				#319	#218	#6246	Spruce
■				#320	#215	#6017	Pistachio Green Med.
■				#322	#978	#7978	Copen Blue
■		◪	◪	#353	#8	#3006	Peach Flesh Med.
■	◪	◪		#355	#1014	#2339	Terra Cotta Very Dk.
■		◪		#368	#214	#6016	Pistachio Green Lt.
■		◪		#433	#358	#5471	Coffee Brown
■				#434	#310	#5000	Darkest Toast
■		◪		#436	#1045	#5943	Toast
■				#646	#8581	#8500	Beaver Grey Dk.
■		◪		#738	#361	#5375	Toast Very Lt.
■				#775	#128	#7031	Baby Blue
■				#778	#968	#3080	Antique Mauve Very Lt.
■		◪		#792	#941	#7150	Cornflower Blue Dk.
■	◪	◪		#797	#132	#7143	Deep Blueberry
■				#798	#131	#7022	Blueberry Dk.
■				#809	#130	#7021	Blueberry Lt.
■				#841	#378	#5376	Pecan Lt.
■			◪	#844	#1041	#8501	Beaver Grey Ultra Dk.
	◪			#938	#381	#5381	Darkest Mahogany
■		◪		#948	#1011	#2331	Peach Flesh Very Lt.
■	◪			#3350	#59	#3004	Dusty Rose Very Dk.
■		◪	◪	#3689	#49	#3086	Mauve Very Lt.
■		◪		#3733	#75	#3126	Dusty Rose Lt.
■		◪		#3753	#1031	#7031	Blue Denim Pale
■		◪		#3755	#140	#7976	Delft Blue Med.
■		◪		White	#2	#1001	White

Present a dear friend with this tender memento of the special relationship you share.

Warm Friendships
Create
Happy Hearts

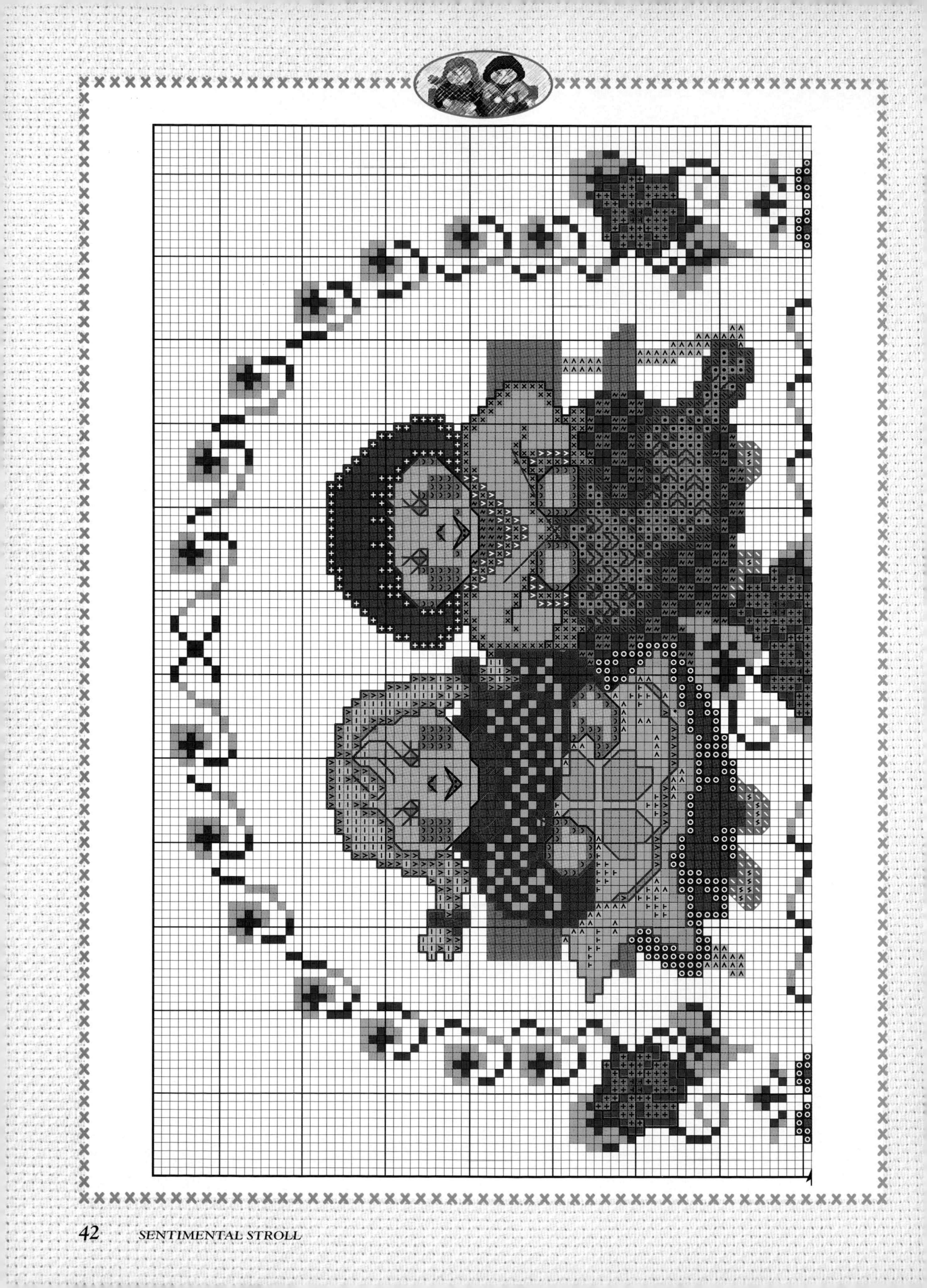

Warm Friendships
Create
Happy Hearts

Fairy Footprints
'Tis not freckles
that I see
Sprinkled on your
precious cheeks.
Tiny footprints
mark the place
Where fairies dance
Upon your face.

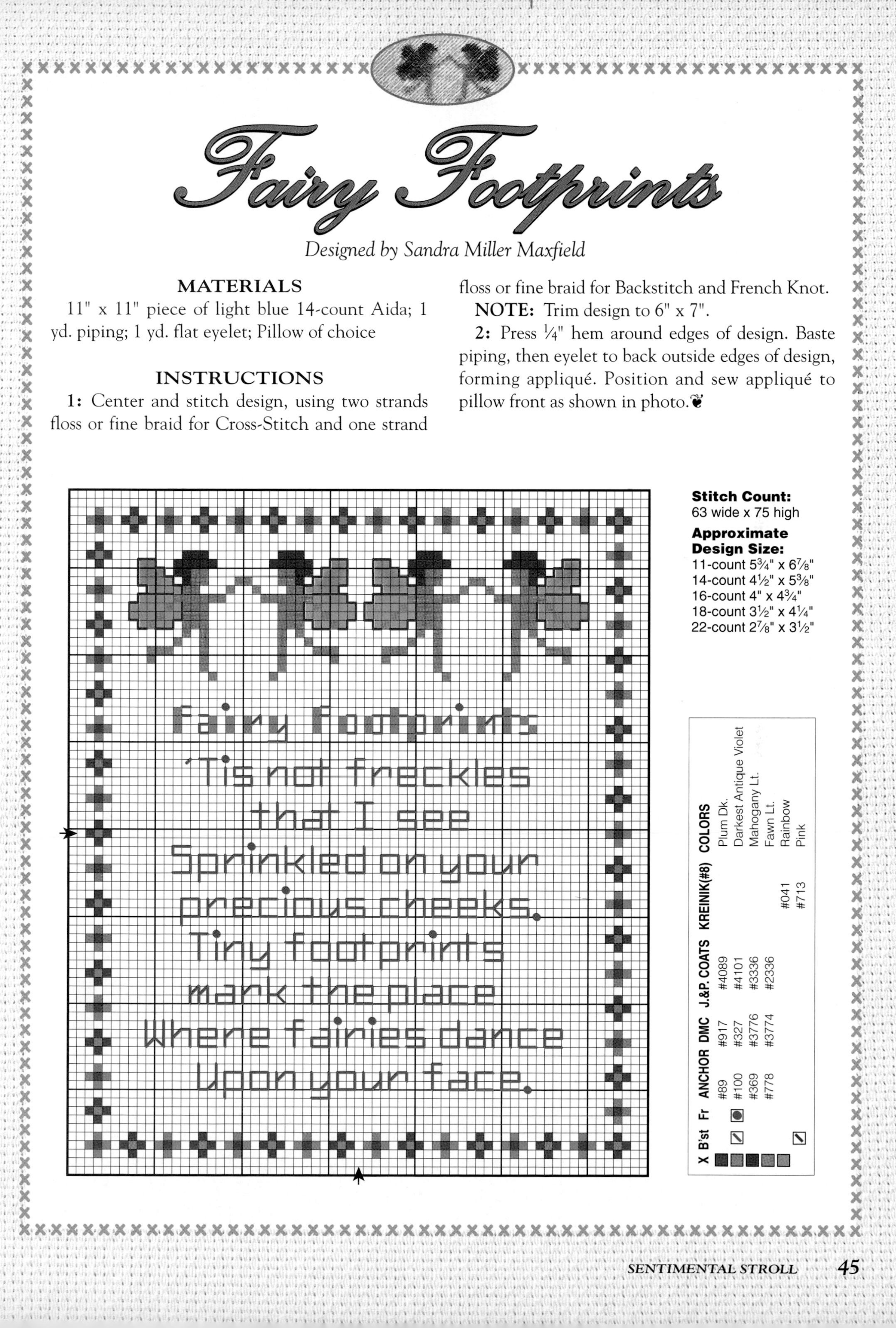

Fairy Footprints

Designed by Sandra Miller Maxfield

MATERIALS

11" x 11" piece of light blue 14-count Aida; 1 yd. piping; 1 yd. flat eyelet; Pillow of choice

INSTRUCTIONS

1: Center and stitch design, using two strands floss or fine braid for Cross-Stitch and one strand floss or fine braid for Backstitch and French Knot.

NOTE: Trim design to 6" x 7".

2: Press ¼" hem around edges of design. Baste piping, then eyelet to back outside edges of design, forming appliqué. Position and sew appliqué to pillow front as shown in photo.❦

Stitch Count:
63 wide x 75 high

Approximate Design Size:
11-count 5¾" x 6⅞"
14-count 4½" x 5⅜"
16-count 4" x 4¾"
18-count 3½" x 4¼"
22-count 2⅞" x 3½"

X	B'st	Fr	ANCHOR	DMC	J.&P. COATS	KREINIK(#8)	COLORS
■			#89	#917	#4089		Plum Dk.
■	▧	●	#100	#327	#4101		Darkest Antique Violet
■			#369	#3776	#3336		Mahogany Lt.
■			#778	#3774	#2336		Fawn Lt.
■						#041	Rainbow
	▧					#713	Pink

Reproduce a profound biblical verse in a divine setting bordered with harmony and beauty.

Where There is No Vision

Designed by Virginia G. Soskin

MATERIALS

12" x 15" piece of oatmeal 18-count Rustico Aida®; Wooden tray with 7" x 10" design area

INSTRUCTIONS

1: Center and stitch design, using two strands floss for Cross-Stitch and Lazy Daisy Stitch. Use one strand floss for Backstitch and French Knot.

2: Position and secure design in tray following manufacturer's instructions.❦

X	B'st	1/4x	3/4x	Fr	DMC	ANCHOR	J.&P. COATS	COLORS
					#310	#403	#8403	Black
					#312	#979	#7979	Azure Blue Dk.
					#315	#972	#3082	Antique Mauve Very Dk.
					#316	#1017	#3081	Antique Mauve Med.
					#319	#218	#6246	Spruce
					#327	#100	#4101	Darkest Antique Violet
					#334	#977	#7977	Delft Blue Dk.
					#368	#214	#6016	Pistachio Green Lt.
					#676	#891	#2305	Honey
					#754	#1012	#2331	Peach Flesh Lt.
					#758	#882	#2337	Terra Cotta Lt.
					#988	#243	#6258	Willow Green Med.

X	B'st	1/4x	3/4x	LzD	Fr	DMC	ANCHOR	J.&P. COATS	COLORS
						#3031	#360	#5472	Coffee Brown Dk.
						#3685	#1028	#3089	Darkest Mauve
						#3804	#63	#3063	Cyclamen Pink Dk.
						#3808	#675	#7227	Wedgewood Dk.
						#3810	#168	#7226	Wedgewood
						#3811	#928	#7053	Wedgewood Very Pale
						#3814	#187	#6186	Aquamarine Very Dk.
						#3822	#295	#2295	Golden Wheat Lt.
						#3826	#349	#5349	Golden Brown Dk.
						#3827	#311	#5351	Golden Brown Lt.
						White	#2	#1001	White
						Ecru	#387	#1002	Ecru

Stitch Count:
156 wide x 108 high

Approximate Design Size:
11-count 14¼" x 9⅞"
14-count 11¼" x 7¾"
16-count 9¾" x 6¾"
18-count 8¾" x 6"
22-count 7⅛" x 5"

X	B'st	1/4x	3/4x	Fr	DMC	ANCHOR	J.&P. COATS	COLORS
					#310	#403	#8403	Black
					#312	#979	#7979	Azure Blue Dk.
					#315	#972	#3082	Antique Mauve Very Dk.
					#316	#1017	#3081	Antique Mauve Med.
					#319	#218	#6246	Spruce
					#327	#100	#4101	Darkest Antique Violet
					#334	#977	#7977	Delft Blue Dk.
					#368	#214	#6016	Pistachio Green Lt.
					#676	#891	#2305	Honey
					#754	#1012	#2331	Peach Flesh Lt.
					#758	#882	#2337	Terra Cotta Lt.
					#988	#243	#6258	Willow Green Med.

X	B'st	1/4x	3/4x	LzD	Fr	DMC	ANCHOR	J.&P. COATS	COLORS
						#3031	#360	#5472	Coffee Brown Dk.
						#3685	#1028	#3089	Darkest Mauve
						#3804	#63	#3063	Cyclamen Pink Dk.
						#3808	#675	#7227	Wedgewood Dk.
						#3810	#168	#7226	Wedgewood
						#3811	#928	#7053	Wedgewood Very Pale
						#3814	#187	#6186	Aquamarine Very Dk.
						#3822	#295	#2295	Golden Wheat Lt.
						#3826	#349	#5349	Golden Brown Dk.
						#3827	#311	#5351	Golden Brown Lt.
						White	#2	#1001	White
						Ecru	#387	#1002	Ecru

Honor the Women

Honor the Women

Designed by Virginia G. Soskin

MATERIALS

13" x 15" piece of white 14-count Aida

INSTRUCTIONS

Center and stitch design, using two strands floss for Cross-Stitch and one strand floss for Backstitch and French Knot.❦

Stitch Count:
100 wide x 121 high

Approximate Design Size:
11-count 9⅛" x 11"
14-count 7¼" x 8¾"
16-count 6¼" x 7⅝"
18-count 5⅝" x 6¾"
22-count 4⅝" x 5½"

X	B'st	¼x	Fr	DMC	ANCHOR	J.&P. COATS	COLORS
×		◪		#367	#217	#6018	Pistachio Green Dk.
■				#368	#214	#6016	Pistachio Green Lt.
I				#415	#398	#8398	Silver
N				#422	#373	#5350	Hazel Nut Lt.
■				#436	#1045	#5943	Toast
C				#471	#266	#6266	Avocado Green Very Lt.
O				#503	#876	#6879	Sage Green Lt.
\				#504	#1042	#6875	Sage Green Very Pale
■	\	◪	●	#647	#1040	#8900	Beaver Grey Med.
□				#747	#158	#7053	Larkspur Very Lt.
∧				#754	#1012	#2331	Peach Flesh Lt.
■				#772	#259	#6250	Celery Green Very Lt.
)				#776	#24	#3281	Rose Pink Lt.
■				#799	#136	#7030	Blueberry Med.
T				#809	#130	#7021	Blueberry Lt.
=				#813	#161	#7161	Sky Blue Med.
■				#818	#23	#3281	Antique Rose Very Lt.
■	\		●	#840	#379	#5379	Pecan Med.
>		◪		#989	#242	#6266	Willow Green
S				#3078	#292	#2292	Yellow Cream
+				#3325	#129	#7976	Delft Blue
	\			#3685	#1028	#3089	Darkest Mauve
■				#3747	#120	#7004	Blue Violet Very Lt.
	\		●	#3790	#393	#5393	Beige Grey Dk.
•				White	#2	#1001	White

GOD BL • FARMERS • HOMEMAKERS • HUMANITARIANS •
MINISTERS • PRESIDENTS • NURSES • DESIGNERS • DANCERS
Hats off to the women who won the vote
And to women who organized,
Cheers to the women who worked the land
Or soared solo in the skies;
Salute the women who guard the rights
Of every race and creed,
Honor the women around the world
Who respond to those in need.
ENGINEERS • WRITERS • ARCHITECTS • POETS • AMBASSADORS •

Iris Place Mat

Designed by Darlene Polachic

MATERIALS

9" x 19" piece of white 14-count Aida; 13" x 18" place mat

INSTRUCTIONS

1: Center and stitch design, using two strands floss for Cross-Stitch and one strand floss for Backstitch.

NOTE: Trim design to 4¼" x 13½".

2: Press ¼" hem around edges of design. Position design on place mat and sew along outside edges as shown in photo.❦

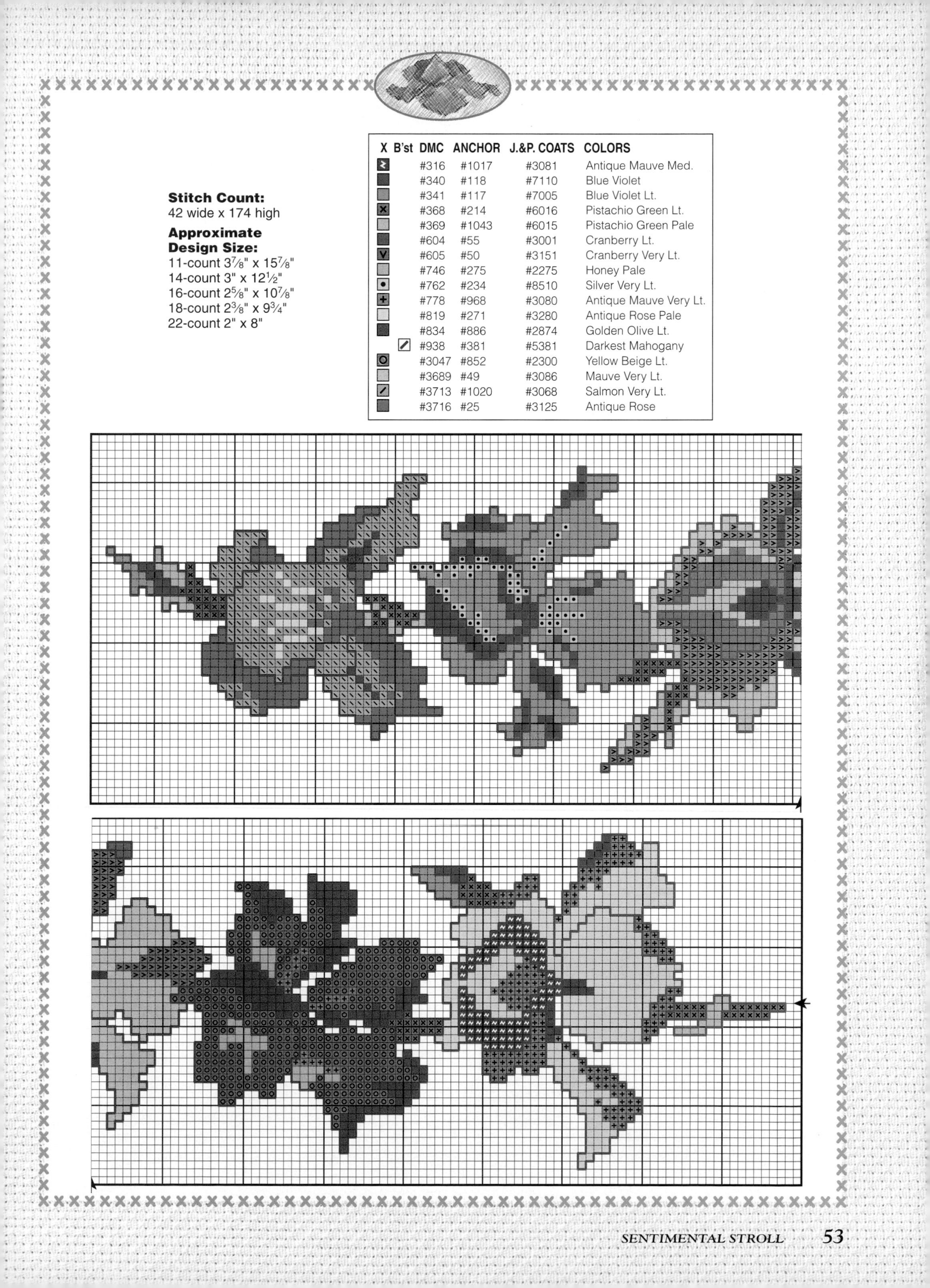

Stitch Count:
42 wide x 174 high

Approximate Design Size:
11-count $3\frac{7}{8}$" x $15\frac{7}{8}$"
14-count 3" x $12\frac{1}{2}$"
16-count $2\frac{5}{8}$" x $10\frac{7}{8}$"
18-count $2\frac{3}{8}$" x $9\frac{3}{4}$"
22-count 2" x 8"

X	B'st	DMC	ANCHOR	J.&P. COATS	COLORS
		#316	#1017	#3081	Antique Mauve Med.
		#340	#118	#7110	Blue Violet
		#341	#117	#7005	Blue Violet Lt.
x		#368	#214	#6016	Pistachio Green Lt.
		#369	#1043	#6015	Pistachio Green Pale
		#604	#55	#3001	Cranberry Lt.
V		#605	#50	#3151	Cranberry Very Lt.
		#746	#275	#2275	Honey Pale
•		#762	#234	#8510	Silver Very Lt.
+		#778	#968	#3080	Antique Mauve Very Lt.
		#819	#271	#3280	Antique Rose Pale
		#834	#886	#2874	Golden Olive Lt.
	/	#938	#381	#5381	Darkest Mahogany
O		#3047	#852	#2300	Yellow Beige Lt.
		#3689	#49	#3086	Mauve Very Lt.
/		#3713	#1020	#3068	Salmon Very Lt.
		#3716	#25	#3125	Antique Rose

Show me Your ways, O
Lord;
Teach me Your paths.
Lead me in Your truth and
teach me,
For You are the God of my
salvation;
On You I wait all the day.
Psalm 25:4-5

Glorify your Heavenly Father with this passionate prayer exquisitely designed on an archaic scroll background.

Meditation

Designed by Pauline Rosenberger

MATERIALS

15" x 18" piece of French blue 30-count Melinda Cloth

INSTRUCTIONS

Center and stitch design, stitching over two threads and using two strands floss for Cross-Stitch and one strand floss or fine braid for Backstitch and French Knot.

Stitch Count:
132 wide x 177 high

Approximate Design Size:
11-count 12" x 16⅛"
14-count 9½" x 12¾"
16-count 8¼" x 11⅛"
18-count 7⅜" x 9⅞"
22-count 6" x 8⅛"
30-count over two threads 8⅞" x 11⅞"

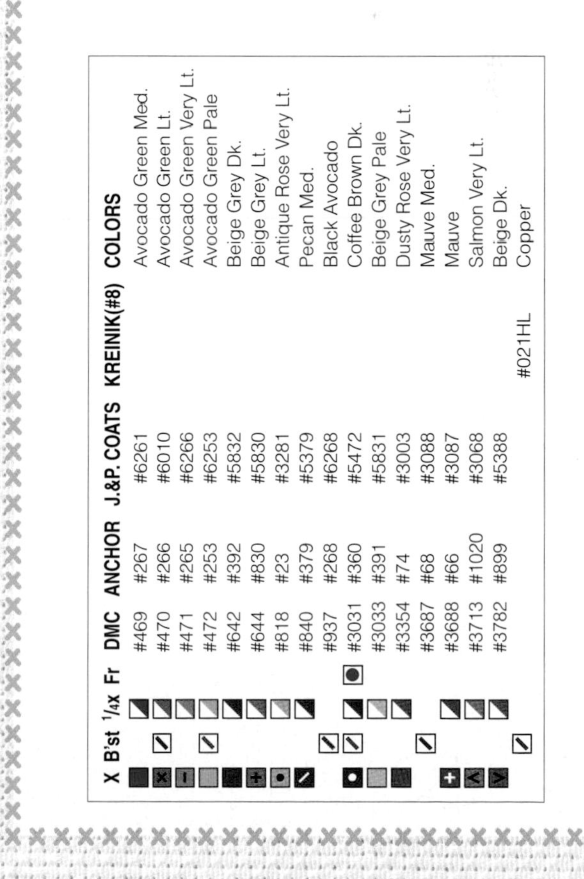

X	B'st	¼x	Fr	DMC	ANCHOR	J.&P. COATS	KREINIK(#8)	COLORS
■		■		#469	#267	#6261		Avocado Green Med.
×	■	■		#470	#266	#6010		Avocado Green Lt.
-		■		#471	#265	#6266		Avocado Green Very Lt.
■	■	■		#472	#253	#6253		Avocado Green Pale
■		■		#642	#392	#5832		Beige Grey Dk.
■		■		#644	#830	#5830		Beige Grey Lt.
+		■		#818	#23	#3281		Antique Rose Very Lt.
•		■		#840	#379	#5379		Pecan Med.
/	■			#937	#268	#6268		Black Avocado
○	■	■	●	#3031	#360	#5472		Coffee Brown Dk.
■		■		#3033	#391	#5831		Beige Grey Pale
■		■		#3354	#74	#3003		Dusty Rose Very Lt.
	■			#3687	#68	#3088		Mauve Med.
+		■		#3688	#66	#3087		Mauve
<		■		#3713	#1020	#3068		Salmon Very Lt.
>		■		#3782	#899	#5388		Beige Dk.
	■						#021HL	Copper

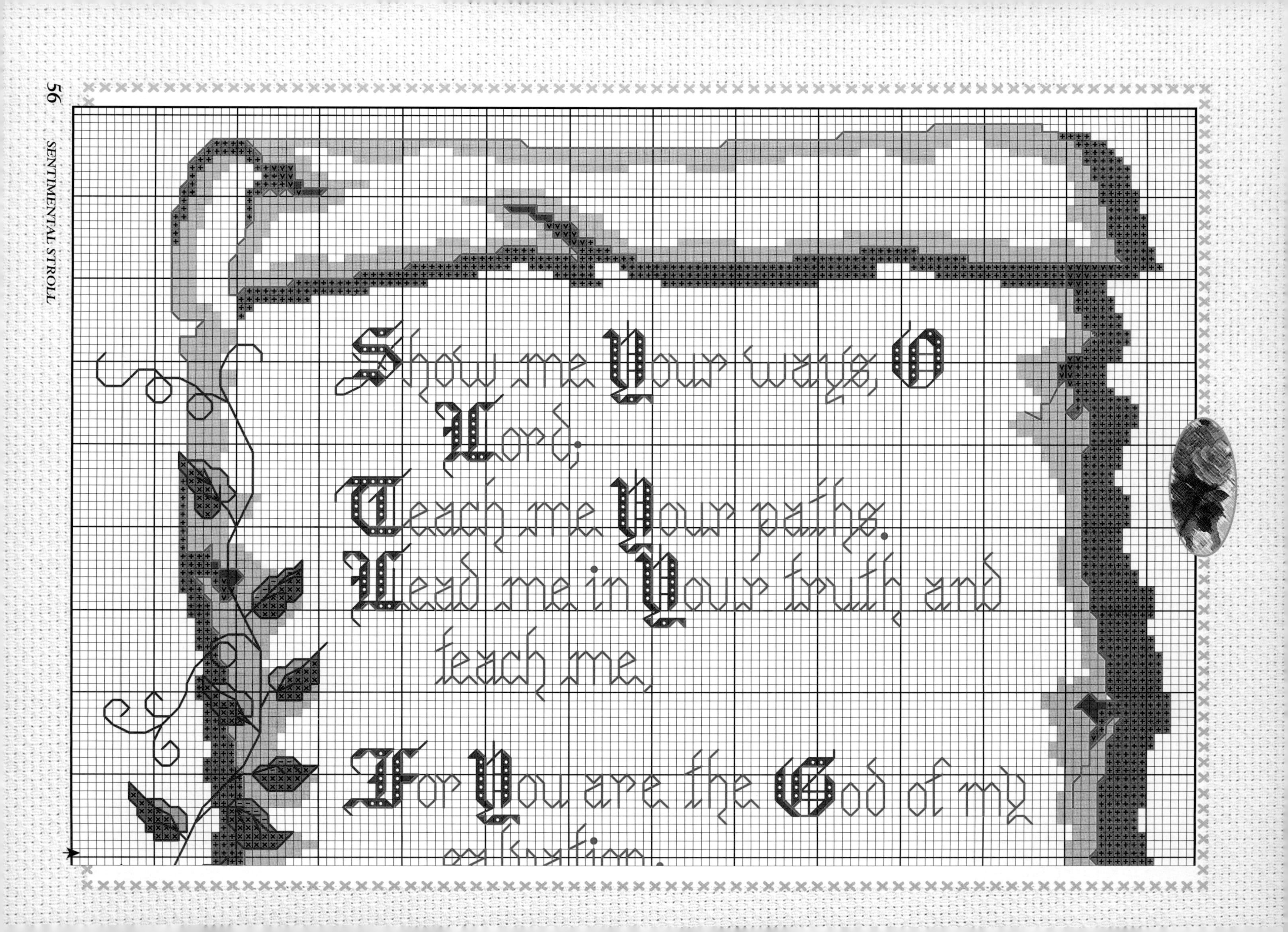
Show me Your ways, O
Lord;
Teach me Your paths.
Lead me in Your truth and
teach me,
For You are the God of my

On You I wait all the day.
Psalm 25:4–5

Antique Auto

Designed by Lois Winston

MATERIALS

11" x 16" piece of tea-dyed 28-count Monaco

INSTRUCTIONS

Center and stitch design, stitching over two threads and using two strands floss for Cross-Stitch and one strand floss for Backstitch.

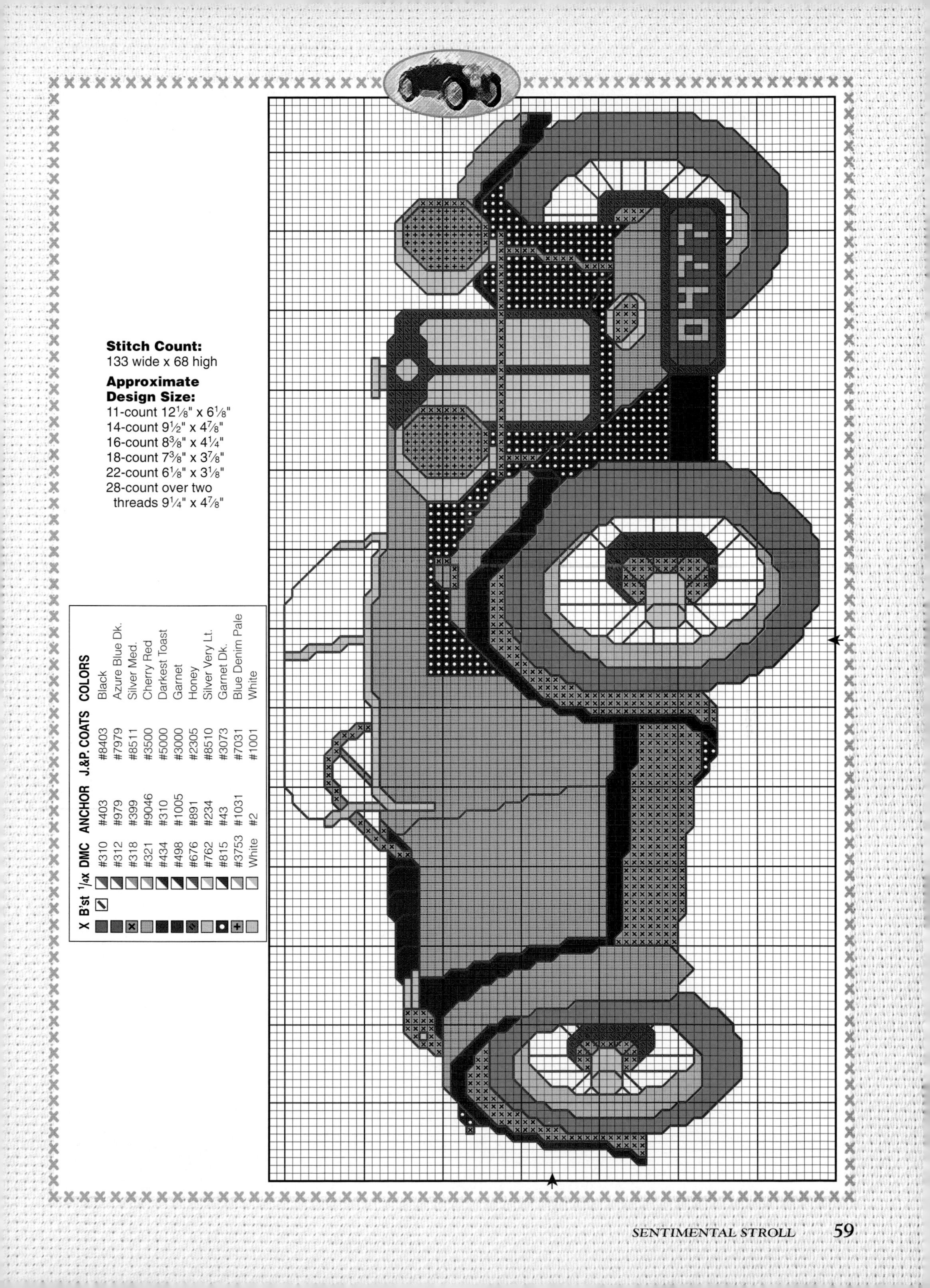

Stitch Count:
133 wide x 68 high

Approximate Design Size:
11-count 12⅛" x 6⅛"
14-count 9½" x 4⅞"
16-count 8⅜" x 4¼"
18-count 7⅜" x 3⅞"
22-count 6⅛" x 3⅛"
28-count over two threads 9¼" x 4⅞"

X	B'st	1/4x	DMC	ANCHOR	J.&P. COATS	COLORS
			#310	#403	#8403	Black
			#312	#979	#7979	Azure Blue Dk.
			#318	#399	#8511	Silver Med.
			#321	#9046	#3500	Cherry Red
			#434	#310	#5000	Darkest Toast
			#498	#1005	#3000	Garnet
			#676	#891	#2305	Honey
			#762	#234	#8510	Silver Very Lt.
			#815	#43	#3073	Garnet Dk.
			#3753	#1031	#7031	Blue Denim Pale
			White	#2	#1001	White

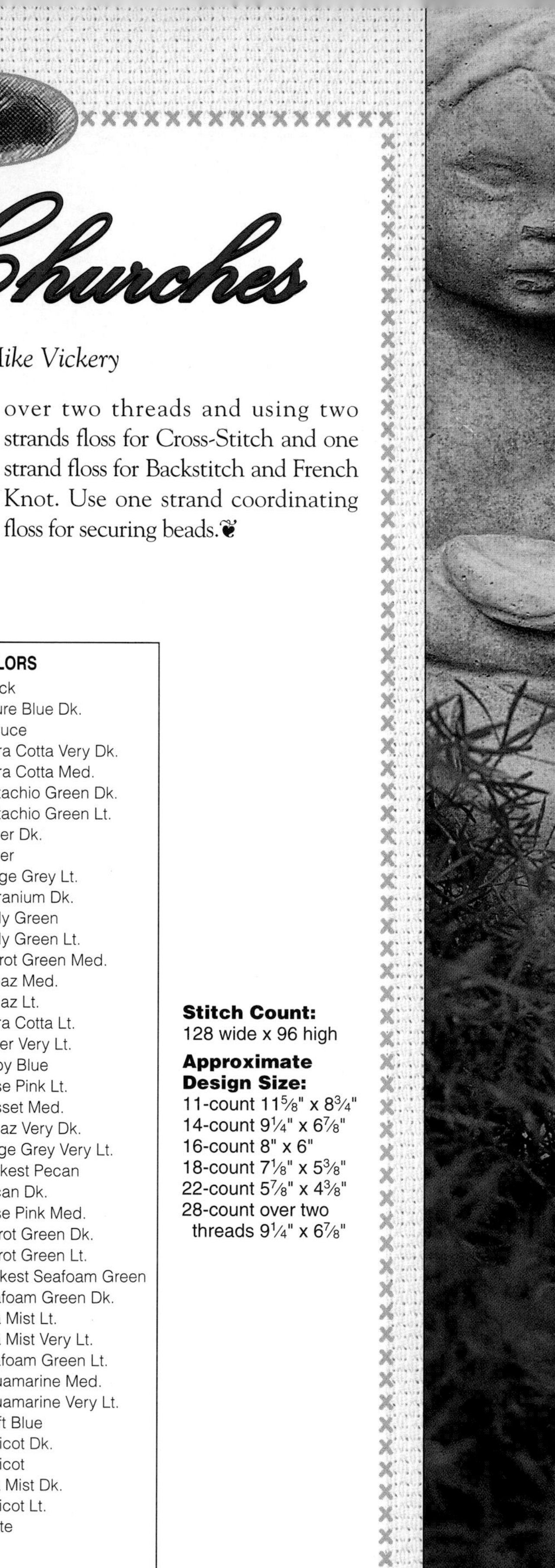

Four Churches

Designed by Mike Vickery

MATERIALS

13" x 15" piece of white 28-count Annabelle®

INSTRUCTIONS

Center and stitch design, stitching over two threads and using two strands floss for Cross-Stitch and one strand floss for Backstitch and French Knot. Use one strand coordinating floss for securing beads.❦

DMC	ANCHOR	J.&P. COATS	COLORS
#310	#403	#8403	Black
#312	#979	#7979	Azure Blue Dk.
#319	#218	#6246	Spruce
#355	#1014	#2339	Terra Cotta Very Dk.
#356	#5975	#2338	Terra Cotta Med.
#367	#217	#6018	Pistachio Green Dk.
#368	#214	#6016	Pistachio Green Lt.
#414	#235	#8513	Silver Dk.
#415	#398	#8398	Silver
#644	#830	#5830	Beige Grey Lt.
#666	#46	#3046	Geranium Dk.
#700	#228	#6227	Kelly Green
#702	#226	#6239	Kelly Green Lt.
#704	#256	#6238	Parrot Green Med.
#725	#305	#2294	Topaz Med.
#727	#293	#2289	Topaz Lt.
#758	#882	#2337	Terra Cotta Lt.
#762	#234	#8510	Silver Very Lt.
#775	#128	#7031	Baby Blue
#776	#24	#3281	Rose Pink Lt.
#781	#309	#5309	Russet Med.
#783	#307	#5307	Topaz Very Dk.
#822	#390	#5933	Beige Grey Very Lt.
#838	#380	#5478	Darkest Pecan
#839	#360	#5360	Pecan Dk.
#899	#52	#3282	Rose Pink Med.
#905	#257	#6258	Parrot Green Dk.
#907	#255	#6001	Parrot Green Lt.
#910	#229	#6031	Darkest Seafoam Green
#912	#209	#6266	Seafoam Green Dk.
#927	#848	#6006	Sea Mist Lt.
#928	#274	#6005	Sea Mist Very Lt.
#954	#203	#6030	Seafoam Green Lt.
#958	#187	#6186	Aquamarine Med.
#964	#185	#6185	Aquamarine Very Lt.
#3325	#129	#7976	Delft Blue
#3340	#329	#2332	Apricot Dk.
#3341	#328	#3008	Apricot
#3768	#779	#6007	Sea Mist Dk.
#3824	#8	#3006	Apricot Lt.
White	#2	#1001	White

(Symbol columns: X, B'st, ¼x, Fr)

SEED BEADS

#02013 Red

Stitch Count:
128 wide x 96 high

Approximate Design Size:
11-count 11⅝" x 8¾"
14-count 9¼" x 6⅞"
16-count 8" x 6"
18-count 7⅛" x 5⅜"
22-count 5⅞" x 4⅜"
28-count over two threads 9¼" x 6⅞"

Stitch a picturesque view of historical churches with architectural appeal.

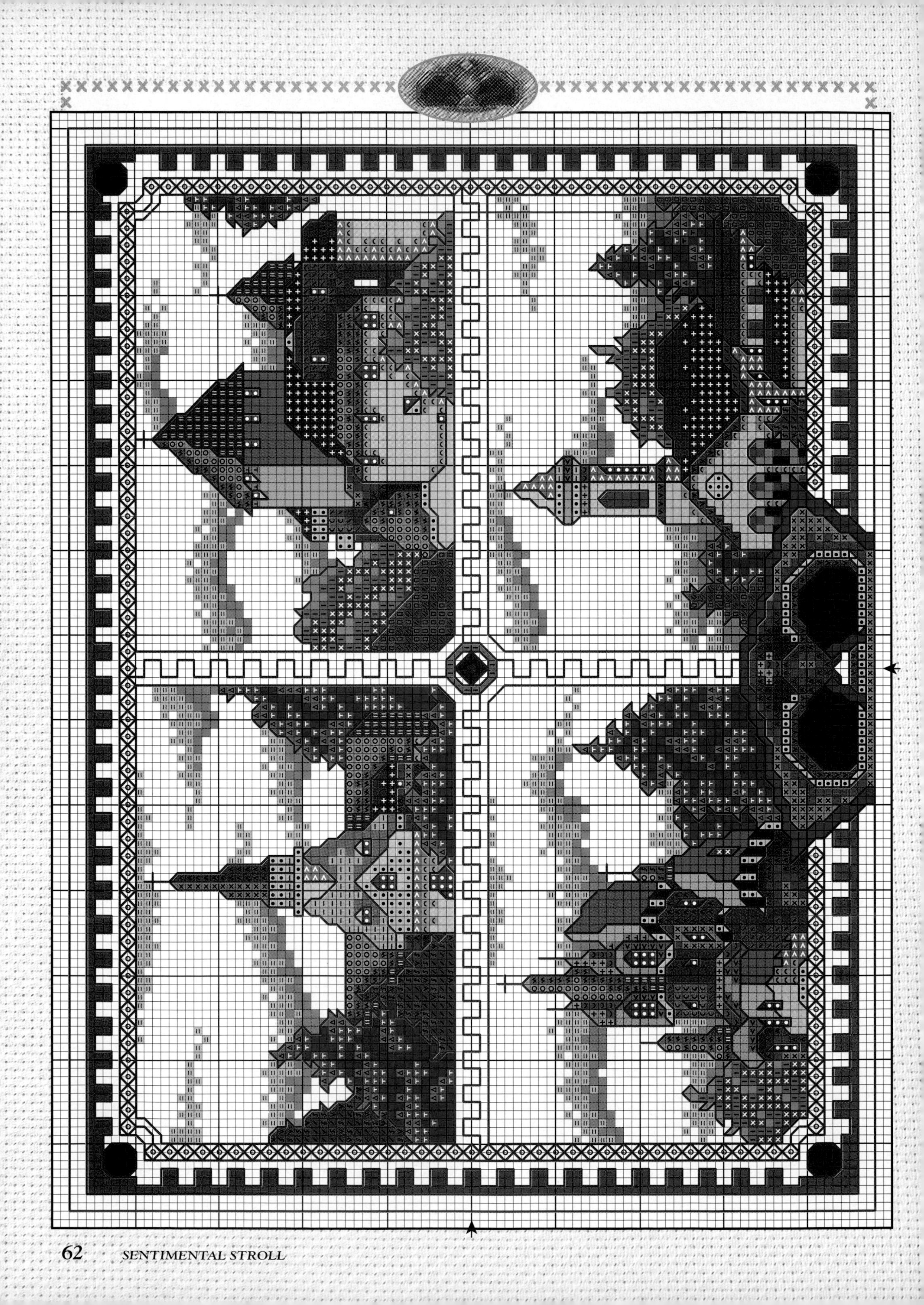

Spindrift

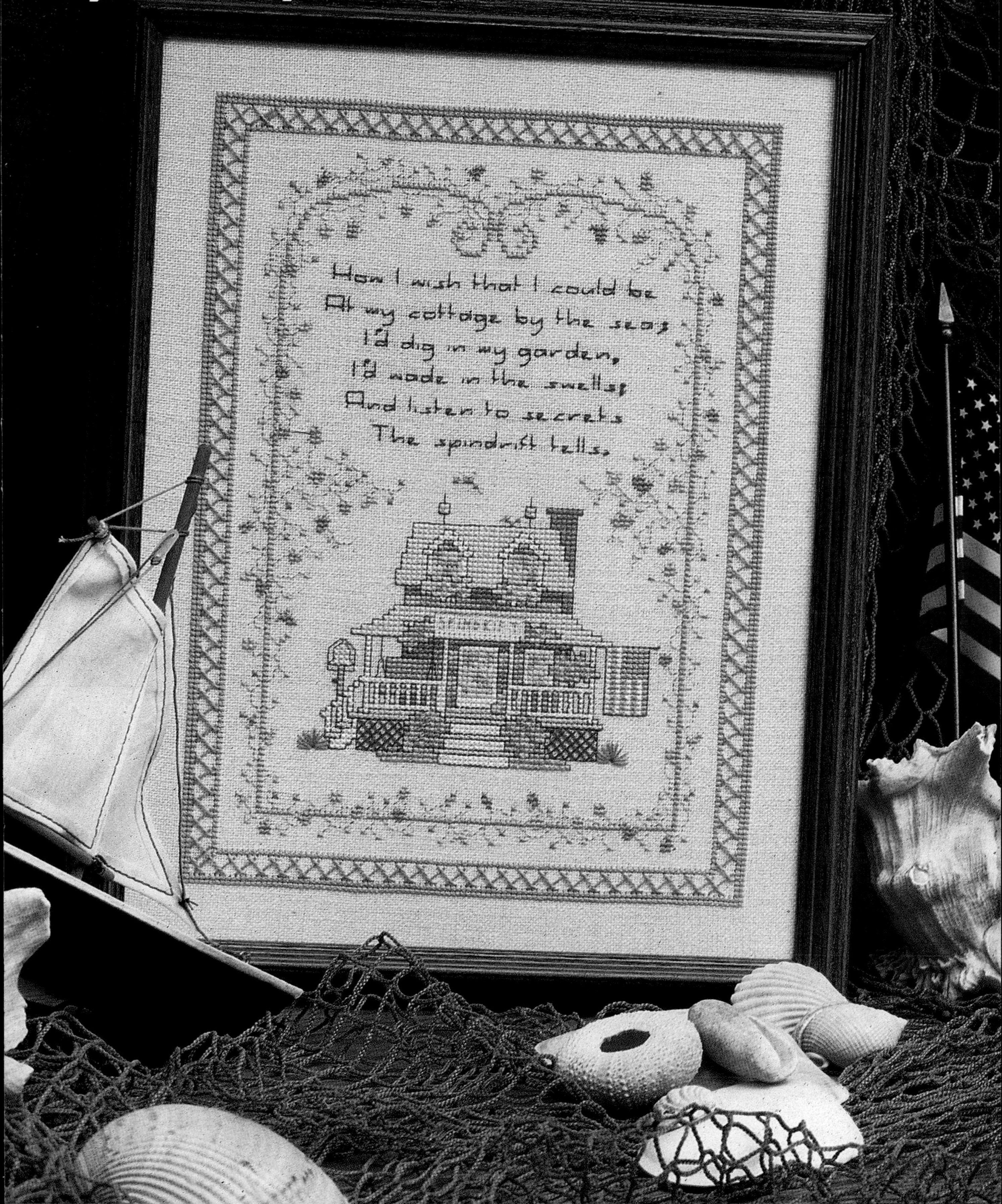
How I wish that I could be
At my cottage by the sea;
I'd dig in my garden,
I'd wade in the swells,
And listen to secrets
The spindrift tells.

Spindrift

Designed by Virginia G. Soskin

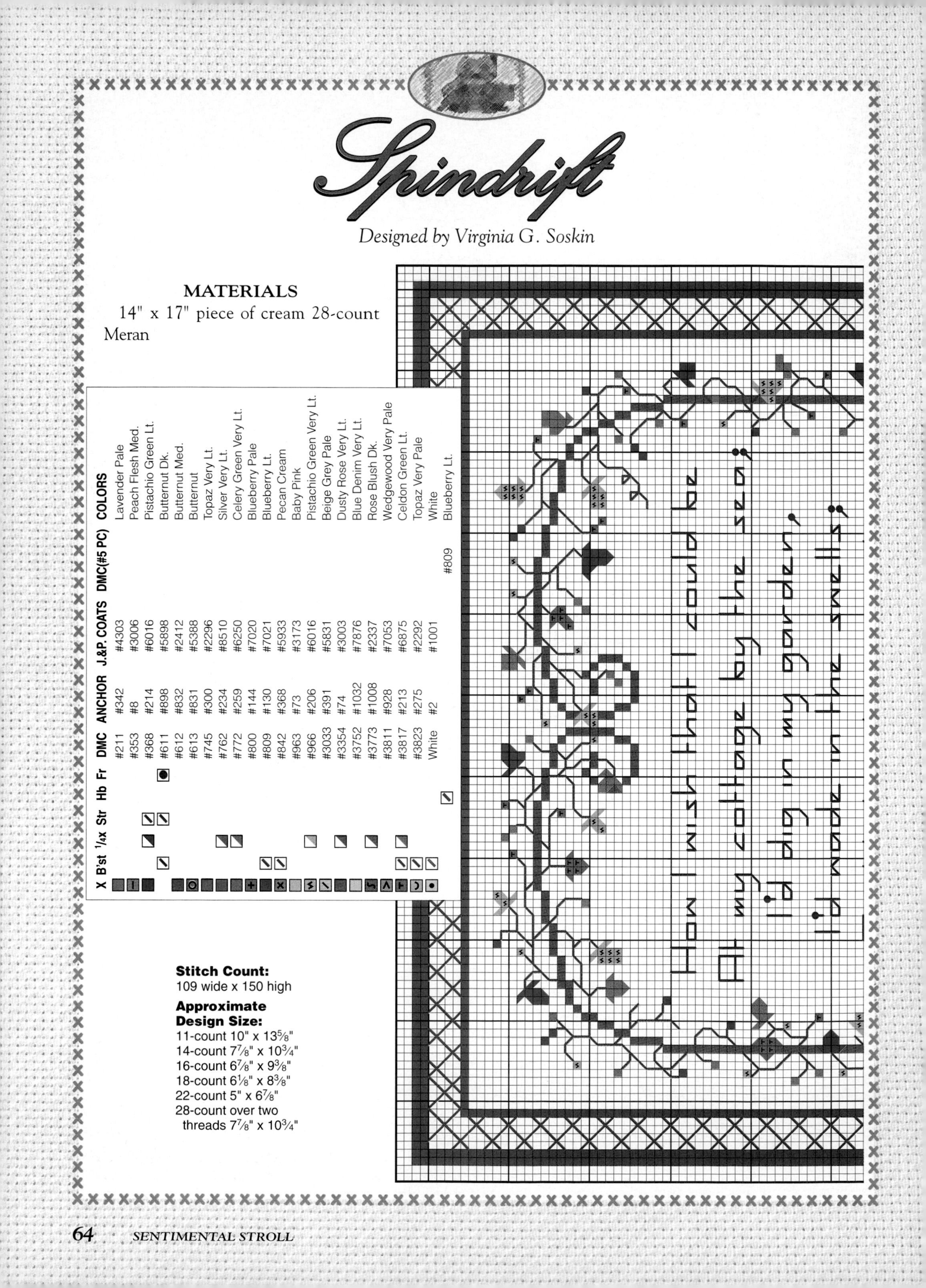

MATERIALS

14" x 17" piece of cream 28-count Meran

X	B'st	1/4x	Str	Hb	Fr	DMC	ANCHOR	J.&P. COATS	DMC(#5 PC)	COLORS
■						#211	#342	#4303		Lavender Pale
■						#353	#8	#3006		Peach Flesh Med.
■		■	■			#368	#214	#6016		Pistachio Green Lt.
	■		■		■	#611	#898	#5898		Butternut Dk.
■						#612	#832	#2412		Butternut Med.
■						#613	#831	#5388		Butternut
■						#745	#300	#2296		Topaz Very Lt.
■		■				#762	#234	#8510		Silver Very Lt.
■		■				#772	#259	#6250		Celery Green Very Lt.
■						#800	#144	#7020		Blueberry Pale
■	■					#809	#130	#7021		Blueberry Lt.
■	■					#842	#368	#5933		Pecan Cream
■						#963	#73	#3173		Baby Pink
■		■				#966	#206	#6016		Pistachio Green Very Lt.
■						#3033	#391	#5831		Beige Grey Pale
■		■				#3354	#74	#3003		Dusty Rose Very Lt.
■						#3752	#1032	#7876		Blue Denim Very Lt.
■		■				#3773	#1008	#2337		Rose Blush Dk.
■						#3811	#928	#7053		Wedgewood Very Pale
■	■	■				#3817	#213	#6875		Celdon Green Lt.
■	■					#3823	#275	#2292		Topaz Very Pale
■	■					White	#2	#1001		White
				■					#809	Blueberry Lt.

Stitch Count:
109 wide x 150 high

Approximate Design Size:
11-count 10" x 13⅝"
14-count 7⅞" x 10¾"
16-count 6⅞" x 9⅜"
18-count 6⅛" x 8⅜"
22-count 5" x 6⅞"
28-count over two threads 7⅞" x 10¾"

INSTRUCTIONS

Center and stitch design, stitching over two threads and using two strands floss for Cross-Stitch and Backstitch and French Knot of lettering. Use two strands floss for Straight Stitch, working lattice detail stitches crosswise above and below in a weaving pattern as indicated on graph. Use one strand pearl cotton for Herringbone Stitch. Use one strand floss for remaining Backstitch.❦

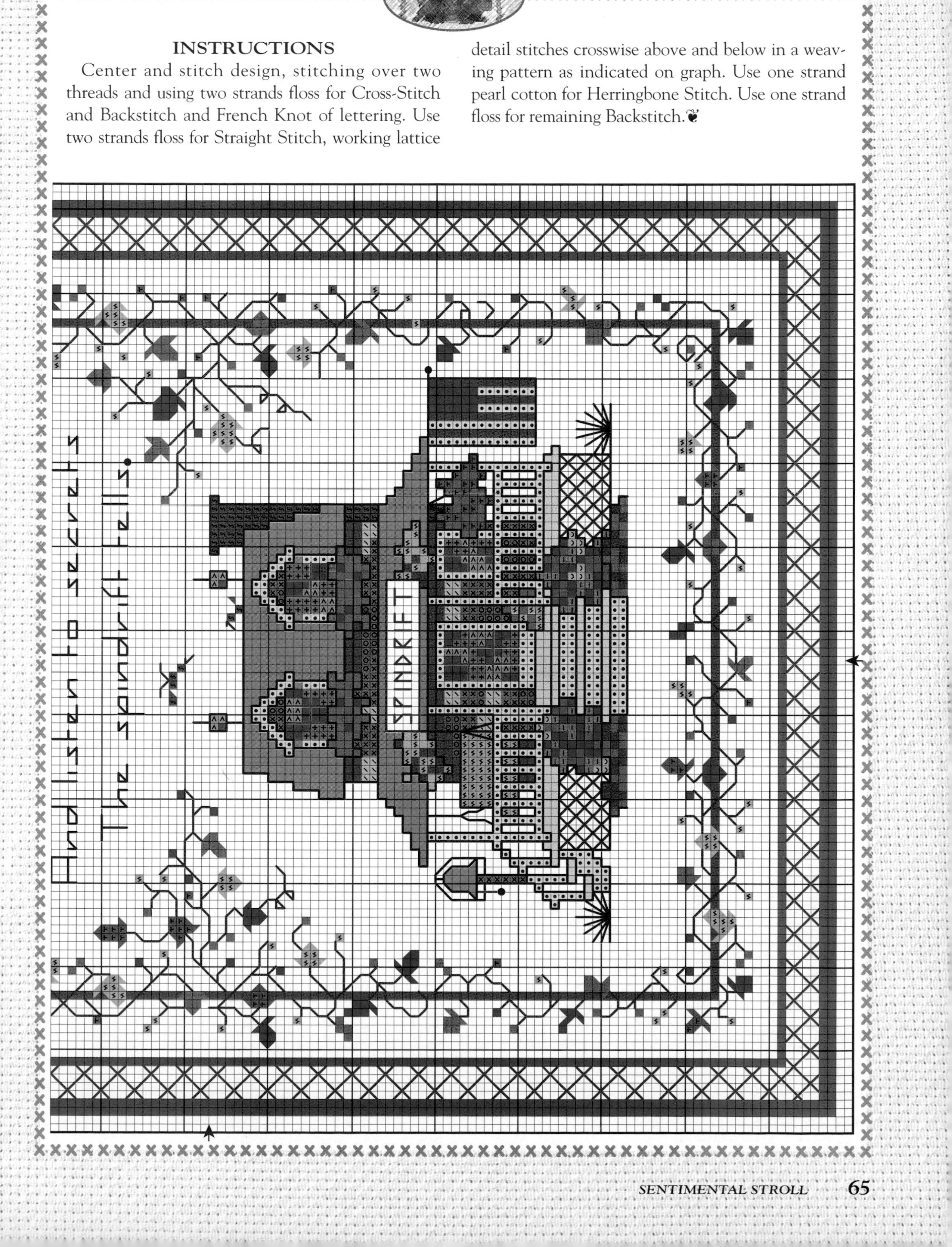

Exclusively Samplers

Create lovely sampler designs to display finely tuned skills and cherished words of kindness. Each stitch becomes a masterpiece as you create your personal rendition of an ages-old form of pattern preservation.

ABCDEFGHIJKLMN
OPQRSTUVWXYZ
A house is made of
brick and stone
A home is made of
Love alone

Somebunny Special

Designed by Jacquelyn Fox

MATERIALS

14" x 17" piece of apricot 25-count Lugana®

INSTRUCTIONS

Selecting desired letters and numbers from Alphabet & Numbers graph, center and stitch design, stitching over two threads and using two strands floss or two strands floss held together with one strand blending filament for Cross-Stitch. Use one strand floss or one strand cord for Backstitch, Modified Eyelet Stitch and Lazy Daisy Stitch.

Alphabet & Numbers

Announcing
the
arrival of
special
Katherine Ruth
July 23, 1996

Announcing
the
arrival of
Somebunny
special
Katherine Ru
July 23, 199
7lbs 1oz

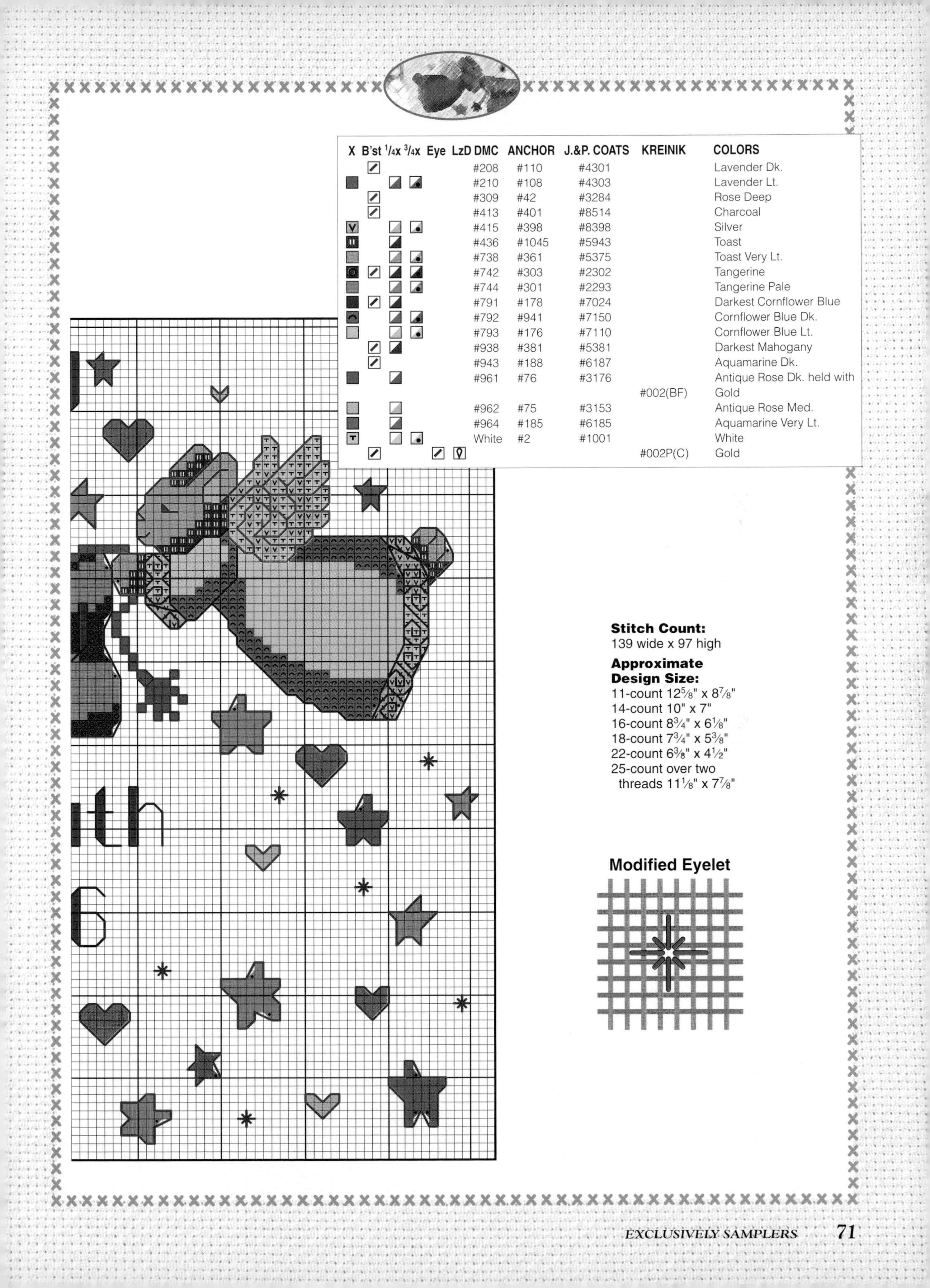

X	B'st	1/4x	3/4x	Eye	LzD	DMC	ANCHOR	J.&P. COATS	KREINIK	COLORS
	■					#208	#110	#4301		Lavender Dk.
■		■	■			#210	#108	#4303		Lavender Lt.
	■					#309	#42	#3284		Rose Deep
	■					#413	#401	#8514		Charcoal
V		■	■			#415	#398	#8398		Silver
II		■				#436	#1045	#5943		Toast
■		■	■			#738	#361	#5375		Toast Very Lt.
■	■	■	■			#742	#303	#2302		Tangerine
■		■	■			#744	#301	#2293		Tangerine Pale
■	■	■				#791	#178	#7024		Darkest Cornflower Blue
■		■	■			#792	#941	#7150		Cornflower Blue Dk.
■		■	■			#793	#176	#7110		Cornflower Blue Lt.
	■	■				#938	#381	#5381		Darkest Mahogany
	■					#943	#188	#6187		Aquamarine Dk.
■		■				#961	#76	#3176		Antique Rose Dk. held with
									#002(BF)	Gold
■		■				#962	#75	#3153		Antique Rose Med.
■		■				#964	#185	#6185		Aquamarine Very Lt.
T		■	■			White	#2	#1001		White
	■			■	■				#002P(C)	Gold

Stitch Count:
139 wide x 97 high

Approximate Design Size:
11-count $12\frac{5}{8}$" x $8\frac{7}{8}$"
14-count 10" x 7"
16-count $8\frac{3}{4}$" x $6\frac{1}{8}$"
18-count $7\frac{3}{4}$" x $5\frac{3}{8}$"
22-count $6\frac{3}{8}$" x $4\frac{1}{2}$"
25-count over two threads $11\frac{1}{8}$" x $7\frac{7}{8}$"

Modified Eyelet

ABCDEFGHIJKLMN
OPQRSTUVWXYZ
A house is made of
brick and stone
A home is made of
Love alone.
1234567890

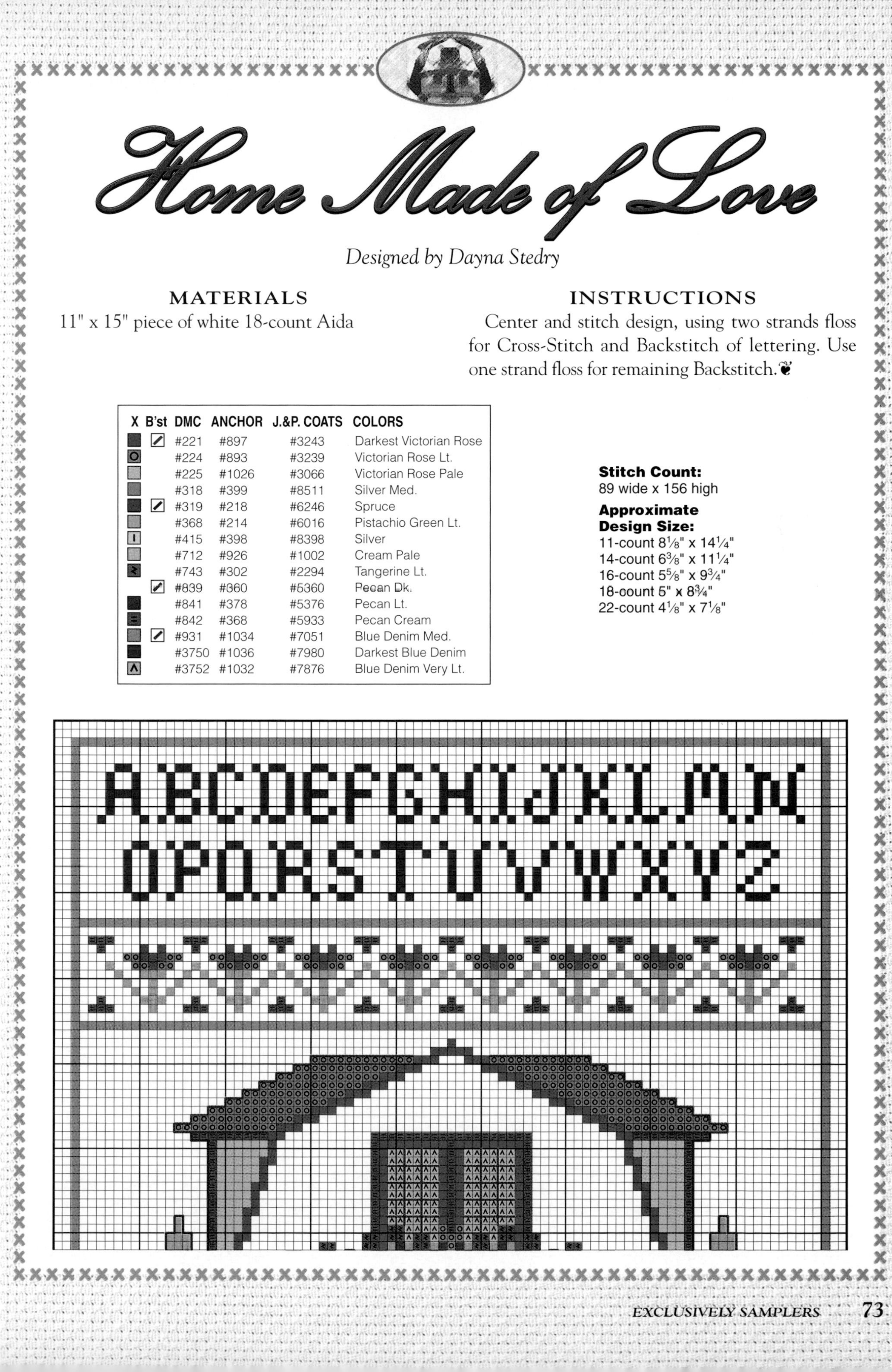

Home Made of Love

Designed by Dayna Stedry

MATERIALS

11" x 15" piece of white 18-count Aida

INSTRUCTIONS

Center and stitch design, using two strands floss for Cross-Stitch and Backstitch of lettering. Use one strand floss for remaining Backstitch.

X	B'st	DMC	ANCHOR	J.&P. COATS	COLORS
■	✓	#221	#897	#3243	Darkest Victorian Rose
O		#224	#893	#3239	Victorian Rose Lt.
■		#225	#1026	#3066	Victorian Rose Pale
■		#318	#399	#8511	Silver Med.
■	✓	#319	#218	#6246	Spruce
■		#368	#214	#6016	Pistachio Green Lt.
I		#415	#398	#8398	Silver
■		#712	#926	#1002	Cream Pale
≷		#743	#302	#2294	Tangerine Lt.
	✓	#839	#360	#5360	Pecan Dk.
■		#841	#378	#5376	Pecan Lt.
≡		#842	#368	#5933	Pecan Cream
■	✓	#931	#1034	#7051	Blue Denim Med.
■		#3750	#1036	#7980	Darkest Blue Denim
Λ		#3752	#1032	#7876	Blue Denim Very Lt.

Stitch Count:
89 wide x 156 high

Approximate Design Size:
11-count 8⅛" x 14¼"
14-count 6⅜" x 11¼"
16-count 5⅝" x 9¾"
18-count 5" x 8¾"
22-count 4⅛" x 7⅛"

X	B'st	DMC	ANCHOR	J.&P. COATS	COLORS
■	✓	#221	#897	#3243	Darkest Victorian Rose
O		#224	#893	#3239	Victorian Rose Lt.
■		#225	#1026	#3066	Victorian Rose Pale
■		#318	#399	#8511	Silver Med.
■	✓	#319	#218	#6246	Spruce
■		#368	#214	#6016	Pistachio Green Lt.
I		#415	#398	#8398	Silver
■		#712	#926	#1002	Cream Pale
■		#743	#302	#2294	Tangerine Lt.
	✓	#839	#360	#5360	Pecan Dk.
■		#841	#378	#5376	Pecan Lt.
■		#842	#368	#5933	Pecan Cream
■	✓	#931	#1034	#7051	Blue Denim Med.
■		#3750	#1036	#7980	Darkest Blue Denim
Λ		#3752	#1032	#7876	Blue Denim Very Lt.

Designed by Patricia Hestand

MATERIALS

15" x 19" piece of ivory 28-count Lugana®

INSTRUCTIONS

Center and stitch design, stitching over two threads and using two strands floss for Cross-Stitch and one strand floss for Backstitch.

Proudly display this wise old proverb and honor your family name.

Stitch Count:
127 wide x 174 high

Approximate Design Size:
11-count 11⅝" x 15⅞"
14-count 9⅛" x 12½"
16-count 8" x 10⅞"
18-count 7⅛" x 9¾"
22-count 5⅞" x 8"
28-count over two threads 9⅛" x 12½"

X	B'st	DMC	ANCHOR	J.&P. COATS	COLORS
■		#223	#895	#3240	Victorian Rose Med.
■		#501	#878	#6878	Sage Green Dk.
■		#930	#1035	#7052	Blue Denim Dk.
■		#931	#1034	#7051	Blue Denim Med.
■		#932	#1033	#7050	Blue Denim Lt.
	⁄	#3750	#1036	#7980	Darkest Blue Denim

A good name is rather
to be chosen than
great riches, and loving
favour rather than
silver and gold. PROVERBS 22:1
1234567890

ABCDEF
GHIJKL
MNOPQR
STUVWX
YZ
12345
67890

Awaken your imagination with colorful beauty and fantasy friends by stitching this charming sampler.

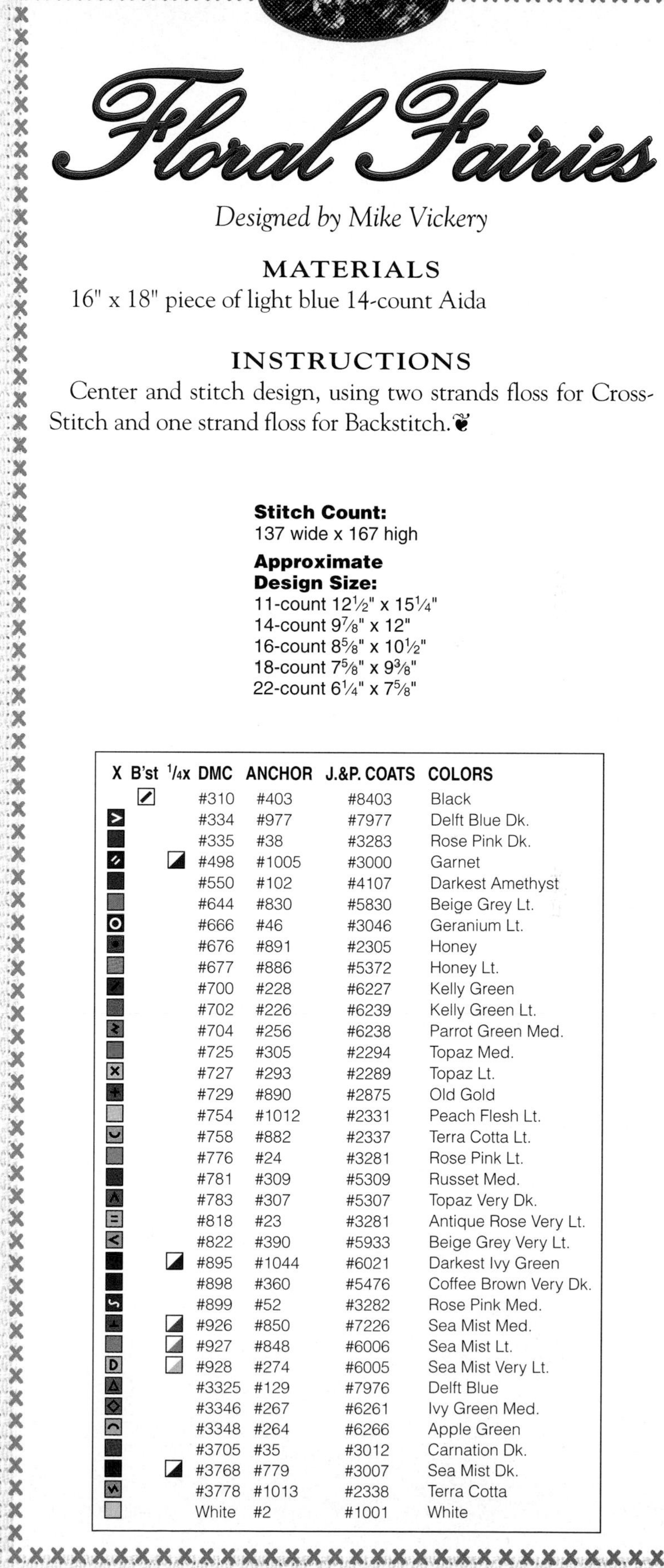

Floral Fairies

Designed by Mike Vickery

MATERIALS

16" x 18" piece of light blue 14-count Aida

INSTRUCTIONS

Center and stitch design, using two strands floss for Cross-Stitch and one strand floss for Backstitch.

Stitch Count:
137 wide x 167 high

Approximate Design Size:
11-count 12½" x 15¼"
14-count 9⅞" x 12"
16-count 8⅝" x 10½"
18-count 7⅝" x 9⅜"
22-count 6¼" x 7⅝"

X	B'st	¼x	DMC	ANCHOR	J.&P. COATS	COLORS
			#310	#403	#8403	Black
			#334	#977	#7977	Delft Blue Dk.
			#335	#38	#3283	Rose Pink Dk.
			#498	#1005	#3000	Garnet
			#550	#102	#4107	Darkest Amethyst
			#644	#830	#5830	Beige Grey Lt.
			#666	#46	#3046	Geranium Lt.
			#676	#891	#2305	Honey
			#677	#886	#5372	Honey Lt.
			#700	#228	#6227	Kelly Green
			#702	#226	#6239	Kelly Green Lt.
			#704	#256	#6238	Parrot Green Med.
			#725	#305	#2294	Topaz Med.
			#727	#293	#2289	Topaz Lt.
			#729	#890	#2875	Old Gold
			#754	#1012	#2331	Peach Flesh Lt.
			#758	#882	#2337	Terra Cotta Lt.
			#776	#24	#3281	Rose Pink Lt.
			#781	#309	#5309	Russet Med.
			#783	#307	#5307	Topaz Very Dk.
			#818	#23	#3281	Antique Rose Very Lt.
			#822	#390	#5933	Beige Grey Very Lt.
			#895	#1044	#6021	Darkest Ivy Green
			#898	#360	#5476	Coffee Brown Very Dk.
			#899	#52	#3282	Rose Pink Med.
			#926	#850	#7226	Sea Mist Med.
			#927	#848	#6006	Sea Mist Lt.
			#928	#274	#6005	Sea Mist Very Lt.
			#3325	#129	#7976	Delft Blue
			#3346	#267	#6261	Ivy Green Med.
			#3348	#264	#6266	Apple Green
			#3705	#35	#3012	Carnation Dk.
			#3768	#779	#3007	Sea Mist Dk.
			#3778	#1013	#2338	Terra Cotta
			White	#2	#1001	White

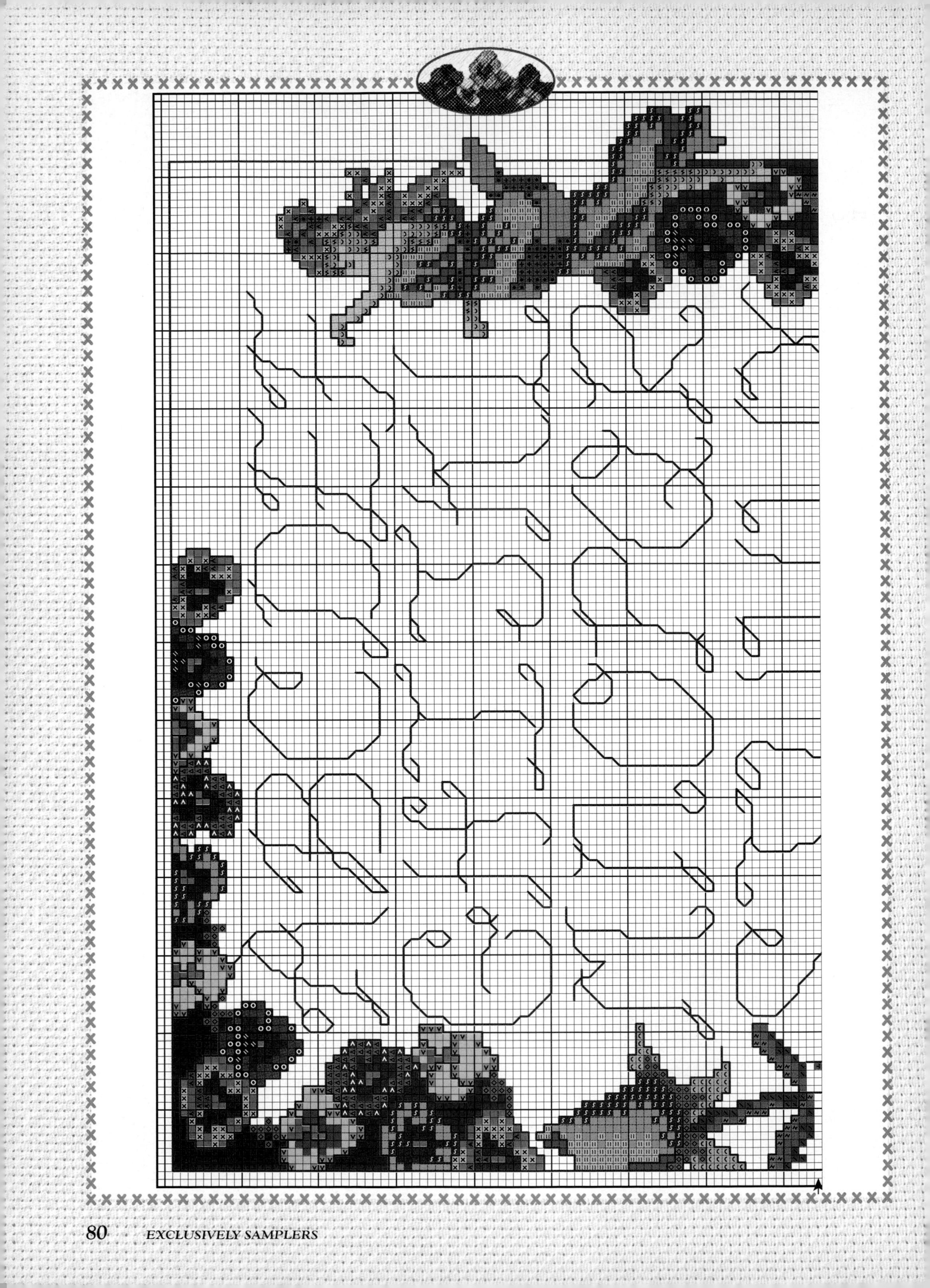

Designed by Jean Higgins

MATERIALS

13" x 14" piece of white 28-count Monaco

INSTRUCTIONS

Selecting desired numbers from Numbers graph, center and stitch design, stitching over two threads and using two strands floss or one strand fine braid or ribbon for Cross-Stitch and Backstitch.❦

Stitch Count:
91 wide x 111 high
Approximate Design Size:
11-count 8⅜" x 10⅛"
14-count 6½" x 8"
16-count 5¾" x 7"
18-count 5⅛" x 6¼"
22-count 4⅛" x 5⅛"
28-count over two threads 6½" x 8"
X B'st DMC ANCHOR J.&P. COATS KREINIK COLORS
#815 #43 #3000 Garnet Dk.
#001(#8) Silver
#001HL(1/16"R) Silver
#002(#8) Gold
Numbers
MERRY MERRY
CHRISTMAS
Christmas Joys
are multiplied
with
Friends & Loved Ones
at your side.
1997

Roses are Red

Designed by Kathy Morris

MATERIALS

15" x 19" piece of white 14-count Aida

INSTRUCTIONS

Center and stitch design, using three strands floss for Cross-Stitch and two strands floss for Backstitch.❦

Stitch Count:
120 wide x 180 high

Approximate Design Size:
11-count 11" x 16⅜"
14-count 8⅝" x 12⅞"
16-count 7½" x 11¼"
18-count 6¾" x 10"
22-count 5½" x 8¼"

Add a romantic touch to any room and stitch this heartwarming sampler featuring poetic charm and floral beauty.

Roses are red,
Violets are blue!

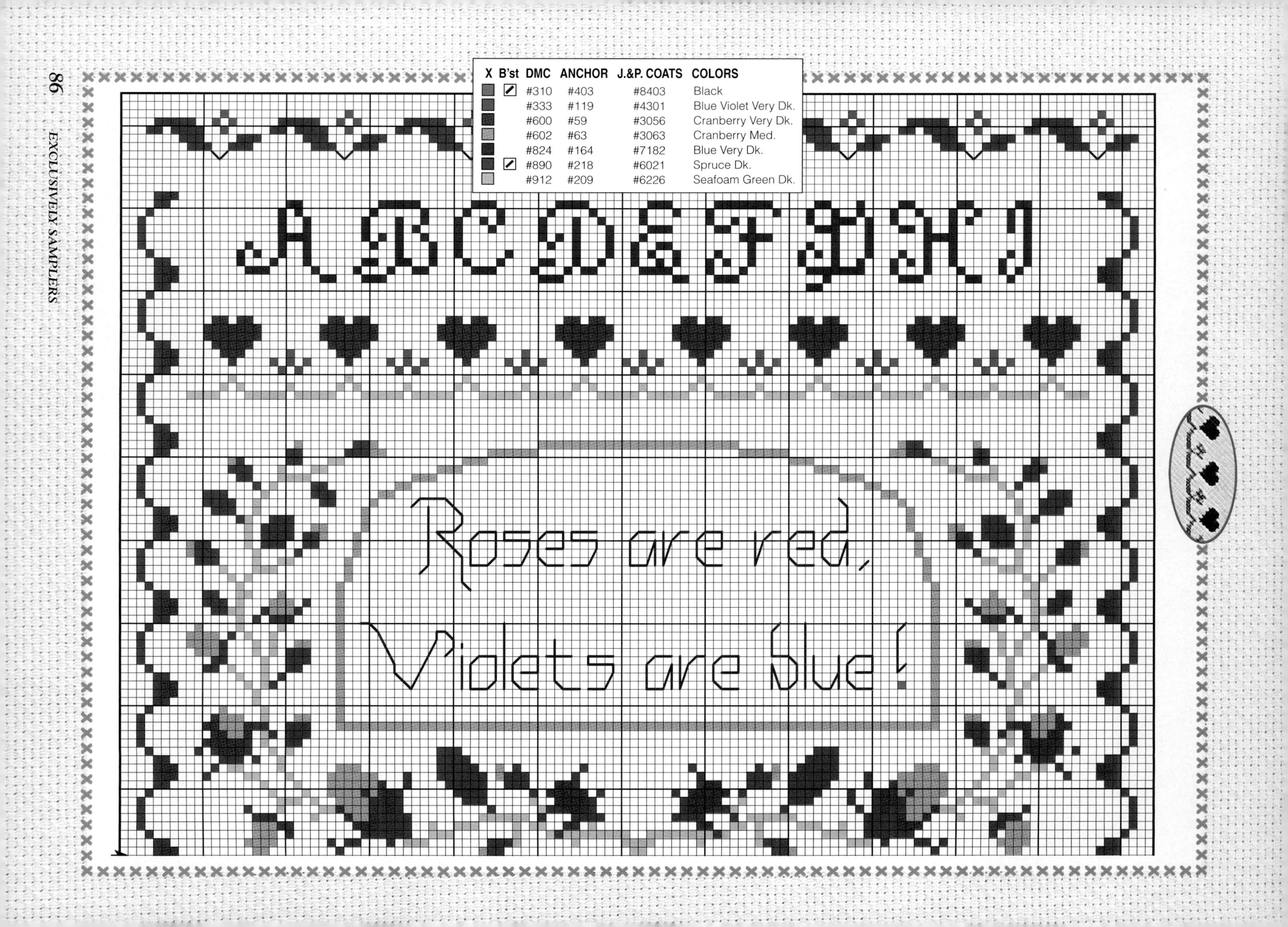

X	B'st	DMC	ANCHOR	J.&P. COATS	COLORS
■	⁄	#310	#403	#8403	Black
■		#333	#119	#4301	Blue Violet Very Dk.
■		#600	#59	#3056	Cranberry Very Dk.
■		#602	#63	#3063	Cranberry Med.
■		#824	#164	#7182	Blue Very Dk.
■	⁄	#890	#218	#6021	Spruce Dk.
■		#912	#209	#6226	Seafoam Green Dk.

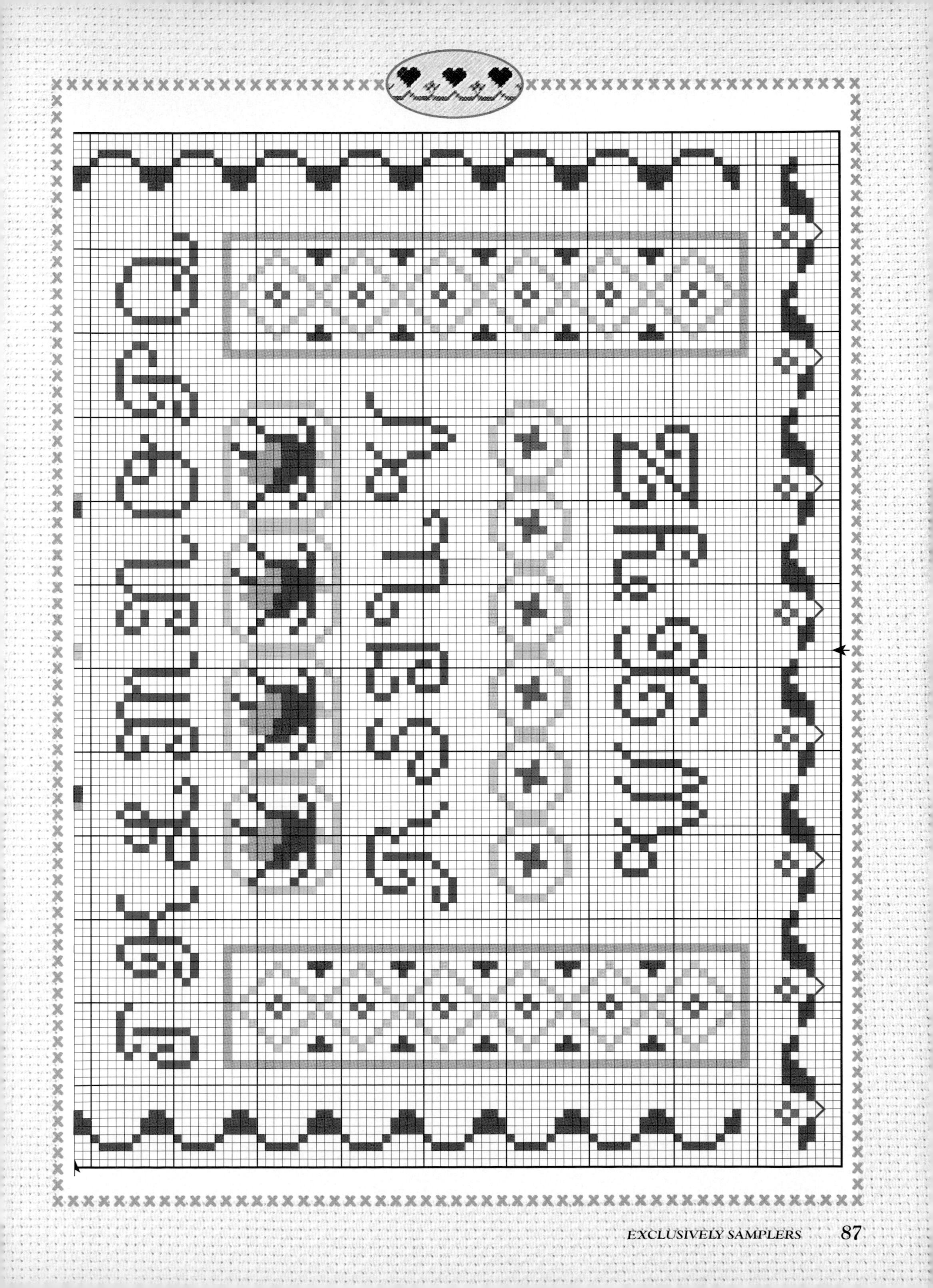

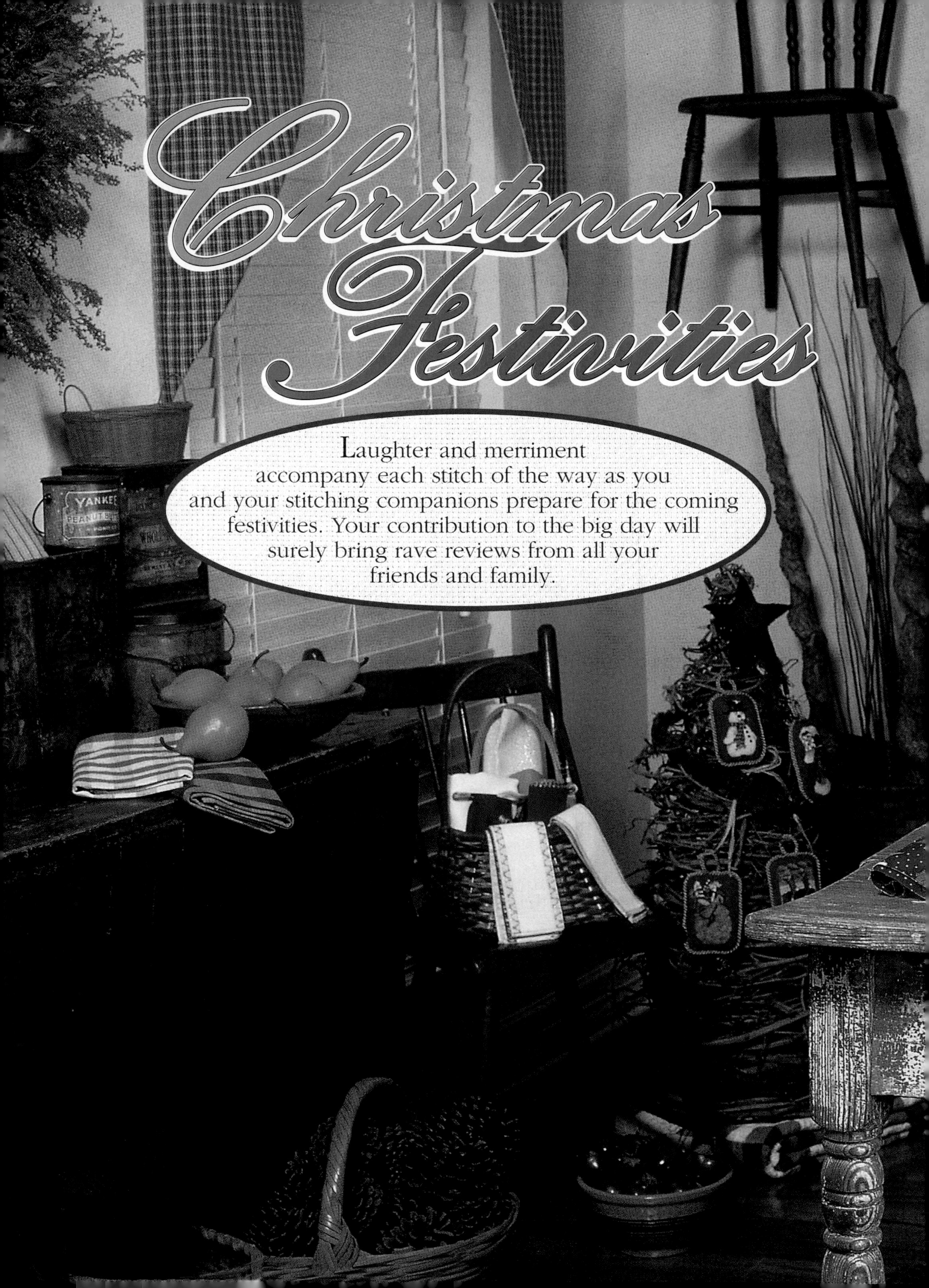

Christmas Festivities

Laughter and merriment accompany each stitch of the way as you and your stitching companions prepare for the coming festivities. Your contribution to the big day will surely bring rave reviews from all your friends and family.

Christmas
Joy is in
my Heart

Christmas Joy

Designed by Ursula Michael

MATERIALS

One 8½" x 11¾" piece and one 11¾" x 18½" piece of silver/white 20-count Valerie; ⅓ yd. fabric; ¾ yd. lining fabric; 1¾ yds. ribbon; 14" dowel rod

INSTRUCTIONS

1: Center and stitch "Message" design onto 11¾" x 18½" piece beginning one inch from top edge and "Angel" design onto 8½" x 11¾" piece of Valerie, stitching over two threads and using three strands floss or one strand fine braid or ombre for Cross-Stitch. Use two strands floss or fine braid for Backstitch and Straight Stitch.

NOTES: From fabric, cut two 2" x 11¾" for A pieces and two 2" x 21½" for B pieces. From lining fabric, cut one 8½" x 11¾" for "Angel" lining and one 13¾" x 21½" for back. Use ½" seam allowance.

2: With right sides facing, sew "Angel" design and "Angel" lining together along top edge, forming pocket. Turn right sides out; press. Baste bottom and side edges of pocket to "Message" design as shown in photo, forming front.

3: For Cardholder, with right sides facing, sew A and B pieces to front according to Assembly Diagram. With right sides facing, sew front and back together, leaving an opening. Turn right sides out; slip stitch opening closed.

4: Cut ribbon into three equal pieces. Sew ribbon to top of Cardholder and attach dowel rod as shown.❦

Angel
Stitch Count:
103 wide x 67 high

Approximate Design Size:
11-count 9⅜" x 6⅛"
14-count 7⅜" x 4⅞"
16-count 6½" x 4¼"
18-count 5¾" x 3¾"
22-count 4¾" x 3⅛"
20-count over two threads 10⅜" x 6¾"

Message
Stitch Count:
105 wide x 99 high

Approximate Design Size:
11-count 9⅝" x 9"
14-count 7½" x 7⅛"
16-count 6⅝" x 6¼"
18-count 5⅞" x 5½"
22-count 4⅞" x 4½"
20-count over two threads 10½" x 10"

DMC	ANCHOR	J.&P. COATS	COLORS
#309	#42	#3284	Rose Deep
#321	#9046	#3500	Cherry Red
#413	#401	#8514	Charcoal
#435	#1046	#5371	Toast Dk.
#700	#228	#6227	Kelly Green
#796	#133	#7100	Royal Blue
#798	#131	#7200	Blueberry Dk.
#809	#130	#7021	Blueberry Lt.
#931	#1034	#7051	Blue Denim Med.

DMC	ANCHOR	J.&P. COATS	KREINIK	COLORS
#951	#1010	#3335		Blush Lt.
#3326	#36	#3126		Rose Pink
#3753	#1031	#7031		Blue Denim Pale
#3760	#161	#7169		Peacock Blue Dk.
White	#2	#1001		White
			#091 (#8)	Star Yellow
			#1800 (Ombre)	Misty Sunrise
			#4639 (#8)	Light Aqua

Message

Angel

Home for the Holidays

Designed by Darlene Polachic

MATERIALS

9" x 10" piece of white 14-count Aida; ½ yd. piping; Mounting board; Batting; Craft glue or glue gun

INSTRUCTIONS

1: Center and stitch design, using two strands floss for Cross-Stitch and one strand floss for Backstitch and French Knot.

NOTE: From batting and mounting board, cut one each 4⅛" x 4½".

2: Center and mount design over batting and board. Glue piping around outside edges of mounted design.

Stitch Count:
45 wide x 50 high

Approximate Design Size:
11-count 4⅛" x 4⅝"
14-count 3¼" x 3⅝"
16-count 2⅞" x 3⅛"
18-count 2½" x 2⅞"
22-count 2⅛" x 2⅜"

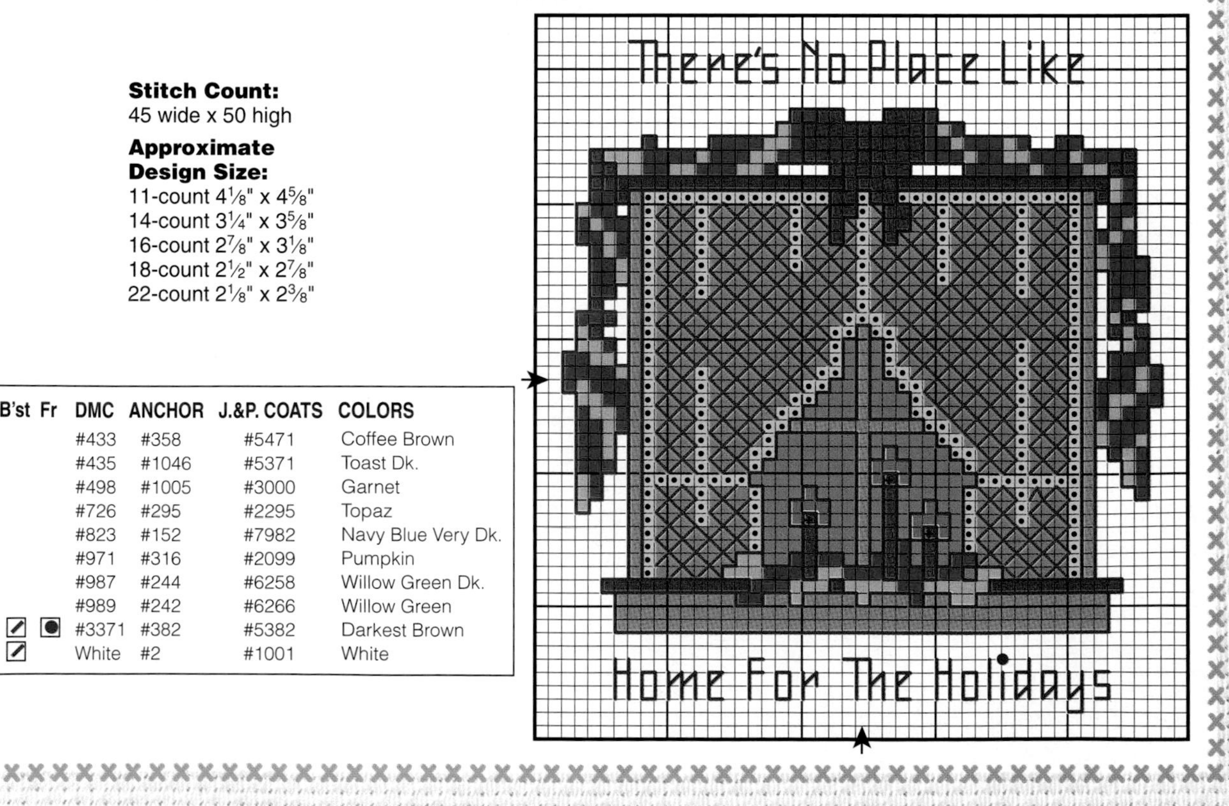

X	B'st	Fr	DMC	ANCHOR	J.&P. COATS	COLORS
■			#433	#358	#5471	Coffee Brown
■			#435	#1046	#5371	Toast Dk.
■			#498	#1005	#3000	Garnet
■			#726	#295	#2295	Topaz
■			#823	#152	#7982	Navy Blue Very Dk.
■			#971	#316	#2099	Pumpkin
■			#987	#244	#6258	Willow Green Dk.
■			#989	#242	#6266	Willow Green
	⁄	●	#3371	#382	#5382	Darkest Brown
•	⁄		White	#2	#1001	White

Complement your Christmas decor with the majestic beauty of winter and this picturesque scene.

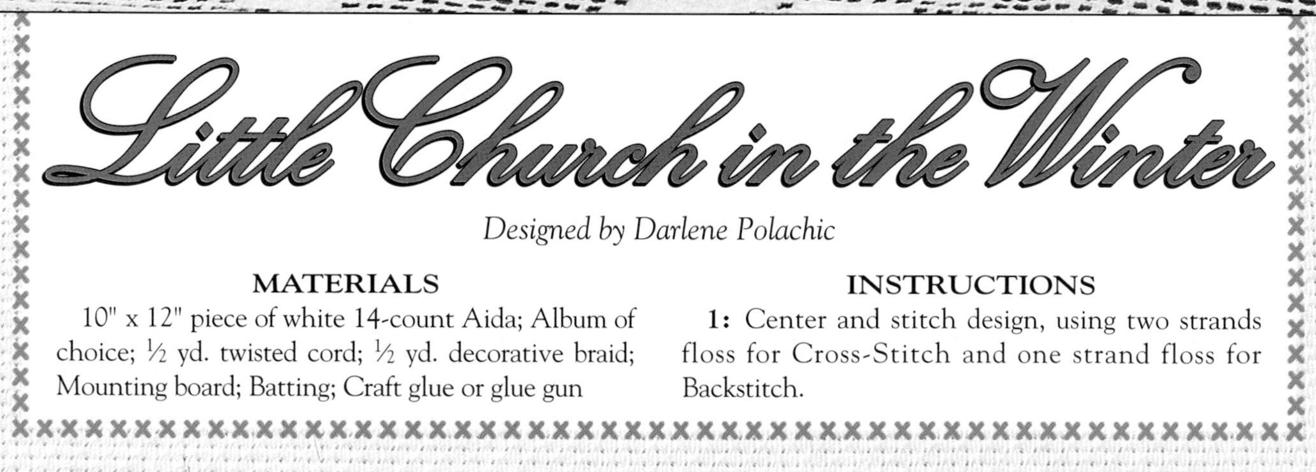

Little Church in the Winter

Designed by Darlene Polachic

MATERIALS

10" x 12" piece of white 14-count Aida; Album of choice; ½ yd. twisted cord; ½ yd. decorative braid; Mounting board; Batting; Craft glue or glue gun

INSTRUCTIONS

1: Center and stitch design, using two strands floss for Cross-Stitch and one strand floss for Backstitch.

NOTE: From batting and mounting board, cut one each 4⅜" x 6¼".

2: Center and mount design over batting and board. Glue cord around outside edges of design.

3: Center and glue mounted design to front of album. Glue braid to album around mounted design as shown in photo.

Stitch Count:
57 wide x 87 high

Approximate Design Size:
11-count 5¼" x 8"
14-count 4⅛" x 6¼"
16-count 3⅝" x 5½"
18-count 3¼" x 4⅞"
22-count 2⅝" x 4"

X	B'st	DMC	ANCHOR	J.&P. COATS	COLORS
■		#309	#42	#3284	Rose Deep
■		#319	#218	#6246	Spruce
■		#433	#358	#5471	Coffee Brown
≷		#435	#1046	#5371	Toast Dk.
■		#437	#362	#5942	Toast Lt.
■		#727	#293	#2289	Topaz Lt.
■		#818	#23	#3281	Antique Rose Very Lt.
V		#828	#158	#7053	Larkspur Lt.
	⁄	#938	#381	#5381	Darkest Mahogany
+		#3328	#1024	#3071	Salmon Dk.
■		White	#2	#1001	White

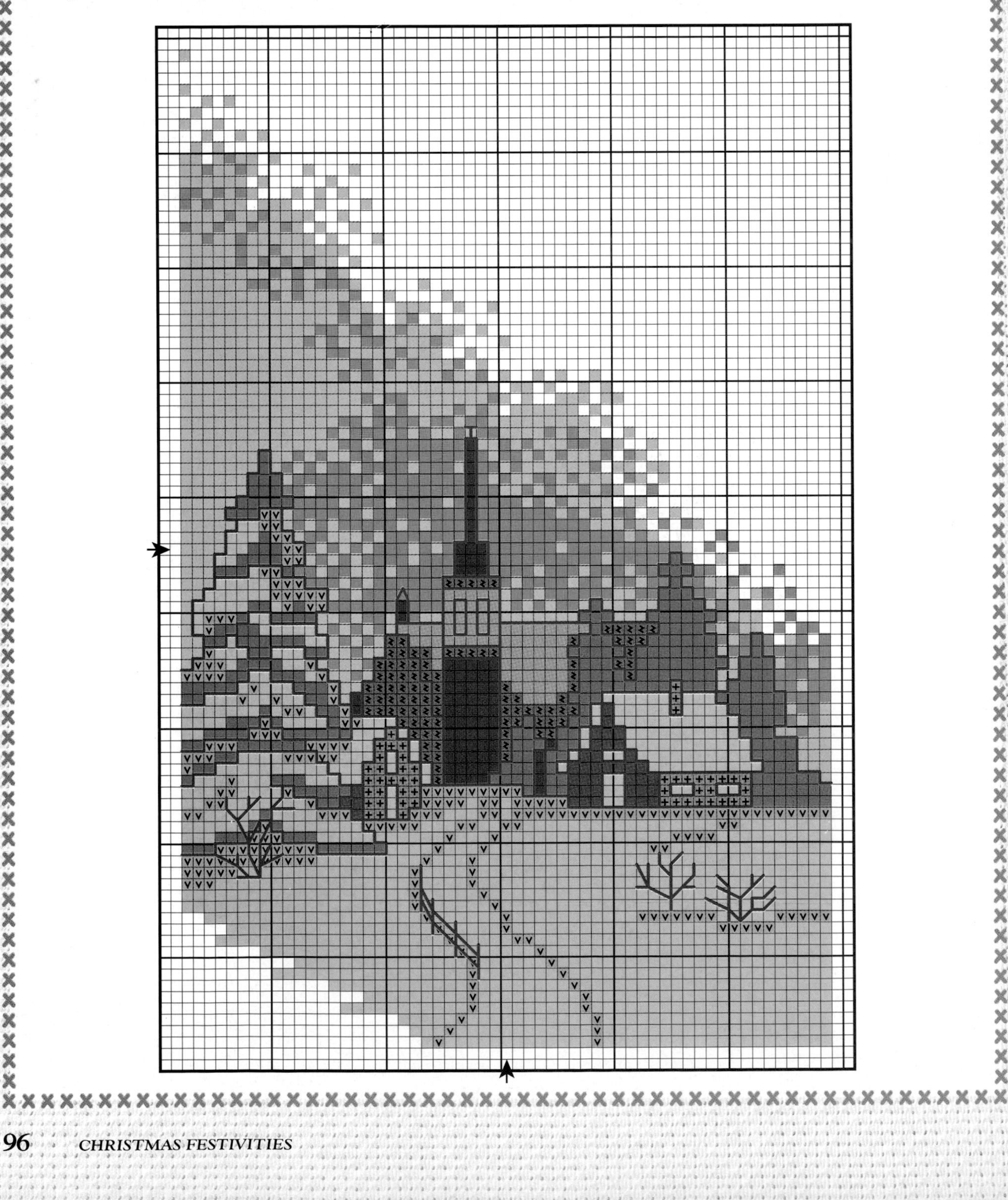

Partridge in a Bear Tree
and a partridge
in a beartree
merry christmas

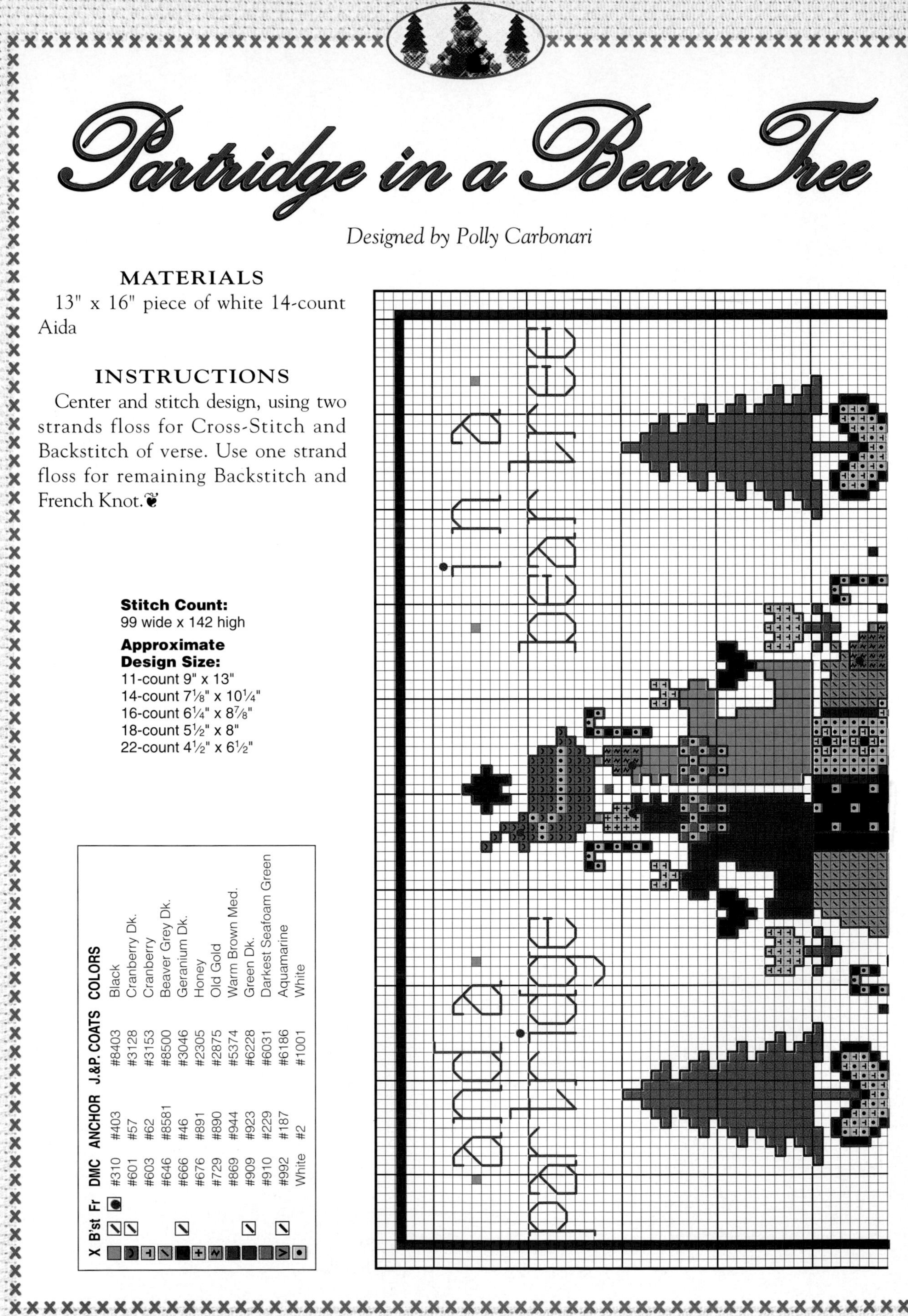

Partridge in a Bear Tree

Designed by Polly Carbonari

MATERIALS

13" x 16" piece of white 14-count Aida

INSTRUCTIONS

Center and stitch design, using two strands floss for Cross-Stitch and Backstitch of verse. Use one strand floss for remaining Backstitch and French Knot.❦

Stitch Count:
99 wide x 142 high

Approximate Design Size:
11-count 9" x 13"
14-count 7⅛" x 10¼"
16-count 6¼" x 8⅞"
18-count 5½" x 8"
22-count 4½" x 6½"

X	B'st	Fr	DMC	ANCHOR	J.&P. COATS	COLORS
	✓	✓	#310	#403	#8403	Black
	✓		#601	#57	#3128	Cranberry Dk.
			#603	#62	#3153	Cranberry
			#646	#8581	#8500	Beaver Grey Dk.
	✓		#666	#46	#3046	Geranium Dk.
			#676	#891	#2305	Honey
			#729	#890	#2875	Old Gold
			#869	#944	#5374	Warm Brown Med.
	✓		#909	#923	#6228	Green Dk.
			#910	#229	#6031	Darkest Seafoam Green
	✓		#992	#187	#6186	Aquamarine
			White	#2	#1001	White

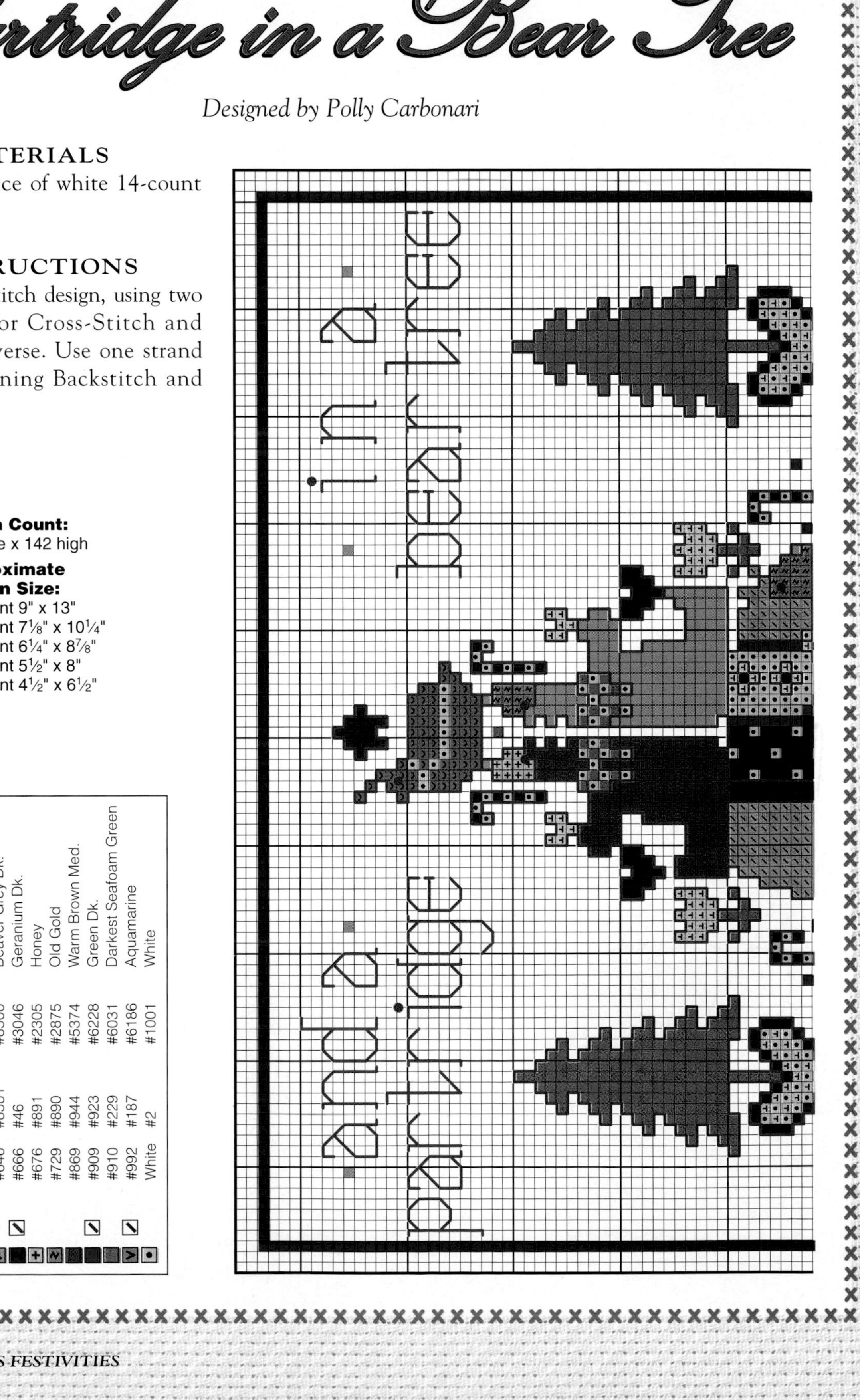

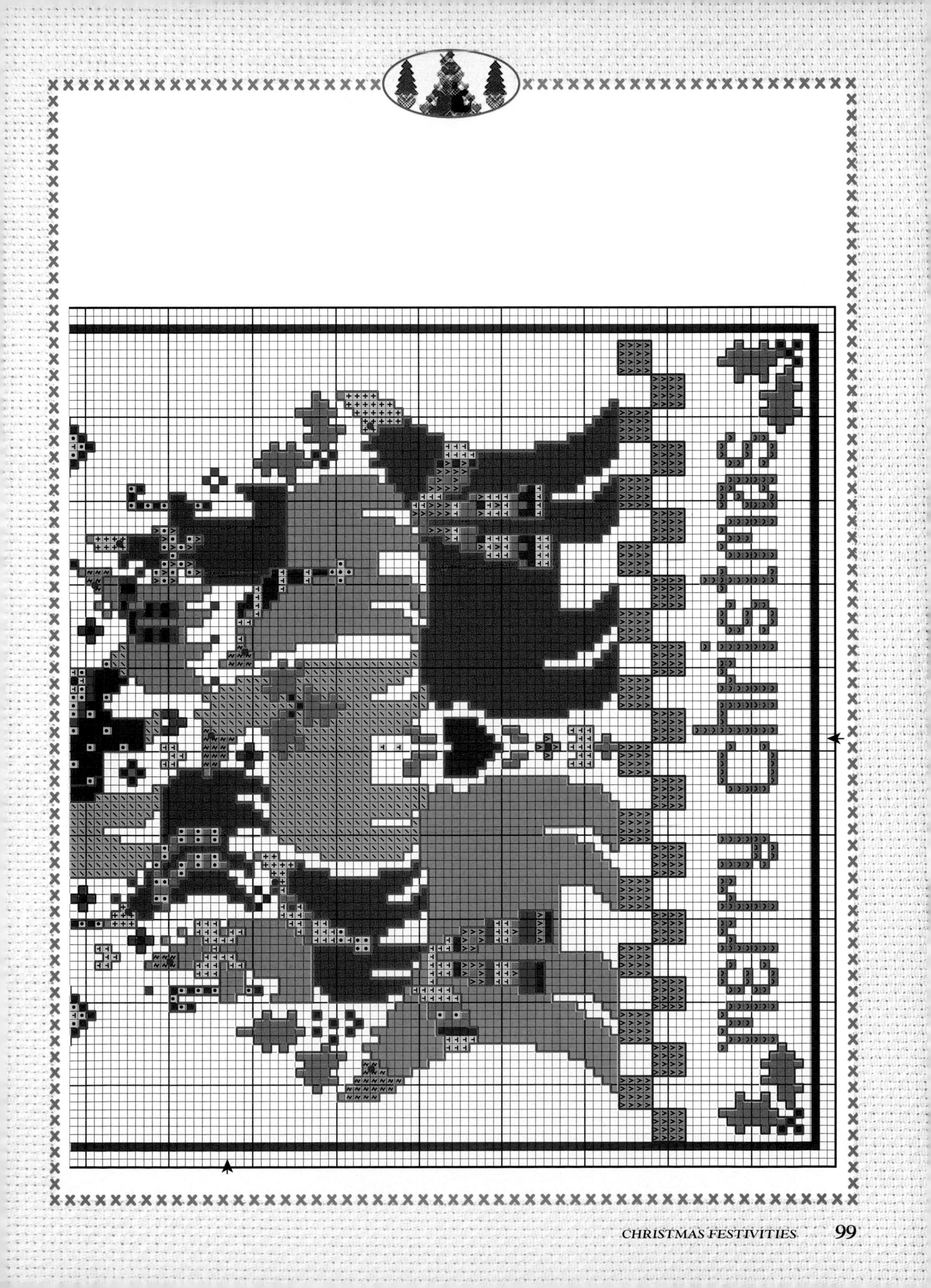
Merry Christmas

Decorate your tree or mantle with sentimental ornaments featuring time-honored Christmas symbols.

Christmas Scenes

Designed by Barbara Core

MATERIALS FOR ONE

10" x 12" piece of white 28-count linen; Scrap of fabric; ⅝ yd. twisted cord; Fiberfill

INSTRUCTIONS

1: Center and stitch design of choice, stitching over two threads and using two strands floss for Cross-Stitch and Straight Stitch. Use one strand floss for Backstitch and French Knot.

NOTES: Trim ½" from design edges. From fabric, cut one same as design for back.

2: With right sides facing and ½" seams, sew design and back together, leaving an opening for turning. Turn right sides out; stuff lightly with fiberfill. Slip stitch opening closed. Beginning at center top, tack cord around outside edges. Form a hanging loop and secure end of cord to back.❦

X	B'st	¼x	¾x	Str	Fr	DMC	ANCHOR	J.&P. COATS	COLORS
						#309	#42	#3284	Rose Deep
						#310	#403	#8403	Black
						#311	#148	#7980	Indigo Blue Dk.
						#312	#979	#7979	Azure Blue Dk.
						#318	#399	#8511	Silver Med.
						#321	#9046	#3500	Cherry Red
						#335	#38	#3283	Rose Pink Dk.
						#414	#235	#8513	Silver Dk.
						#415	#398	#8398	Silver
						#433	#358	#5471	Coffee Brown
						#434	#310	#5000	Darkest Toast
						#435	#1046	#5371	Toast Dk.
						#436	#1045	#5943	Toast
						#437	#362	#5942	Toast Lt.
						#498	#1005	#3000	Garnet
						#699	#923	#6228	Kelly Green Dk.
						#699	#923	#6228	Kelly Green Dk. held with
						#310	#403	#8403	Black
						#700	#228	#6227	Kelly Green
						#701	#227	#6226	Kelly Green Med.
						#702	#226	#6239	Kelly Green Lt.
						#703	#238	#6238	Parrot Green
						#704	#256	#6001	Parrot Green Med.
						#738	#361	#5375	Toast Very Lt.
						#739	#387	#5369	Toast Pale
						#740	#316	#2327	Pumpkin Bright
						#741	#304	#2314	Tangerine Dk.
						#742	#303	#2302	Tangerine
						#743	#302	#2294	Tangerine Lt.
						#744	#301	#2293	Tangerine Pale
						#762	#234	#8510	Silver Very Lt.
						#762	#234	#8510	Silver Very Lt. held with
						White	#2	#1001	White
						#814	#45	#3044	Garnet Very Dk.
						#814	#45	#3044	Garnet Very Dk. held with
						#310	$403	#8403	Black
						#815	#43	#3000	Garnet Dk.
						#816	#20	#3021	Garnet Med.
						#899	#52	#3282	Rose Pink Med.
						#938	#381	#5381	Darkest Mahogany
						#939	#152	#7160	Navy Blue Ultra Very Dk.
						#3371	#382	#5382	Darkest Brown
						White	#2	#1001	White

Stockings
Stitch Count:
49 wide x 65 high

Approximate Design Size:
11-count 4½" x 6"
14-count 3½" x 4¾"
16-count 3⅛" x 4⅛"
18-count 2¾" x 3⅝"
22-count 2¼" x 3"
28-count over two threads 3½" x 4¾"

Snowman
Stitch Count:
45 wide x 65 high

Approximate Design Size:
11-count 4⅛" x 6"
14-count 3¼" x 4¾"
16-count 2⅞" x 4⅛"
18-count 2½" x 3⅝"
22-count 2⅛" x 3"
28-count over two threads 3¼" x 4¾"

Mailbox
Stitch Count:
51 wide x 78 high

Approximate Design Size:
11-count 4⅝" x 7⅛"
14-count 3¾" x 5⅝"
16-count 3¼" x 4⅞"
18-count 2⅞" x 4⅜"
22-count 2⅜" x 3⅝"
28-count over two threads 3¾" x 5⅝"

Gifts
Stitch Count:
54 wide x 74 high

Approximate Design Size:
11-count 5" x 6¾"
14-count 3⅞" x 5⅜"
16-count 3⅜" x 4⅝"
18-count 3" x 4⅛"
22-count 2½" x 3⅜"
28-count over two threads 3⅞" x 5⅜"

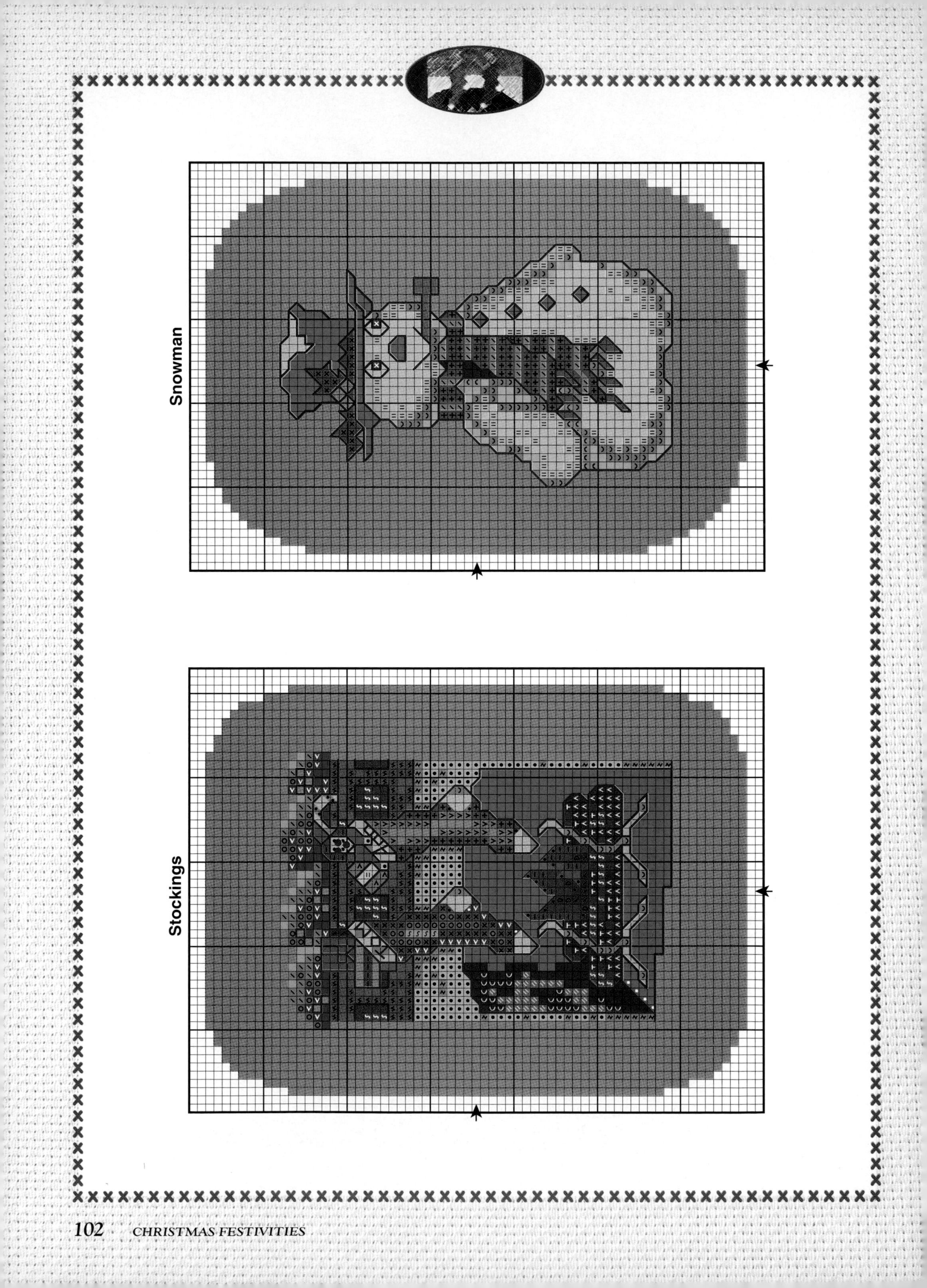
Snowman
Stockings

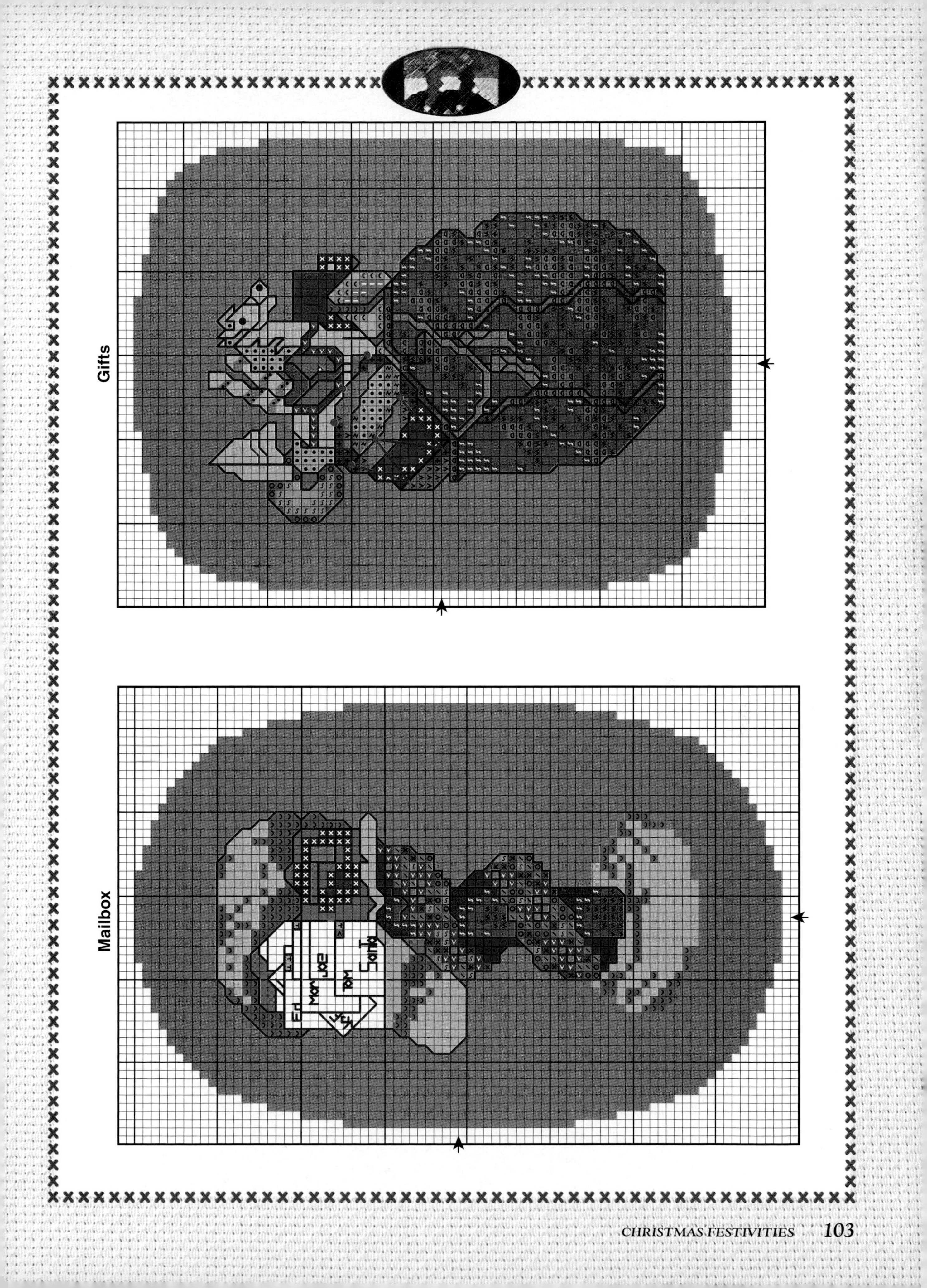
Gifts
Mailbox

Designed by Alice Okon

MATERIALS FOR ONE

9" x 11" piece of white 14-count Aida; ½ yd. flat lace; ⅝ yd. metallic cord; Mounting board; Batting; Craft glue or glue gun

INSTRUCTIONS

1: Center and stitch design of choice, using two strands floss or one strand fine braid for Cross-Stitch and one strand floss for Backstitch.

NOTE: From batting and mounting board, cut one each according to Angel Pattern.

2: Center and mount design over batting and board. Beginning at top center, glue cord around outside edges of design. Form a hanging loop with excess cord; secure end to back. Glue lace to back outside edges of mounted design.

X	B'st	DMC	ANCHOR	J.&P. COATS	KREINIK(#8)	COLORS
■		#301	#1049	#5365		Cinnamon Lt.
^		#309	#42	#3284		Rose Deep
■		#341	#117	#7005		Blue Violet Lt.
V		#519	#1038	#7159		Sky Blue
≥		#743	#302	#2294		Tangerine Lt.
□		#745	#300	#2296		Topaz Very Lt.
⊥		#776	#24	#3281		Rose Pink Lt.
■		#799	#136	#7030		Blueberry Med.
T		#800	#144	#7020		Blueberry Pale
	/	#838	#380	#5478		Darkest Pecan
■		#839	#360	#5360		Pecan Dk.
◡		#899	#52	#3282		Rose Pink Med.
X		#909	#923	#6228		Green Dk.
■		#912	#209	#6266		Seafoam Green Dk.
□		#948	#1011	#2331		Peach Flesh Very Lt.
■		#3326	#36	#3126		Rose Pink
M		#3733	#75	#3001		Dusty Rose Lt.
■		#3815	#216	#6876		Celdon Green Dk.
>		#3816	#215	#6879		Celdon Green
O		#3817	#213	#6875		Celdon Green Lt.
•		White	#2	#1001		White
■					#002HL	Gold

Angel #1

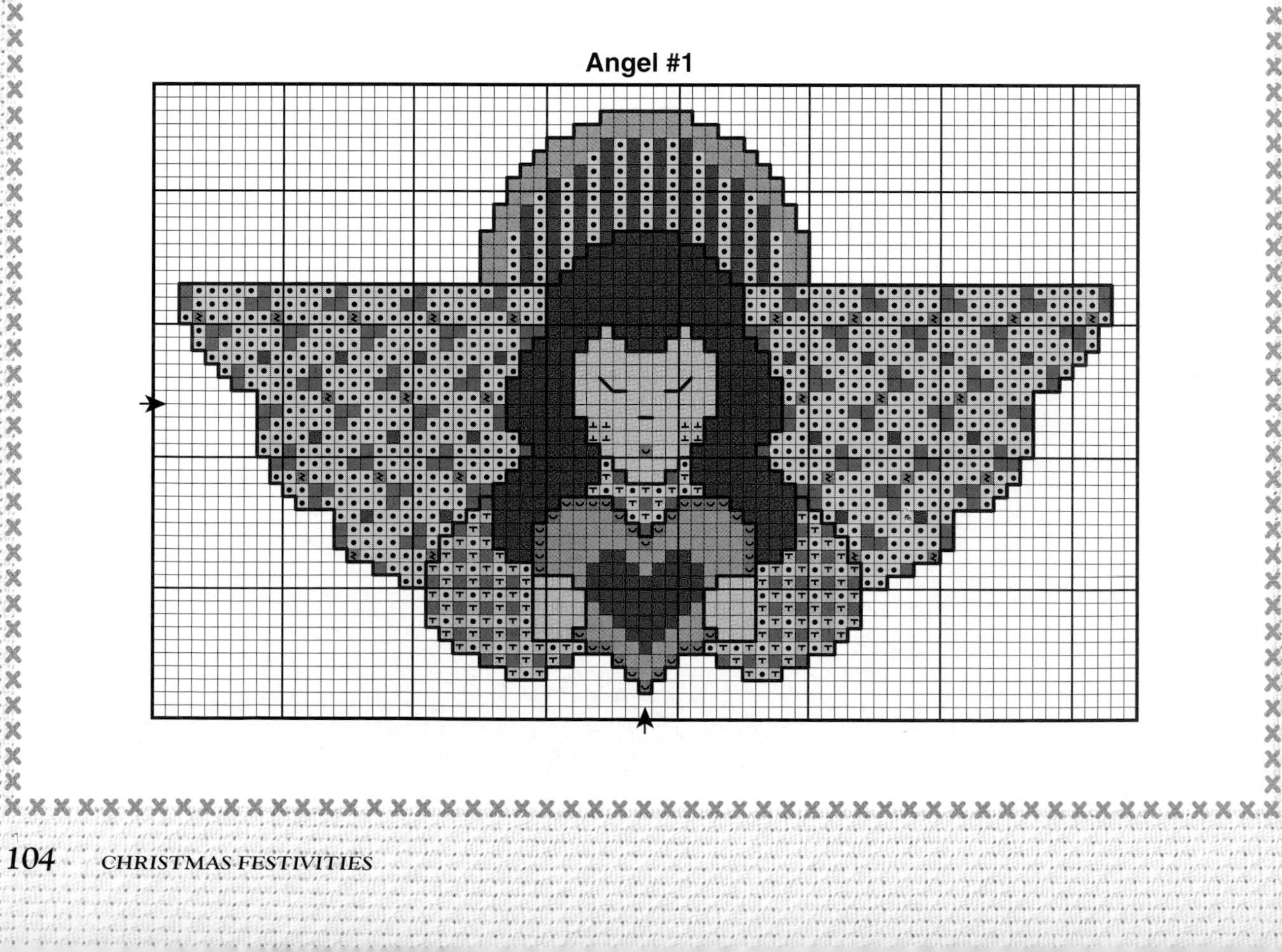

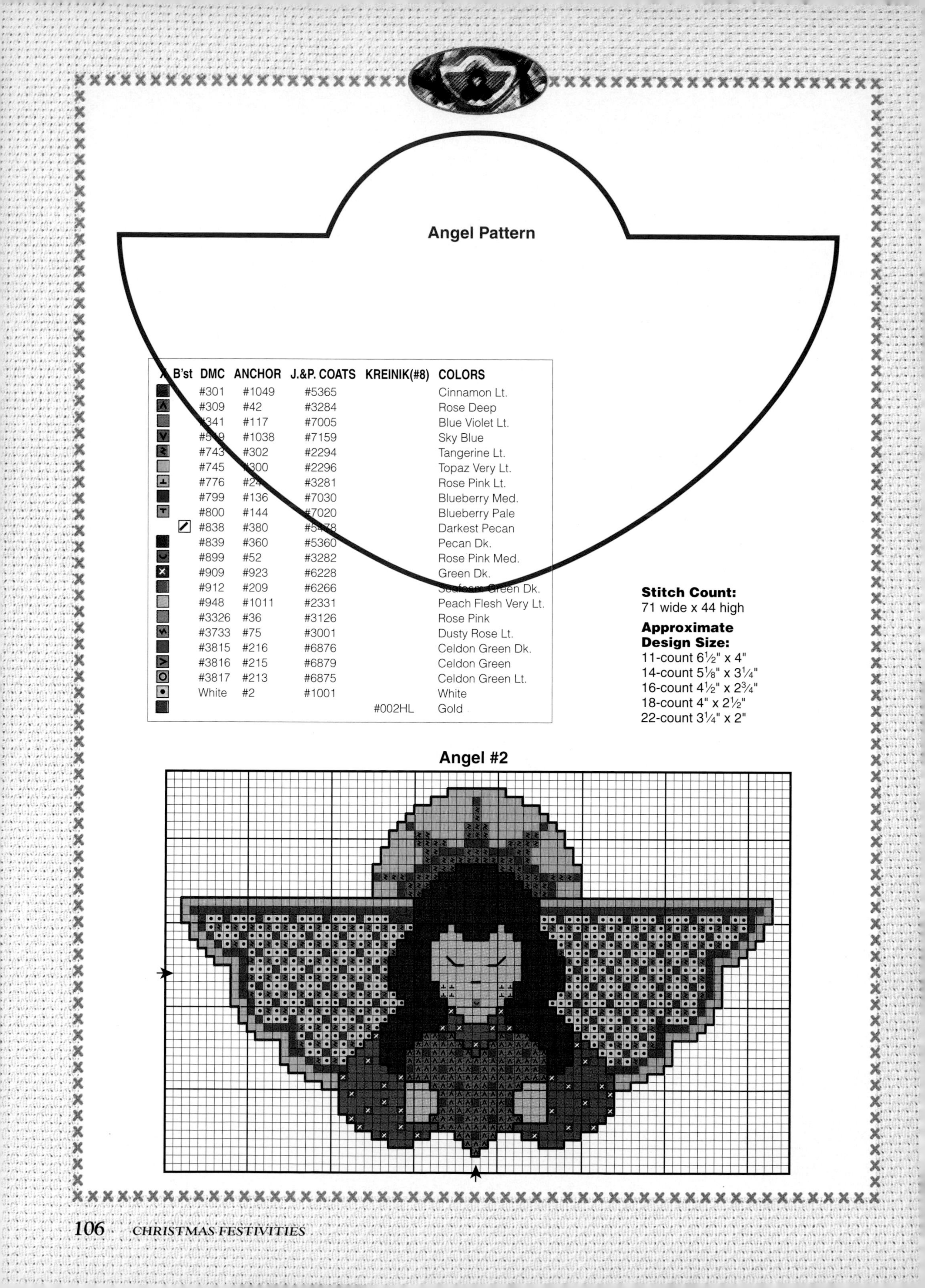

Angel Pattern

X	B'st	DMC	ANCHOR	J.&P. COATS	KREINIK(#8)	COLORS
		#301	#1049	#5365		Cinnamon Lt.
		#309	#42	#3284		Rose Deep
		#341	#117	#7005		Blue Violet Lt.
		#519	#1038	#7159		Sky Blue
		#743	#302	#2294		Tangerine Lt.
		#745	#300	#2296		Topaz Very Lt.
		#776	#24	#3281		Rose Pink Lt.
		#799	#136	#7030		Blueberry Med.
		#800	#144	#7020		Blueberry Pale
		#838	#380	#5478		Darkest Pecan
		#839	#360	#5360		Pecan Dk.
		#899	#52	#3282		Rose Pink Med.
		#909	#923	#6228		Green Dk.
		#912	#209	#6266		Seafoam Green Dk.
		#948	#1011	#2331		Peach Flesh Very Lt.
		#3326	#36	#3126		Rose Pink
		#3733	#75	#3001		Dusty Rose Lt.
		#3815	#216	#6876		Celdon Green Dk.
		#3816	#215	#6879		Celdon Green
		#3817	#213	#6875		Celdon Green Lt.
		White	#2	#1001		White
					#002HL	Gold

Stitch Count:
71 wide x 44 high

Approximate Design Size:
11-count 6½" x 4"
14-count 5⅛" x 3¼"
16-count 4½" x 2¾"
18-count 4" x 2½"
22-count 3¼" x 2"

Angel #2

Angel #3
Angel #4

Surprise and excite children and friends with these precious gift bags they'll treasure as much as the gifts themselves.

Merry Christmice

Designed by Barbara Sestok

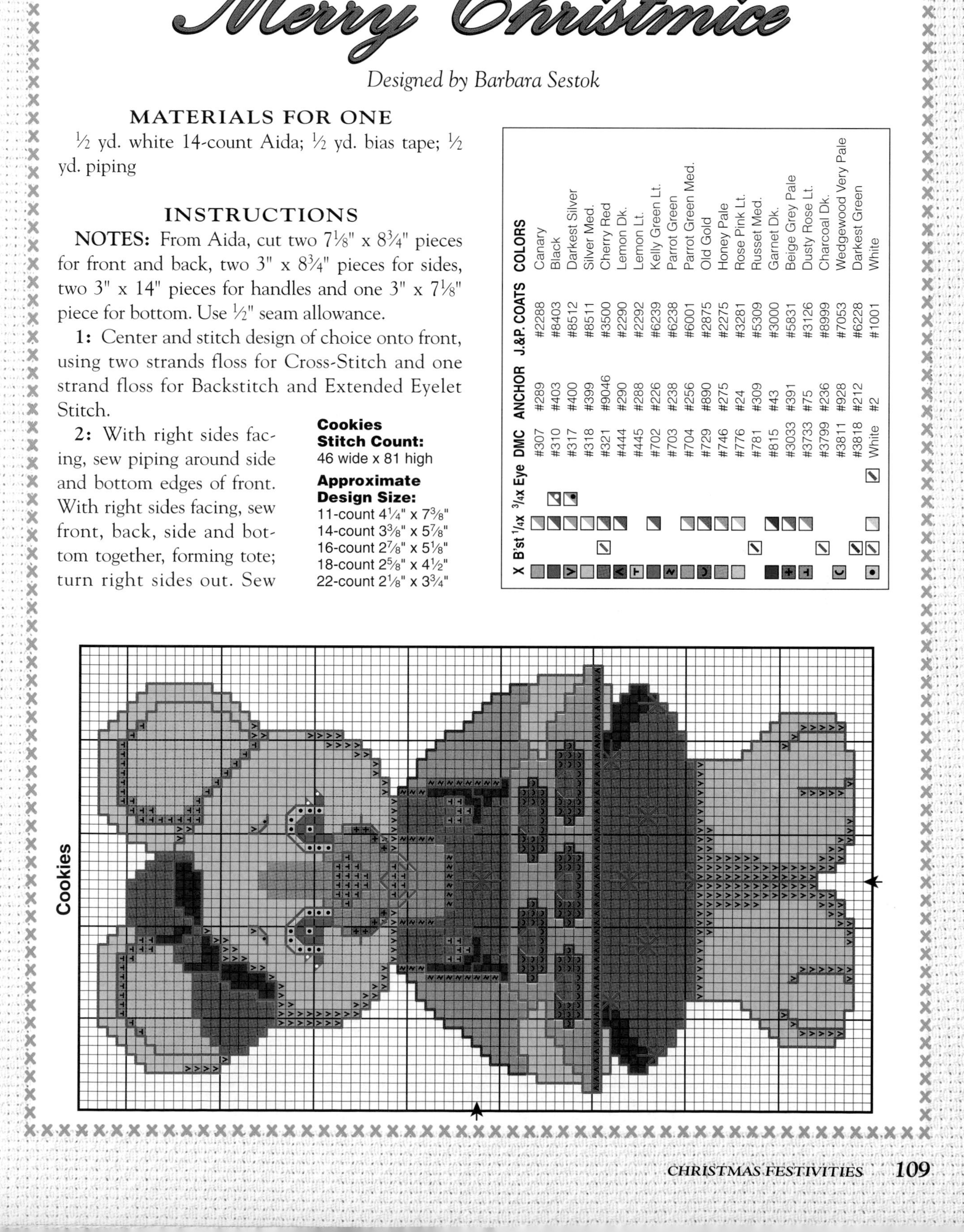

MATERIALS FOR ONE

½ yd. white 14-count Aida; ½ yd. bias tape; ½ yd. piping

INSTRUCTIONS

NOTES: From Aida, cut two 7⅛" x 8¾" pieces for front and back, two 3" x 8¾" pieces for sides, two 3" x 14" pieces for handles and one 3" x 7⅛" piece for bottom. Use ½" seam allowance.

1: Center and stitch design of choice onto front, using two strands floss for Cross-Stitch and one strand floss for Backstitch and Extended Eyelet Stitch.

2: With right sides facing, sew piping around side and bottom edges of front. With right sides facing, sew front, back, side and bottom together, forming tote; turn right sides out. Sew

Cookies Stitch Count:
46 wide x 81 high

Approximate Design Size:
11-count 4¼" x 7⅜"
14-count 3⅜" x 5⅞"
16-count 2⅞" x 5⅛"
18-count 2⅝" x 4½"
22-count 2⅛" x 3¾"

X	B'st	¼x	¾x	Eye	DMC	ANCHOR	J.&P. COATS	COLORS
■		■			#307	#289	#2288	Canary
■		■	■		#310	#403	#8403	Black
■		■	■		#317	#400	#8512	Darkest Silver
■		■			#318	#399	#8511	Silver Med.
■	■	■			#321	#9046	#3500	Cherry Red
■		■			#444	#290	#2290	Lemon Dk.
■					#445	#288	#2292	Lemon Lt.
■		■			#702	#226	#6239	Kelly Green Lt.
■					#703	#238	#6238	Parrot Green
■		■			#704	#256	#6001	Parrot Green Med.
■		■			#729	#890	#2875	Old Gold
■		■			#746	#275	#2275	Honey Pale
■		■			#776	#24	#3281	Rose Pink Lt.
	■				#781	#309	#5309	Russet Med.
■		■			#815	#43	#3000	Garnet Dk.
■		■			#3033	#391	#5831	Beige Grey Pale
■		■			#3733	#75	#3126	Dusty Rose Lt.
	■				#3799	#236	#8999	Charcoal Dk.
■					#3811	#928	#7053	Wedgewood Very Pale
	■				#3818	#212	#6228	Darkest Green
■	■	■		■	White	#2	#1001	White

Cookies

Mischievous Mice

Designed by Ursula Michael

MATERIALS

12" x 13" piece of white 14-count Aida; 1 yd. piping; 1/3 yd. ribbon; Pillow of choice

INSTRUCTIONS

1: Center and stitch design, using two strands floss or two strands floss held together with one strand blending filament for Cross-Stitch and Backstitch.

NOTE: Trim design to 7¾" x 9¼" for appliqué.

2: Press ¼" hem around edges of appliqué; sew piping to back outside edges. Position and sew Appliqué to front of pillow as shown in photo. Tie ribbon into a bow; tack to corner of Appliqué as shown.

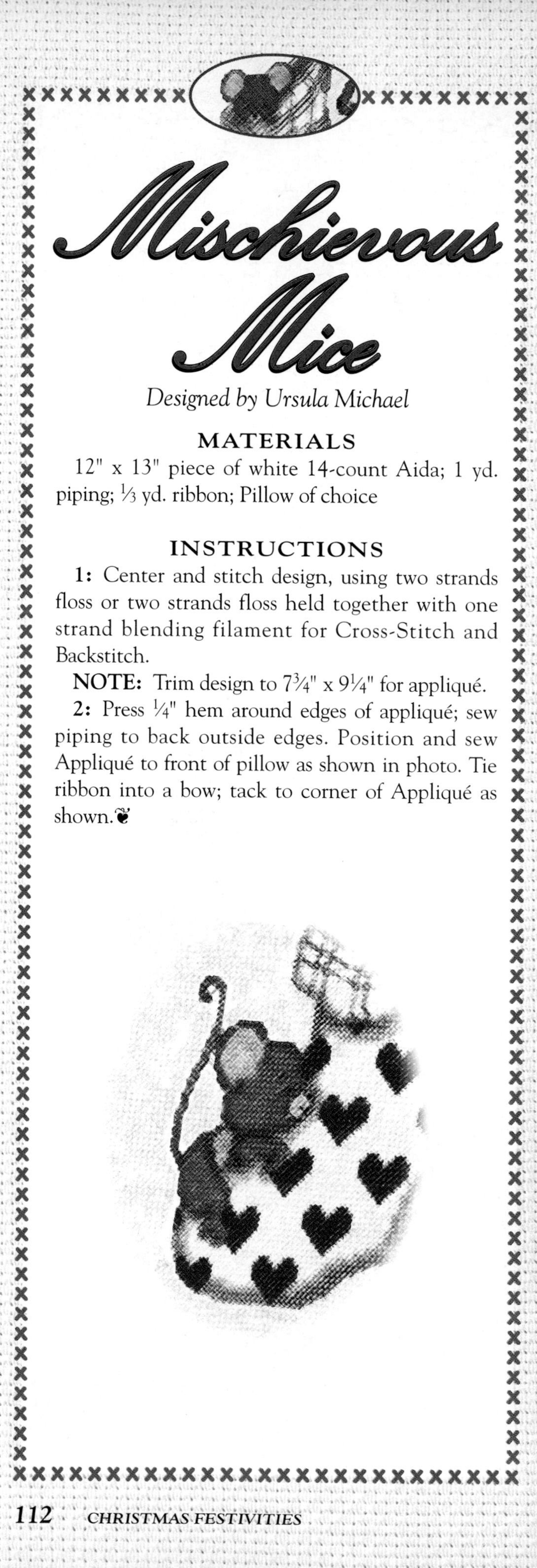

Stitch this playful design on a perky holiday pillow to warm up your home with festive fun.

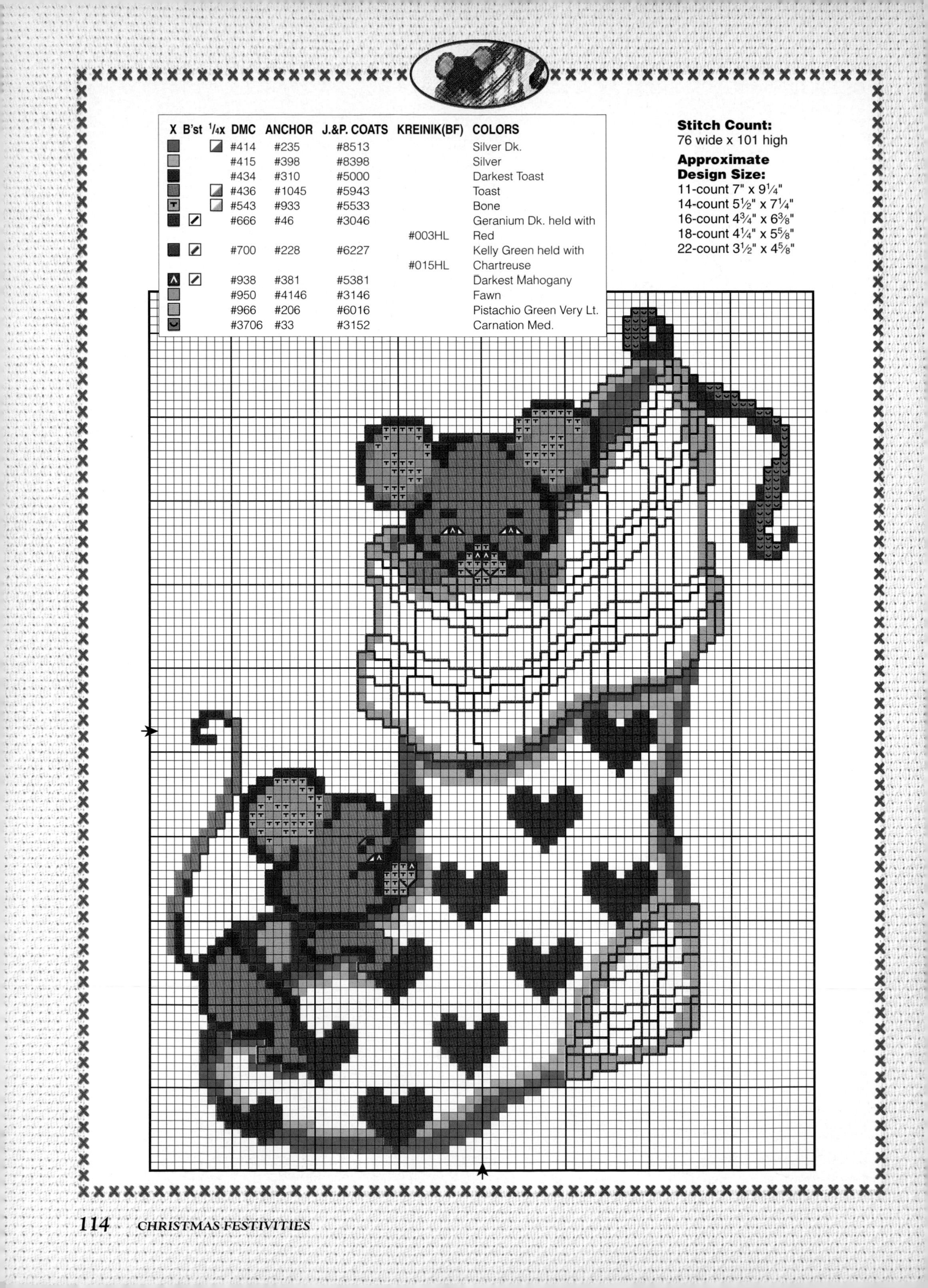

X	B'st	1/4x	DMC	ANCHOR	J.&P. COATS	KREINIK(BF)	COLORS
■		◪	#414	#235	#8513		Silver Dk.
■			#415	#398	#8398		Silver
■			#434	#310	#5000		Darkest Toast
■		◪	#436	#1045	#5943		Toast
T		◪	#543	#933	#5533		Bone
■	/		#666	#46	#3046		Geranium Dk. held with
						#003HL	Red
■	/		#700	#228	#6227		Kelly Green held with
						#015HL	Chartreuse
Λ	/		#938	#381	#5381		Darkest Mahogany
■			#950	#4146	#3146		Fawn
■			#966	#206	#6016		Pistachio Green Very Lt.
◡			#3706	#33	#3152		Carnation Med.

Stitch Count:
76 wide x 101 high

Approximate Design Size:
11-count 7" x 9¼"
14-count 5½" x 7¼"
16-count 4¾" x 6⅜"
18-count 4¼" x 5⅝"
22-count 3½" x 4⅝"

Dear Santa

Make a personalized stocking that will be cherished each year with this traditional design stitched on 14-count Aida.

Dear Santa

Designed by Mona Eno

MATERIALS

18" x 22" piece of white 14-count Aida; 1 yd. fabric; 1½ yds. piping; 1½ yds. decorative braid

INSTRUCTIONS

1: Selecting desired letters from Alphabet graph, center and stitch design, using two strands floss or two strands floss held together with one strand blending filament for Cross-Stitch. Use one strand floss or floss amounts indicated on Backstitch Instructions for Backstitch.

NOTES: Trim design into a stocking shape as shown in photo for front. From fabric, cut one same as front for back. Use ¼" seam allowance.

2: With right sides facing, sew piping, then braid to outside edges of front. Sew ¼" hem along top edge of back. With right sides facing, sew front and back together, leaving top open; turn right sides out. Hang as desired.❦

Backstitch Instructions

DMC	B'st
#310	Santa boots, Bear eyes & nose, Boy Shoes
#312	Boy bow tie & pants
#318	Boy shirt
#321	Gift detail on white stripes
#334	Border around name (two strands)
#413	Santa belt
#414	Santa fur trim
#415	Girl leg
#433	Santa buckle, Bear, Boy vest
#561	Girl dress & bow, Upper case lettering, Lower case lettering (two strands)
#642	Santa facial hair
#699	Holly, Chair cushion, Gift bow
#702	Girl dress yoke leaves
#729	Gift gold stripes, Girl hair
#814	Border bows, Holly berries
#815	Santa suit, Bear bow
#838	Chair, Ball, Bear vest, Boy hair, Doll eyes
#839	Gift box, Girls eyes, Doll hair
#840	Girl flesh, Boy flesh, Doll flesh, Doll dress
#3328	Santa mouth, Girl mouth
White	All eye highlights

X	B'st	½x	¼x	DMC	ANCHOR	J.&P. COATS	KREINIK(BF)	COLORS
■	✓		◪	#310	#403	#8403		Black
■	✓		◪	#312	#979	#7979		Azure Blue Dk.
+	✓		◪	#318	#399	#8511		Silver Med.
O	✓		◪	#321	#9046	#3500		Cherry Red
■			◪	#322	#978	#7978		Copen Blue
/	✓		◪	#334	#977	#7977		Delft Blue Dk.
<			◪	#353	#8	#3006		Peach Flesh Med.
/	✓		◪	#413	#401	#8514		Charcoal
S	✓		◪	#414	#235	#8513		Silver Dk.
O	✓		◪	#415	#398	#8398		Silver
	✓			#433	#358	#5471		Coffee Brown
■			◪	#434	#310	#5000		Darkest Toast
T			◪	#435	#1046	#5371		Toast Dk.
■			◪	#437	#362	#5942		Toast Lt.
■			◪	#498	#1005	#3000		Garnet
\	✓		◪	#561	#212	#6211		Jade Very Dk.
W			◪	#562	#210	#6213		Jade Med.
X			◪	#563	#208	#6210		Jade Lt.
Z	✓		◪	#642	#392	#5832		Beige Grey Dk.
X			◪	#644	#830	#5830		Beige Grey Lt.
■			◪	#666	#46	#3046		Geranium Dk.
■			◪	#676	#891	#2305		Honey
V			◪	#677	#886	#5372		Honey Lt.
−			◪	#680	#901	#2876	#002HL	Old Gold Dk. held with Gold
■	✓		◪	#699	#923	#6228		Kelly Green Dk.
−			◪	#701	#227	#6226		Kelly Green Med.
■	✓		◪	#702	#226	#6239		Kelly Green Lt.
Z	✓		◪	#729	#890	#2875		Old Gold
>			◪	#729	#890	#2875	#002HL	Old Gold held with Gold
⊥			◪	#754	#1012	#2336		Peach Flesh Lt.
■			◪	#760	#1022	#3069		Salmon
\			◪	#761	#1021	#3068		Salmon Lt.
■			◪	#762	#234	#8510		Silver Very Lt.
O		◪	◪	#775	#128	#7031		Baby Blue
−			◪	#776	#24	#3281		Rose Pink Lt.
•	✓		◪	#814	#45	#3073		Garnet Very Dk.
	✓			#815	#43	#3044		Garnet Dk.
■			◪	#822	#390	#5933		Beige Grey Very Lt.
■	✓		◪	#838	#380	#5478		Darkest Pecan
•	✓		◪	#839	#360	#5360		Pecan Dk.
■	✓		◪	#840	#379	#5379		Pecan Med.
O			◪	#945	#881	#3335		Blush
■			◪	#948	#1011	#2331		Peach Flesh Very Lt.
S			◪	#950	#4146	#3146		Fawn
W			◪	#962	#75	#3153		Antique Rose Med.
	✓			#3328	#1024	#3071		Salmon Dk.
Λ			◪	#3716	#25	#3125		Antique Rose
■			◪	#3755	#140	#7976		Delft Blue Med.
•	✓		◪	White	#2	#1001		White

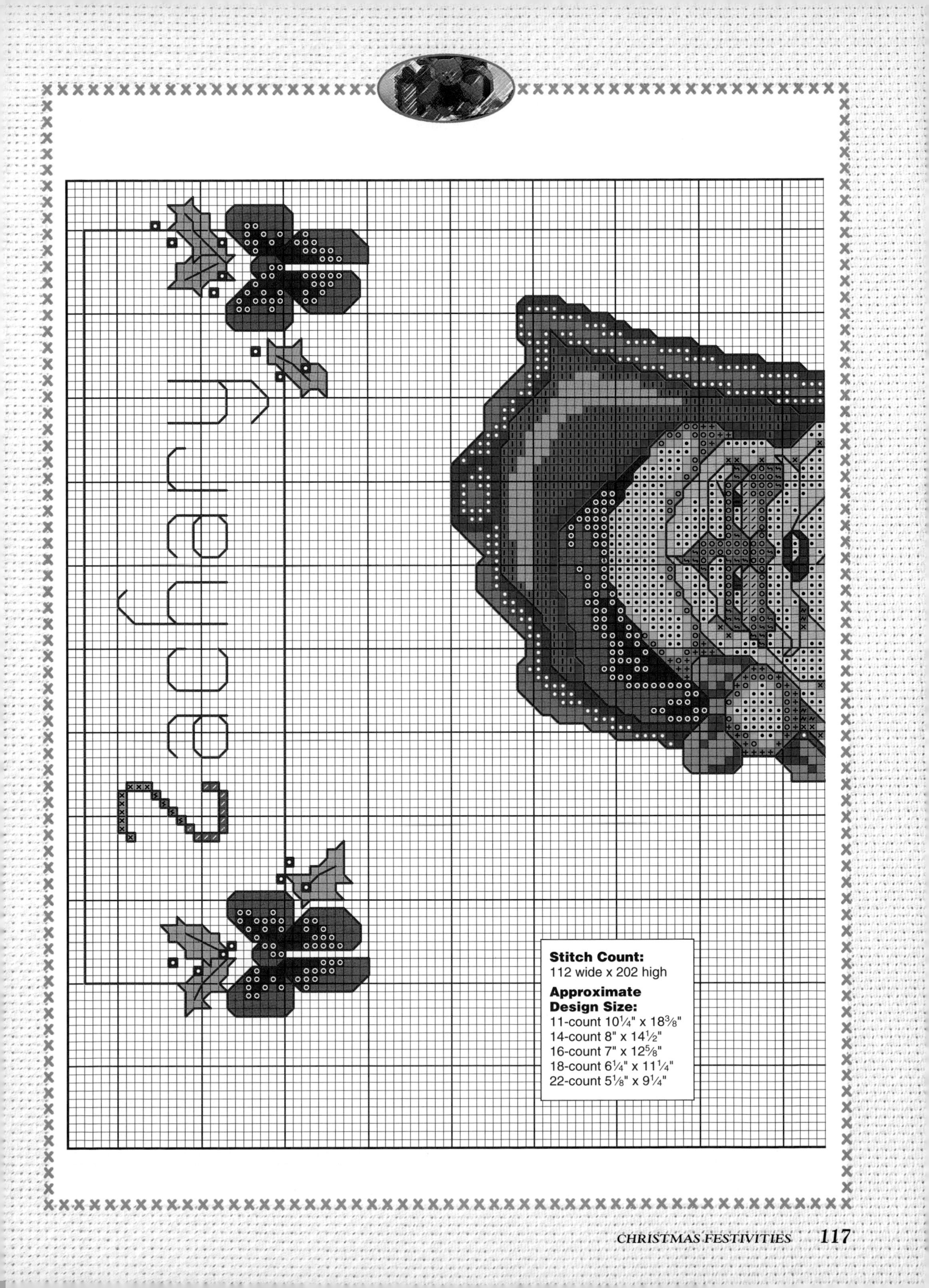

Stitch Count:
112 wide x 202 high

Approximate Design Size:
11-count 10¼" x 18⅜"
14-count 8" x 14½"
16-count 7" x 12⅝"
18-count 6¼" x 11¼"
22-count 5⅛" x 9¼"

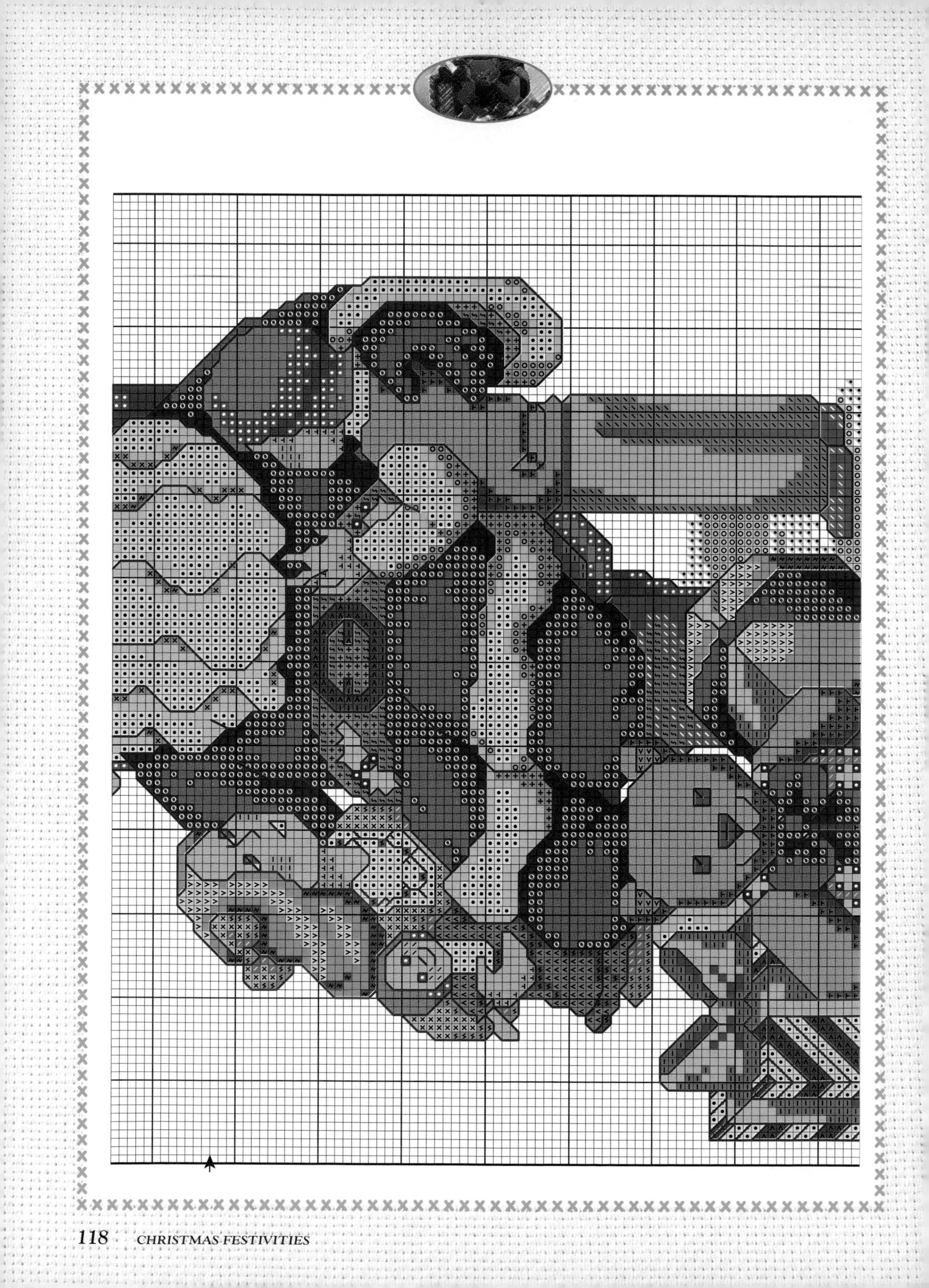

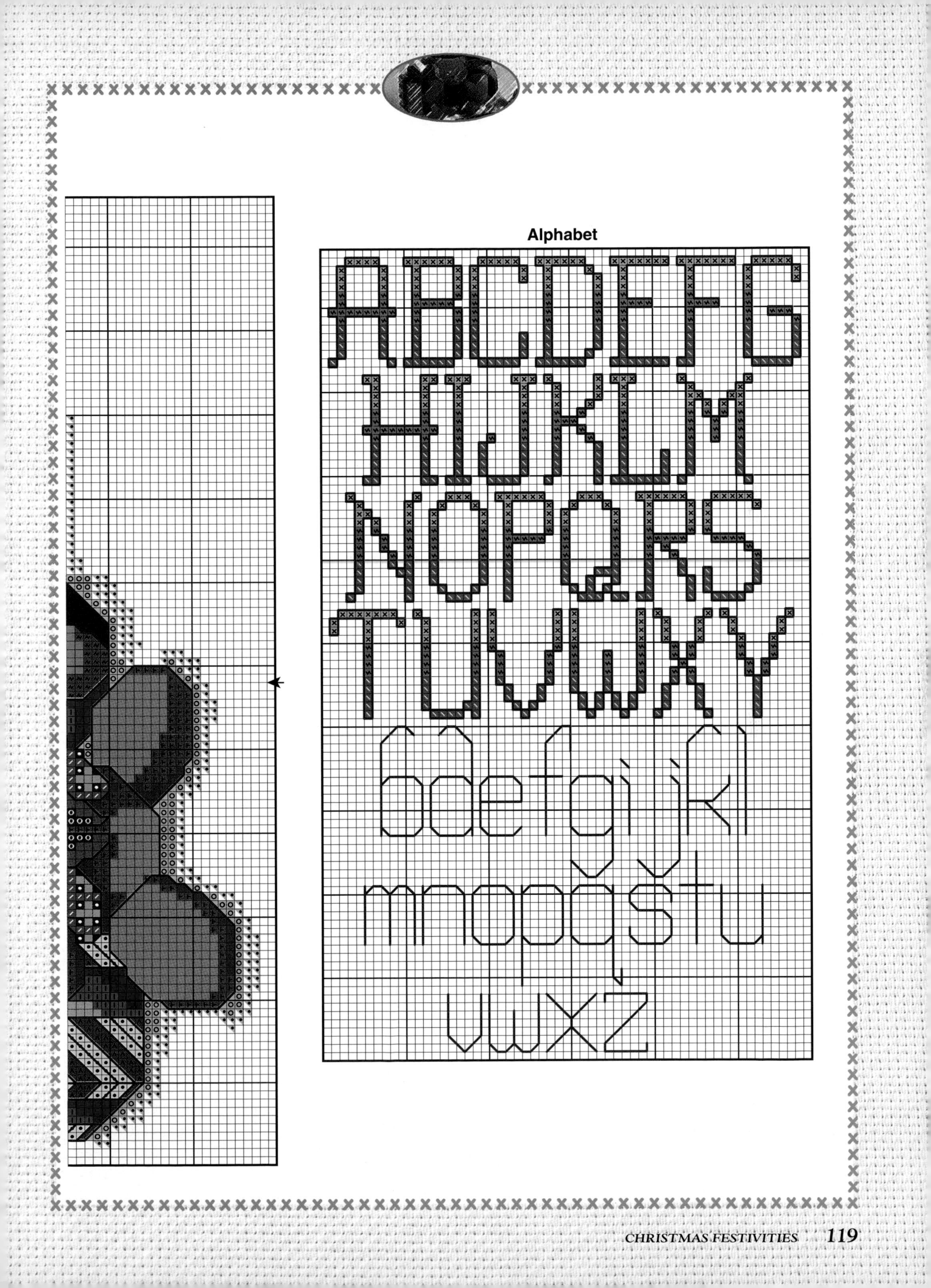
Alphabet

Merry Christmas

Designed by Ursula Michael

MATERIALS

10" x 12" piece of celery green 27-count Linda® ; ¾ yd. piping; ¾ yd. lace; Mounting board; Craft glue or glue gun.

INSTRUCTIONS

1: Center and stitch design, stitching over two threads and using two strands floss for Cross-Stitch, Straight Stitch and Backstitch of lettering. Use one strand floss for remaining Backstitch.

NOTE: From mounting board, cut one according to Trim Pattern.

2: Center and mount design over board. Glue piping, then lace around outside edges of mounted design.❦

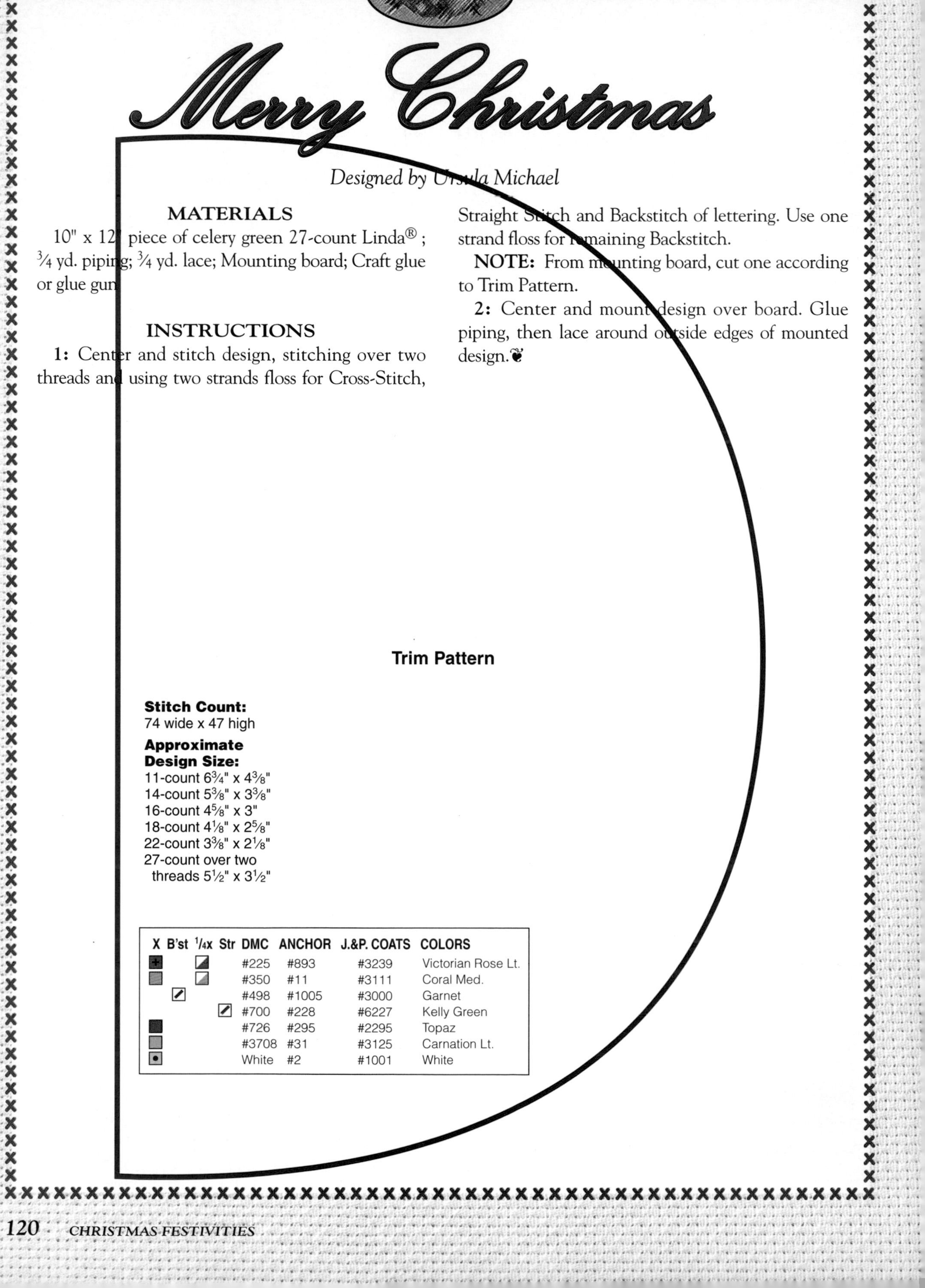

Trim Pattern

Stitch Count:
74 wide x 47 high

Approximate Design Size:
11-count 6¾" x 4⅜"
14-count 5⅜" x 3⅜"
16-count 4⅝" x 3"
18-count 4⅛" x 2⅝"
22-count 3⅜" x 2⅛"
27-count over two threads 5½" x 3½"

X	B'st	¼x	Str	DMC	ANCHOR	J.&P. COATS	COLORS
■		◪		#225	#893	#3239	Victorian Rose Lt.
■		◪		#350	#11	#3111	Coral Med.
	⧄			#498	#1005	#3000	Garnet
			⧄	#700	#228	#6227	Kelly Green
■				#726	#295	#2295	Topaz
■				#3708	#31	#3125	Carnation Lt.
■				White	#2	#1001	White

HERSHEY'S
COCOA
MERRY
Christmas

Collective Comforts
Without the loving hands of
a master, a student longs for the comfort of
encouraging words and the strokes of genius that come
only from experience. Select a design to teach and join
with those before you that found comfort in
preserving a beloved art form.

May your stay
May you take

Tender Loving Care

Designed by Mary T. Cosgrove

MATERIALS

Apron of choice; Pinafore of choice; 14-count waste canvas

INSTRUCTIONS

1: For Apron, apply waste canvas to front of bib and across bottom edge as shown in photo, following manufacturer's instructions. Center and stitch "Apron Bib" design and "Apron Border" design as indicated on graph, using two strands floss for Cross-Stitch. Remove waste canvas after stitching following manufacturer's instructions.

2: For Pinafore, apply waste canvas to top front and across bottom edge as shown, following manufacturer's instructions. Center and stitch "Pinafore Top" design and "Pinafore Border" design, using two strands floss for Cross-Stitch. Remove waste canvas after stitching following manufacturer's instructions.❦

X	DMC	ANCHOR	J.&P. COATS	COLORS
■	#798	#131	#7022	Blueberry Dk.
■	#915	#1029	#3065	Plum Very Dk.
■	#3806	#76	#3001	Cyclamen Pink Lt.

Apron Bib

Apron Bib Stitch Count:
79 wide x 69 high

Approximate Design Size:
11-count 7¼" x 6⅜"
14-count 5¾" x 5"
16-count 5" x 4⅜"
18-count 4⅜" x 3⅞"
22-count 3⅝" x 3⅛"

Encourage togetherness between mother and daughter with a little TLC and homemade fun.

Pinafore Border
Stitch Count:
189 wide x 25 high

Approximate
Design Size:
11-count 17¼" x 2⅜"
14-count 13½" x 1⅞"
16-count 11⅞" x 1⅝"
18-count 10½" x 1⅜"
22-count 8⅝" x 1⅛"

Pinafore Top
Stitch Count:
49 wide x 16 high

Approximate
Design Size:
11-count 4½" x 1½"
14-count 3½" x 1¼"
16-count 3⅛" x 1"
18-count 2¾" x 1"
22-count 2¼" x ¾"

Pinafore Top

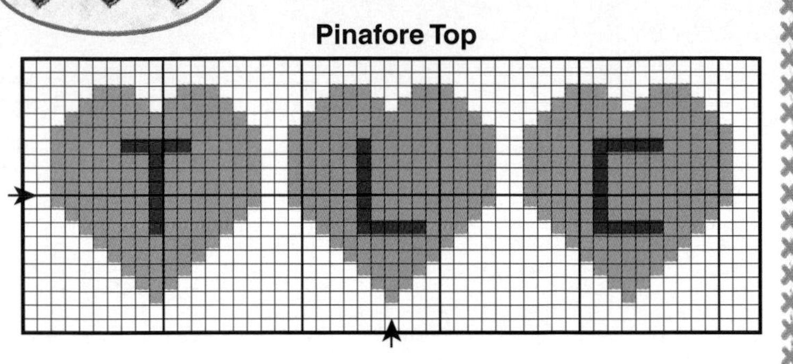

X	DMC	ANCHOR	J.&P. COATS	COLORS
	#798	#131	#7022	Blueberry Dk.
	#915	#1029	#3065	Plum Very Dk.
	#3806	#76	#3001	Cyclamen Pink Lt.

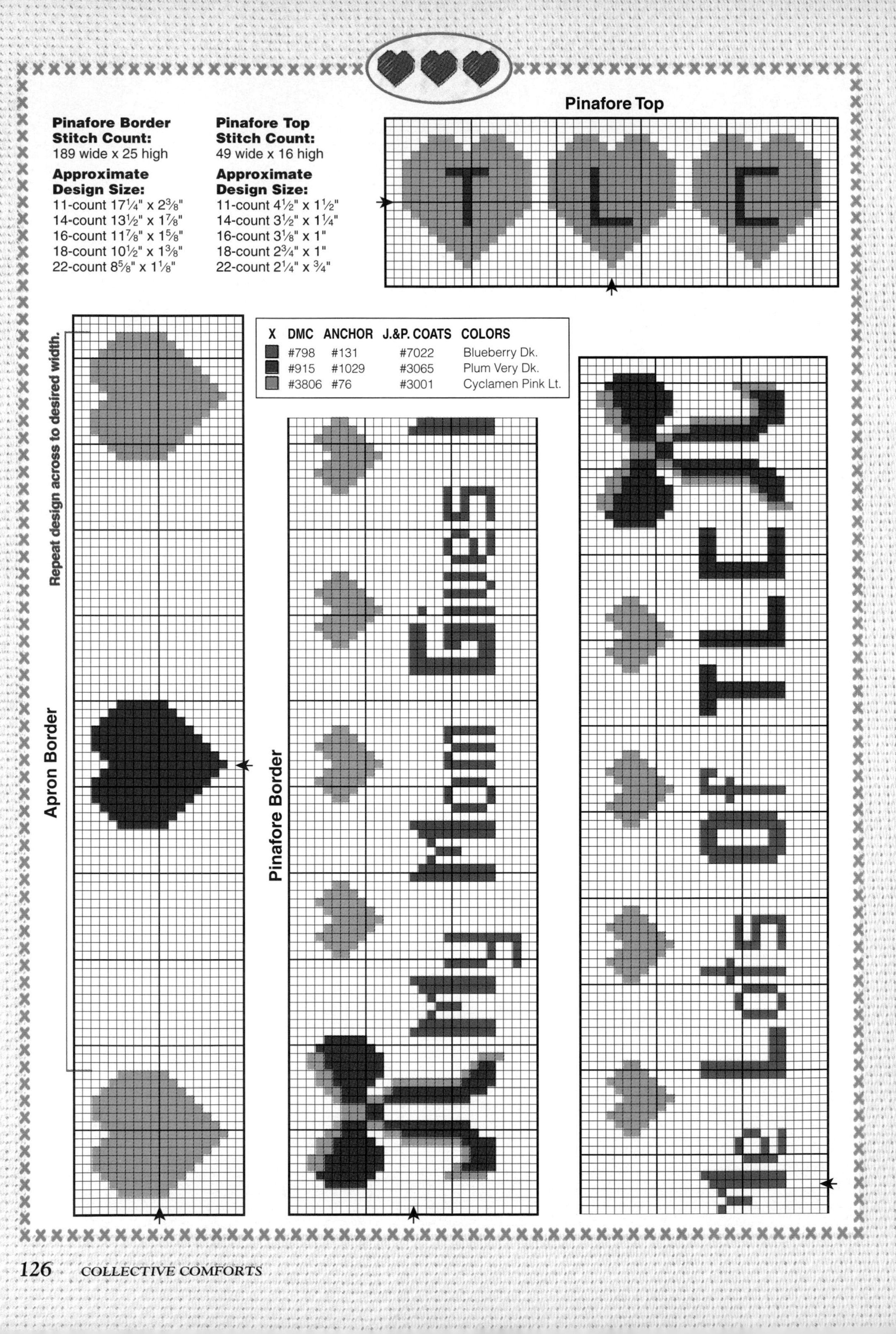

Designed by Janelle Giese of Janelle Marie Designs

MATERIALS

One 9" x 11" piece, one 10" x 10" piece, one 7" x 8" piece and two 5" x 5" pieces of glass blue 28-count Monaco; Wooden box with 3" x 5" design area; White #8 pearl cotton; Four ceramic buttons of choice; Scrap of raffia straw; 3" square piece of medium-weight cardboard; Fiberfill; Craft glue or glue gun

INSTRUCTIONS

1: Center and stitch "Box" design onto 9" x 11" piece, "Pincushion" design onto 10" x 10" piece and "Scissors" design onto 7" x 8" piece of Monaco, stitching over two threads and using two strands floss or amounts indicated on color key for Cross-Stitch, Backstitch, Straight Stitch and French Knot.

2: For Box, sew three ceramic buttons to design

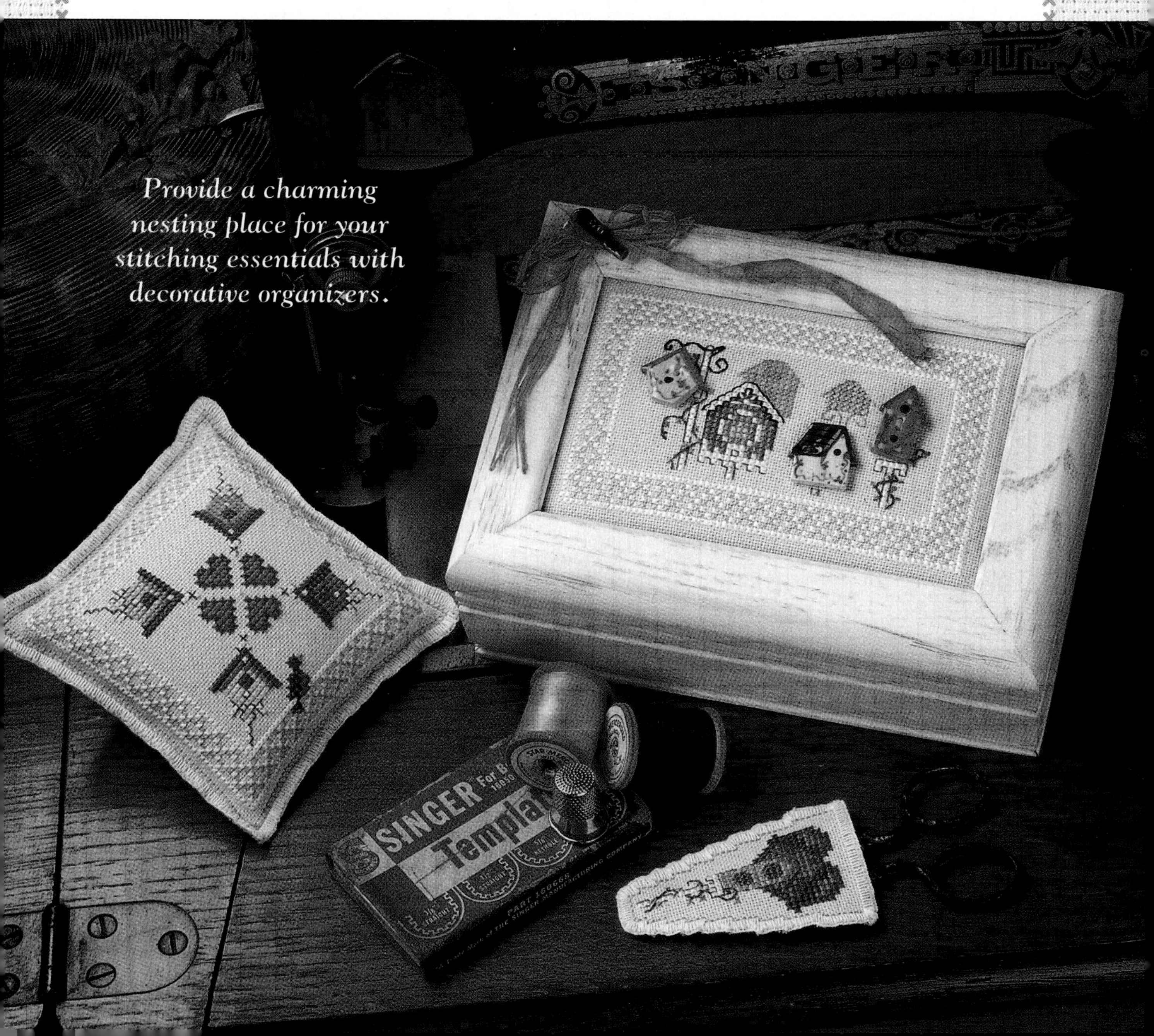

as shown in photo. Position and secure design in box following manufacturer's instructions. Tie raffia straw into bow; glue bow and remaining button to corner of box as shown.

3: For Pincushion, trim design to 5" x 5" for front. Center and glue cardboard to wrong side of one 5" x 5" piece of Monaco for back. With wrong sides facing and beginning four threads from design edge, using one strand blue denim lt. floss and Two-sided Cross-Stitch (see illustration Step 1), stitch front and back together, leaving an opening for stuffing. Stuff with fiberfill and continue with Two-sided Cross-Stitch (see illustration Steps 2 & 3). Trim four threads from stitched edge. Finish edges stitching over both thicknesses using one strand pearl cotton and Buttonhole Stitch.

4: For Scissors Case, carefully trim design following cutting line on graph for front. Cut remaining 5" x 5" piece of Monaco same as design for back. Finish front and back top edges, using one strand pearl cotton and Buttonhole Stitch. With wrong sides facing and using two strands blue denim lt. floss and Backstitch, stitch front and back together as indicated on graph. Finish remaining edges stitching over both thicknesses using one strand pearl cotton and Buttonhole Stitch.❦

X	B'st	¼x	¾x	Str	Fr	DMC	ANCHOR	J.&P. COATS	COLORS
■						#223	#895	#3240	Victorian Rose Med.
	■					#310	#403	#8403	Black
■						#327	#100	#4101	Darkest Antique Violet
	■				■	#413	#401	#8514	Charcoal (one strand)
				■		#413	#401	#8514	Charcoal (two strands)
■			■			#535	#815	#8400	Ash Grey Very Dk.
■	■	■	■			#642	#392	#5832	Beige Grey Dk. (one strand)
■						#642	#392	#5832	Beige Grey Dk. (two strands)
■						#644	#830	#5830	Beige Grey Lt.
■		■				#676	#891	#2305	Honey (one strand)
■						#721	#324	#2324	Orange Spice Med.
■	■		■			#725	#305	#2294	Topaz Med.
■		■				#727	#293	#2289	Topaz Lt.
■						#797	#132	#7143	Deep Blueberry
■		■				#931	#1034	#7051	Blue Denim Med. (one strand)
■						#931	#1034	#7051	Blue Denim Med. (two strands)
■						#932	#1033	#7050	Blue Denim Lt. (one strand)
■	■					#932	#1033	#7050	Blue Denim Lt. (two strands)
■						#963	#73	#3173	Baby Pink
■						#3041	#871	#4222	Antique Violet
■						#3072	#847	#6005	Pearl Grey
	■					#3362	#263	#6317	Darkest Celery Green
■						#3363	#262	#6316	Celery Green Med. (one strand)
	■					#3363	#262	#6316	Celery Green Med. (two strands)
■		■				#3778	#1013	#2338	Terra Cotta
■						#3830	#341	#2339	Terra Cotta Dk.
■	■	■	■	■		White	#2	#1001	White

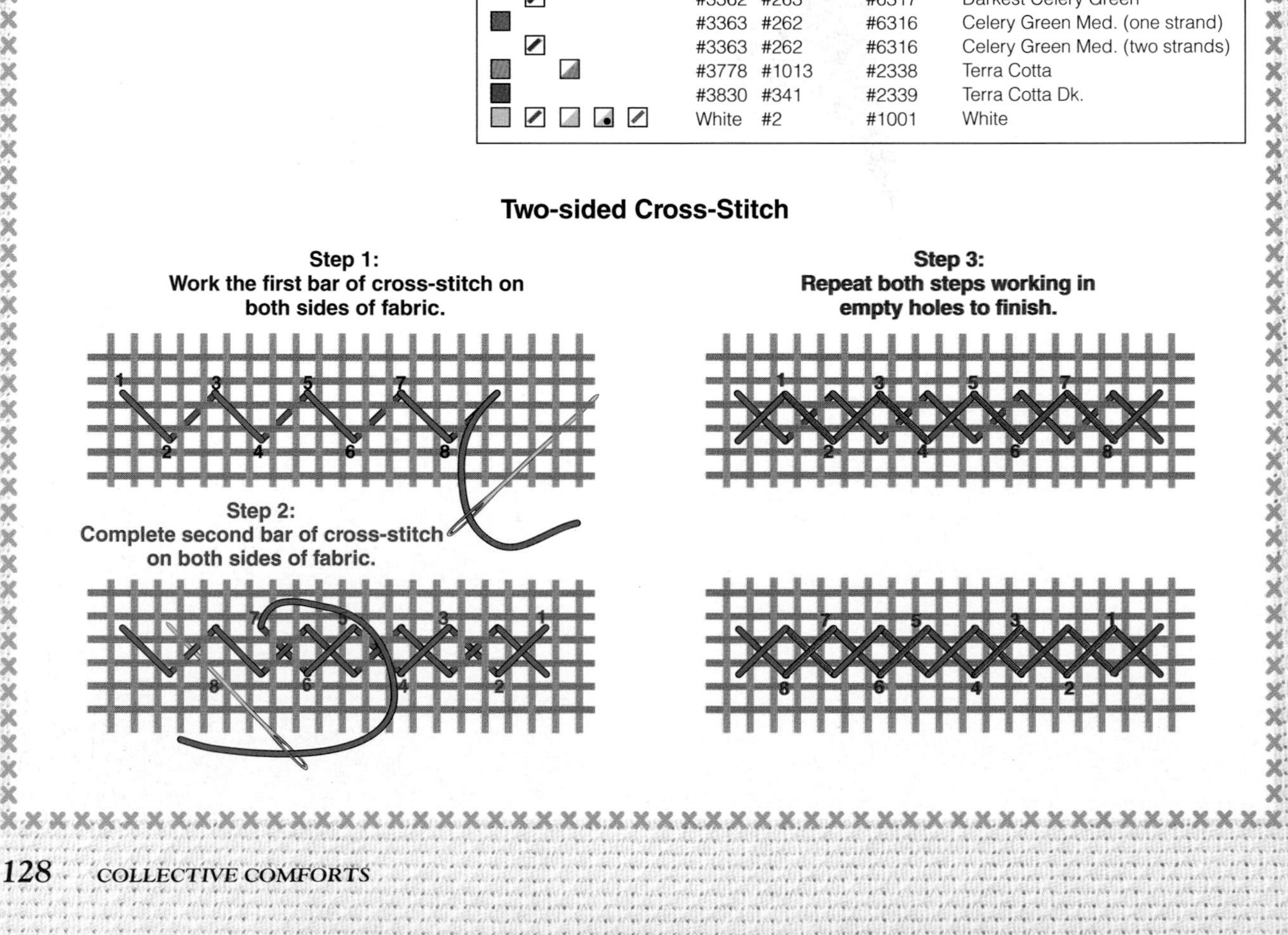

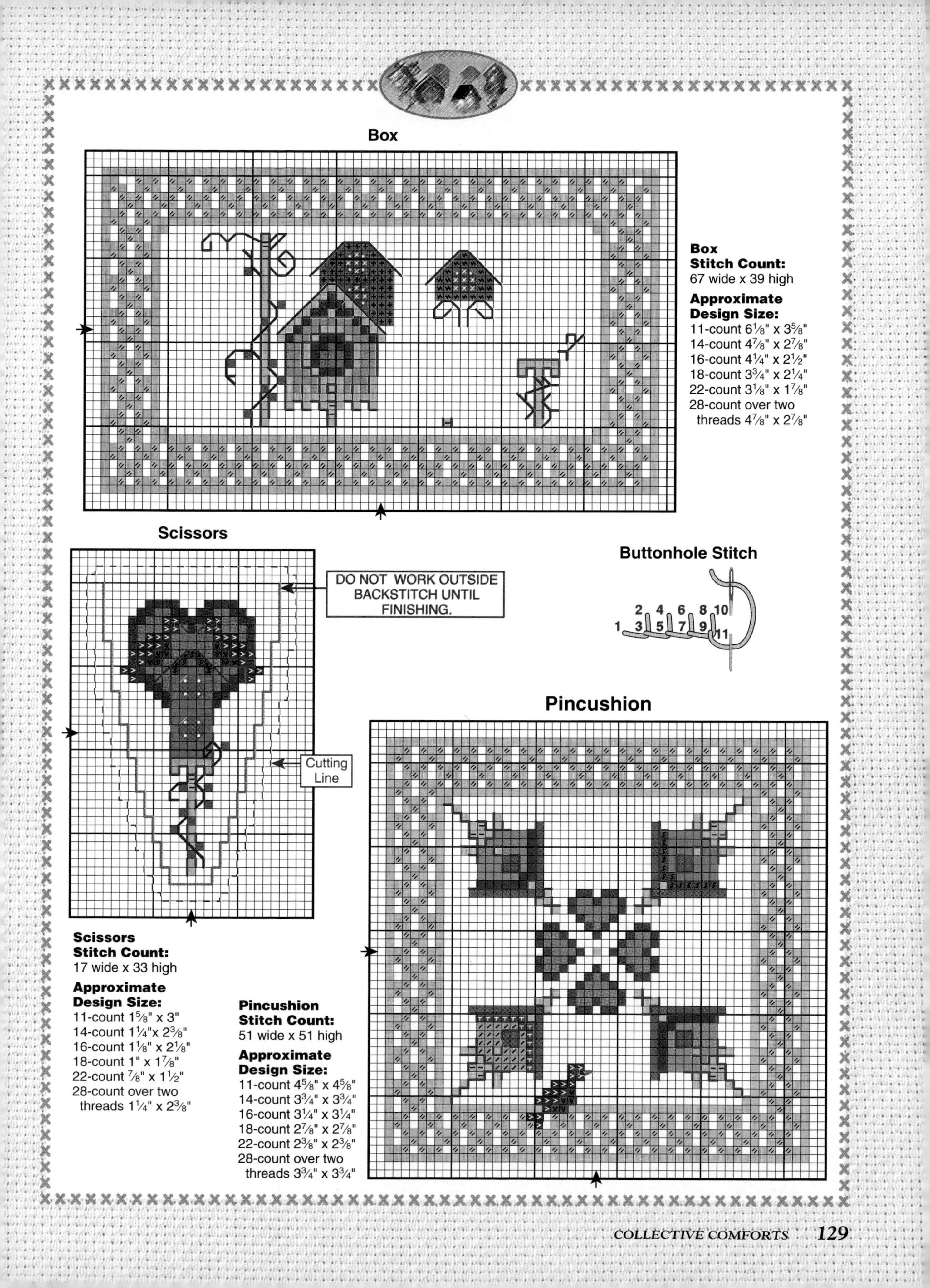

Box
Stitch Count:
67 wide x 39 high

Approximate Design Size:
11-count $6\frac{1}{8}$" x $3\frac{5}{8}$"
14-count $4\frac{7}{8}$" x $2\frac{7}{8}$"
16-count $4\frac{1}{4}$" x $2\frac{1}{2}$"
18-count $3\frac{3}{4}$" x $2\frac{1}{4}$"
22-count $3\frac{1}{8}$" x $1\frac{7}{8}$"
28-count over two threads $4\frac{7}{8}$" x $2\frac{7}{8}$"

Scissors
Stitch Count:
17 wide x 33 high

Approximate Design Size:
11-count $1\frac{5}{8}$" x 3"
14-count $1\frac{1}{4}$"x $2\frac{3}{8}$"
16-count $1\frac{1}{8}$" x $2\frac{1}{8}$"
18-count 1" x $1\frac{7}{8}$"
22-count $\frac{7}{8}$" x $1\frac{1}{2}$"
28-count over two threads $1\frac{1}{4}$" x $2\frac{3}{8}$"

Pincushion
Stitch Count:
51 wide x 51 high

Approximate Design Size:
11-count $4\frac{5}{8}$" x $4\frac{5}{8}$"
14-count $3\frac{3}{4}$" x $3\frac{3}{4}$"
16-count $3\frac{1}{4}$" x $3\frac{1}{4}$"
18-count $2\frac{7}{8}$" x $2\frac{7}{8}$"
22-count $2\frac{3}{8}$" x $2\frac{3}{8}$"
28-count over two threads $3\frac{3}{4}$" x $3\frac{3}{4}$"

Designed by Linda Hebert

MATERIALS

15" x 18" piece of almond 14-count Aida

INSTRUCTIONS

Center and stitch design, using two strands floss for Cross-Stitch and Backstitch.❦

Designed by Marsha J. Coroso

MATERIALS

10" x 10" piece of white 14-count Aida; Wooden box with 7½" x 7½" design area

INSTRUCTIONS

1: Center and stitch design, using two strands floss or two strands floss held together with one strand blending filament for Cross-Stitch. Use two strands floss for Straight Stitch and French Knot.

2: Position and secure design in box following manufacturer's instructions.❦

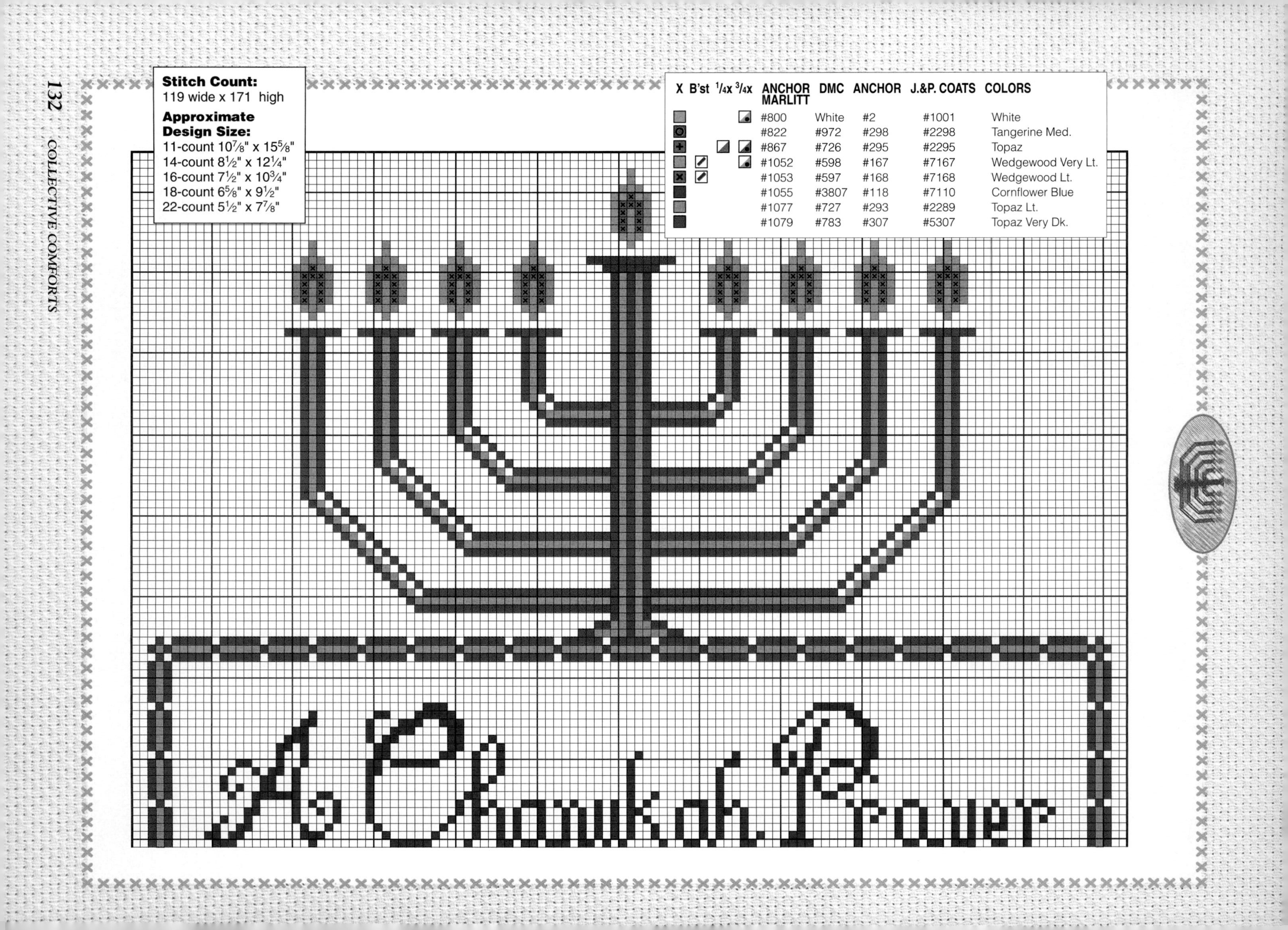

Stitch Count:
119 wide x 171 high

Approximate Design Size:
11-count $10\frac{7}{8}$" x $15\frac{5}{8}$"
14-count $8\frac{1}{2}$" x $12\frac{1}{4}$"
16-count $7\frac{1}{2}$" x $10\frac{3}{4}$"
18-count $6\frac{5}{8}$" x $9\frac{1}{2}$"
22-count $5\frac{1}{2}$" x $7\frac{7}{8}$"

X	B'st	1/4x	3/4x	ANCHOR MARLITT	DMC	ANCHOR	J.&P. COATS	COLORS
■			■	#800	White	#2	#1001	White
■				#822	#972	#298	#2298	Tangerine Med.
■		■	■	#867	#726	#295	#2295	Topaz
■	■		■	#1052	#598	#167	#7167	Wedgewood Very Lt.
■	■			#1053	#597	#168	#7168	Wedgewood Lt.
■				#1055	#3807	#118	#7110	Cornflower Blue
■				#1077	#727	#293	#2289	Topaz Lt.
■				#1079	#783	#307	#5307	Topaz Very Dk.

For all the miracles
and for the salvation
and for the victories
and for the battles that
You performed for our fathers
years ago at this time,
we thank You.

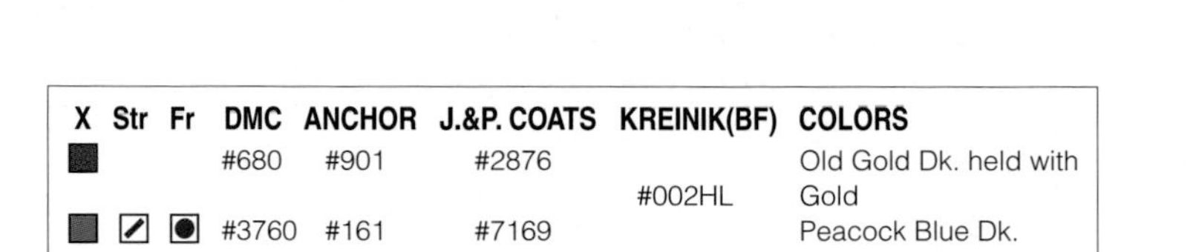

X	Str	Fr	DMC	ANCHOR	J.&P. COATS	KREINIK(BF)	COLORS
■			#680	#901	#2876		Old Gold Dk. held with
						#002HL	Gold
■	⁄	●	#3760	#161	#7169		Peacock Blue Dk.

Stitch Count:
61 wide x 61 high

Approximate Design Size:
11-count 5⅝" x 5⅝"
14-count 4⅜" x 4⅜"
16-count 3⅞" x 3⅞"
18-count 3⅜" x 3⅜"
22-count 2⅞" x 2⅞"

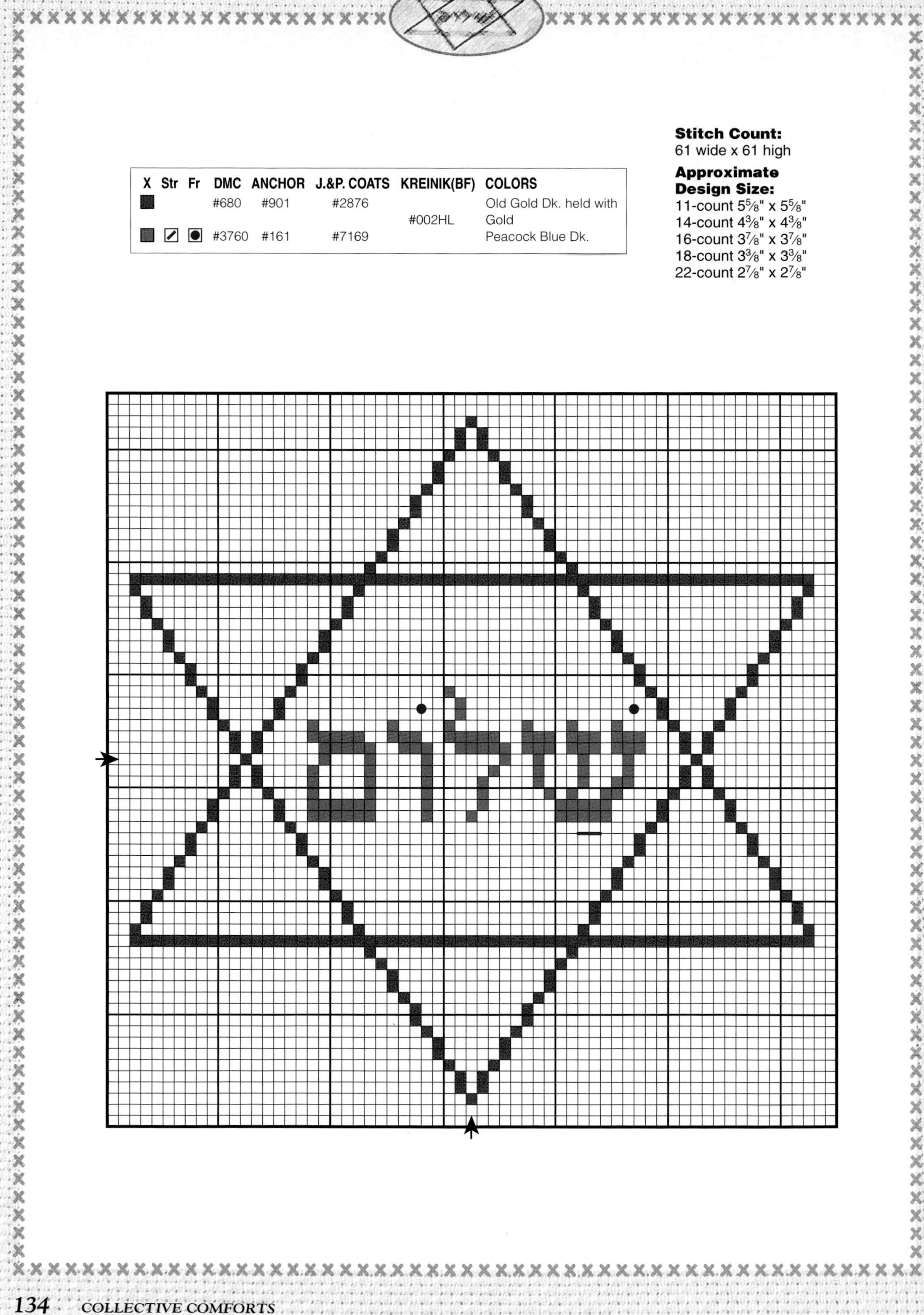

Welcome Friends

Add a welcoming touch to your guest room with this heartwarming design.

Welcome Friends

Designed by Dayna Stedry

MATERIALS

13" x 14" piece of antique white 14-count Aida; 1 yd. fabric #1; ¼ yd. fabric #2; Small amount fabric #3; Batting

INSTRUCTIONS

1: Center and stitch design, using two strands floss for Cross-Stitch and Backstitch.

NOTES: Trim design to 9½" wide x 8½" tall. From fabric #1, cut eighteen 1½" x 3" for A pieces, one 13½" x 14½" piece for back and two 1" x 30" bias strips. From fabric #2, cut sixteen 1½" x 3" for B pieces and four 3" x 3" pieces for corners. From fabric #3, cut four according to Heart Pattern. From batting, cut one 13½" x 14½". Use ¼" seam allowance.

2: Center and sew one heart to each corner piece. With right sides facing, sew design, A, B and corner pieces together according to Assembly Diagram, forming front.

3: With wrong sides facing and batting between, baste front and back together. Machine stitch around edge of Aida.

4: With right sides facing, sew one short edge of bias strips together, forming binding. Press under ¼" on each long edge. With right sides facing, sew binding to front outside edges of wall hanging, folding corners as you sew. Fold binding to back and slip stitch in place. Hang as desired.❦

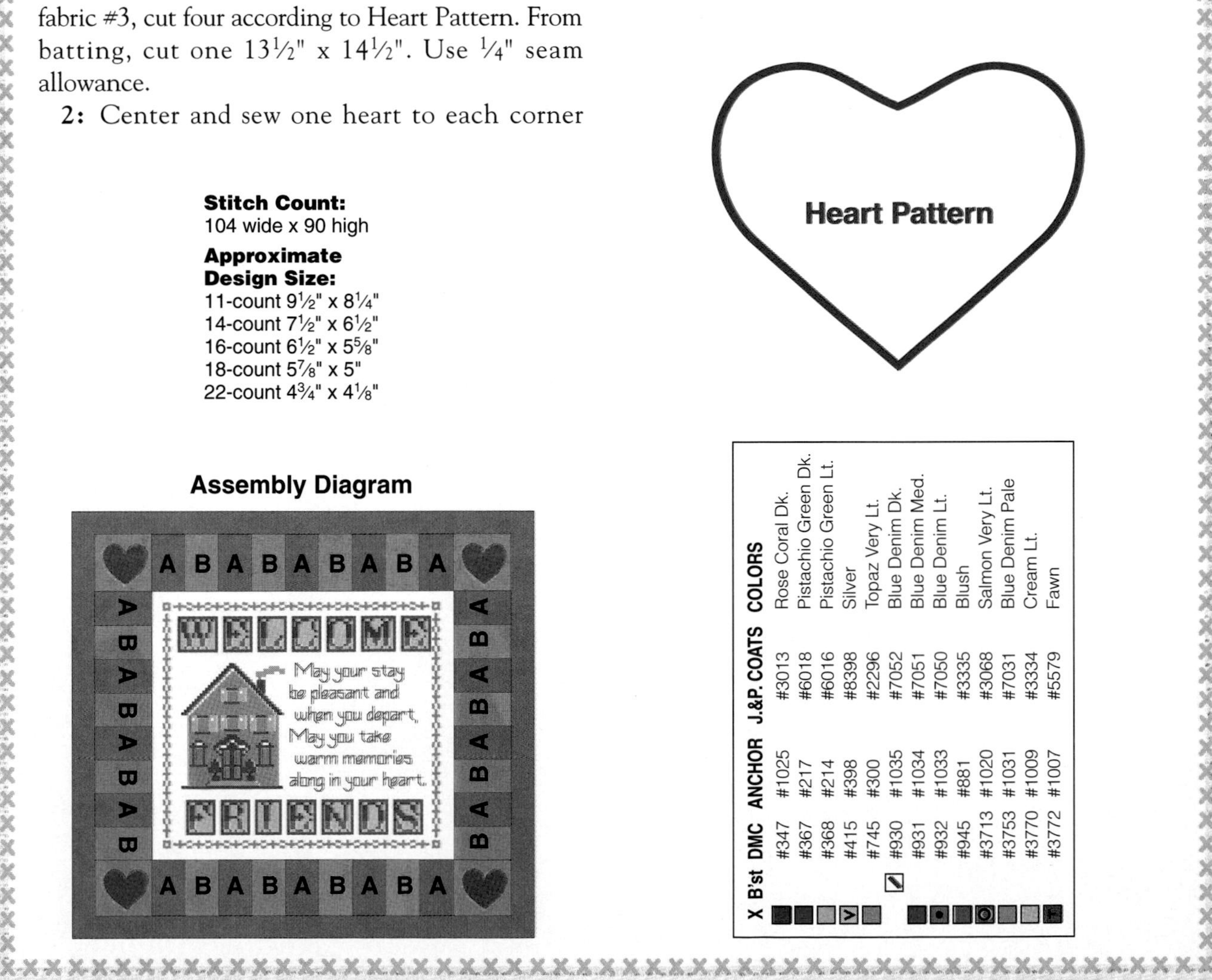

Stitch Count:
104 wide x 90 high

Approximate Design Size:
11-count 9½" x 8¼"
14-count 7½" x 6½"
16-count 6½" x 5⅝"
18-count 5⅞" x 5"
22-count 4¾" x 4⅛"

Assembly Diagram

X	B'st	DMC	ANCHOR	J.&P. COATS	COLORS
■		#347	#1025	#3013	Rose Coral Dk.
■		#367	#217	#6018	Pistachio Green Dk.
■		#368	#214	#6016	Pistachio Green Lt.
>		#415	#398	#8398	Silver
■		#745	#300	#2296	Topaz Very Lt.
	/	#930	#1035	#7052	Blue Denim Dk.
■		#931	#1034	#7051	Blue Denim Med.
•		#932	#1033	#7050	Blue Denim Lt.
■		#945	#881	#3335	Blush
O		#3713	#1020	#3068	Salmon Very Lt.
■		#3753	#1031	#7031	Blue Denim Pale
■		#3770	#1009	#3334	Cream Lt.
■		#3772	#1007	#5579	Fawn

WELCOME
May your stay
be pleasant and
when you depart,
May you take
warm memories
along in your heart.
FRIENDS

Musical Duet

Designed by Mona Eno

MATERIALS

15" x 17" piece of 28-count Annabelle®

INSTRUCTIONS

Center and stitch design, stitching over two threads and using two strands floss for Cross-Stitch and Backstitch of detail on stool cushion. Use one strand floss for remaining Backstitch.

X	B'st	1/2x	1/4x	3/4x	DMC	ANCHOR	J.&P. COATS	COLORS
■			◪		#209	#109	#4302	Lavender Med.
■			◪		#210	#108	#4303	Lavender Lt.
V			◪		#301	#1049	#5365	Cinnamon Lt.
	⁄				#310	#403	#8403	Black
■			◪		#317	#400	#8512	Darkest Silver
+			◪		#318	#399	#8511	Silver Med.
■					#340	#118	#7110	Blue Violet
Λ			◪		#353	#8	#3006	Peach Flesh Med.
■			◪		#415	#398	#8398	Silver
■			◪		#420	#374	#5374	Hazel Nut Dk.
■			◪		#470	#267	#6010	Avocado Green Lt.
■			◪		#471	#266	#6266	Avocado Green Very Lt.
■			◪		#561	#212	#6211	Jade Very Dk.
×			◪		#562	#210	#6213	Jade Med.
■			◪		#563	#208	#6210	Jade Lt.
■			◪		#604	#55	#3001	Cranberry Lt.
⊥			◪		#605	#50	#3151	Cranberry Very Lt.
	⁄				#632	#936	#5936	Fawn Dk.
O			◪		#676	#891	#2305	Honey
/			◪		#677	#886	#5372	Honey Lt.
	⁄				#722	#323	#2323	Orange Spice Lt.
■			◪		#725	#305	#2294	Topaz Med.
S			◪		#727	#293	#2289	Topaz Lt.
–			◪		#754	#1012	#3868	Peach Flesh Lt.
■		◇	◪		#775	#128	#7031	Baby Blue
■			◪		#783	#307	#5307	Topaz Very Dk.
	⁄				#838	#380	#5478	Darkest Pecan
■		△	◪	◪	#840	#379	#5379	Pecan Med.
O			◪		#869	#944	#5475	Warm Brown Med.
	⁄				#890	#218	#6021	Spruce Dk.
■			◪		#931	#1034	#7051	Blue Denim Med.
=			◪		#932	#1033	#7050	Blue Denim Lt.
■			◪		#948	#1011	#2331	Peach Flesh Very Lt.
■		D	◪		#3047	#852	#2300	Yellow Beige Lt.
■	⁄		◪		#3347	#266	#6010	Ivy Green
■			◪		#3687	#68	#3088	Mauve Med.
<			◪		#3688	#66	#3087	Mauve
■			◪		#3689	#49	#3086	Mauve Very Lt.
■			◪		#3746	#1030	#7150	Blue Violet Med.
■			◪		#3776	#1048	#3336	Mahogany Lt.
•			◪	◪	#3799	#236	#8999	Charcoal Dk.
I	⁄		◪		#3803	#69	#3089	Mauve Dk.
■			◪		#3828	#888	#5371	Hazel Nut
•			◪		White	#2	#1001	White

Show your appreciation for the sound of music and display this beautifully orchestrated piece in your home.

MUSICAL

Stitch Count:
127 wide x 157 high
Approximate Design Size:
11-count 11 5/8" x 14 3/8"
14-count 9 1/8" x 11 1/4"
16-count 8" x 9 7/8"
18-count 7 1/8" x 8 3/4"
22-count 5 7/8" x 7 1/8"
28-count over two threads 9 1/8" x 11 1/4"

Zen Garden

Designed by Stephen L. Wendling

MATERIALS

One 9" x 10" piece and one 15" x 19" piece of dawn grey 28-count Jubilee; Hand mirror with 5" design area; 1¾ yds. decorative cord; Craft glue or glue gun

INSTRUCTIONS

1: Center and stitch "Hand Mirror" design onto 9" x 10" piece and "Dresser Scarf" design onto 15" x 19" piece of Jubilee, stitching over two threads and using two strands floss or one strand fine braid for Cross-Stitch and one strand floss for Backstitch.

2: For Hand Mirror, cover design area following manufacturer's instructions. Glue decorative cord around outside edge of mounted design.

3: For Dresser Scarf, trim design to 14" wide x 11" tall. Press edges under ¼". Sew decorative cord around outside edges.❦

X	B'st	¼x	¾x	DMC	ANCHOR	J.&P. COATS	KREINIK(#8)	COLORS
■	/	◢		#310	#403	#8403		Black
+		◢		#414	#235	#8513		Silver Dk.
	/			#434	#310	#5000		Darkest Toast
	/			#699	#923	#6228		Kelly Green Dk.
■	/	◢	◢	#700	#228	#6227		Kelly Green
■	/	◢		#702	#226	#6239		Kelly Green Lt.
O		◢		#704	#256	#6238		Parrot Green Med.
	/			#791	#178	#7024		Darkest Cornflower Blue
	/			#815	#43	#3000		Garnet Dk.
■	/	◢	◢	#817	#13	#2335		Nasturtium
X		◢	◢	#905	#257	#6258		Parrot Green Dk.
V		◢		#3340	#329	#2332		Apricot Dk.
■		◢	◢	#3716	#25	#3125		Antique Rose
T	/	◢		#3807	#118	#7110		Cornflower Blue
■		◢		#3824	#8	#3008		Apricot Lt.
■							#002	Gold

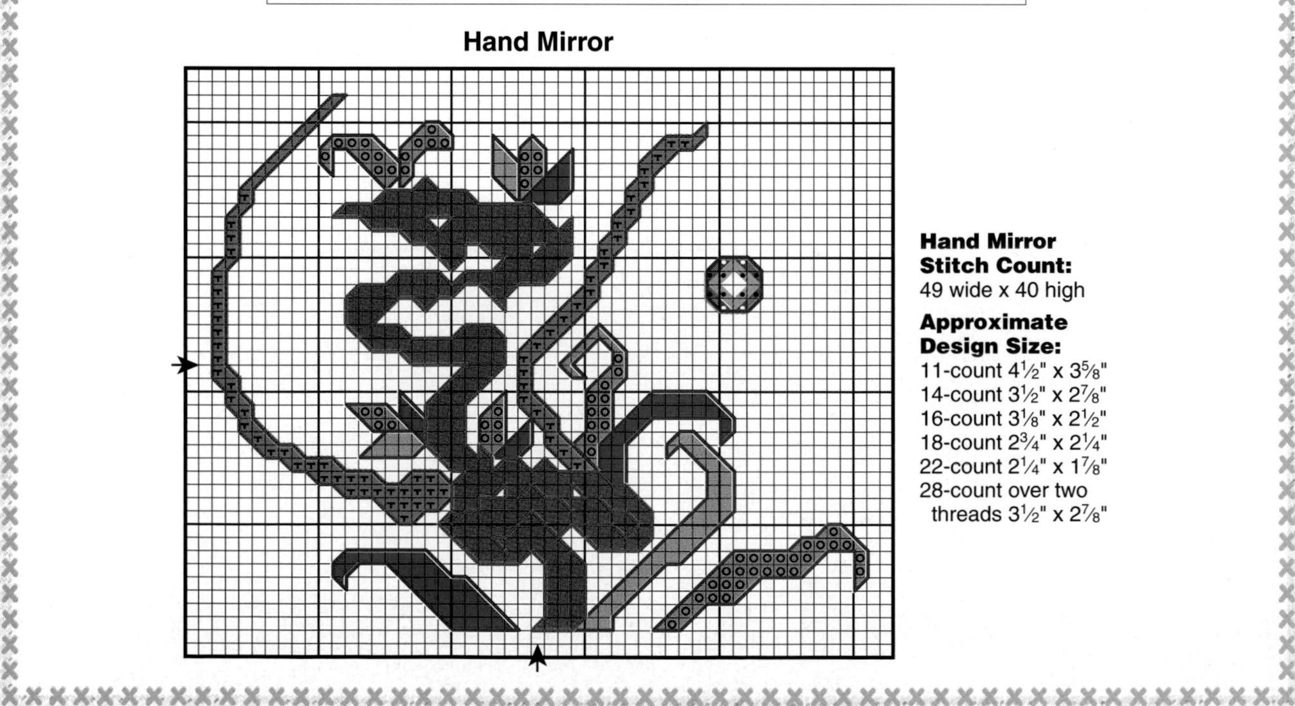

Hand Mirror Stitch Count:
49 wide x 40 high

Approximate Design Size:
11-count 4½" x 3⅝"
14-count 3½" x 2⅞"
16-count 3⅛" x 2½"
18-count 2¾" x 2¼"
22-count 2¼" x 1⅞"
28-count over two threads 3½" x 2⅞"

Oriental beauty is at your fingertips when you stitch this enchanting dresser scarf and hand mirror.

DMC	ANCHOR	J.&P. COATS	KREINIK(#8)	COLORS
#310	#403	#8403		Black
#414	#235	#8513		Silver Dk.
#434	#310	#5000		Darkest Toast
#699	#923	#6228		Kelly Green Dk.
#700	#228	#6227		Kelly Green
#702	#226	#6239		Kelly Green Lt.
#704	#256	#6238		Parrot Green Med.
#791	#178	#7024		Darkest Cornflower Blue
#815	#43	#3000		Garnet Dk.
#817	#13	#2335		Nasturtium
#905	#257	#6258		Parrot Green Dk.
#3340	#329	#2332		Apricot Dk.
#3716	#25	#3125		Antique Rose
#3807	#118	#7110		Cornflower Blue
#3824	#8	#3008		Apricot Lt.
			#002	Gold

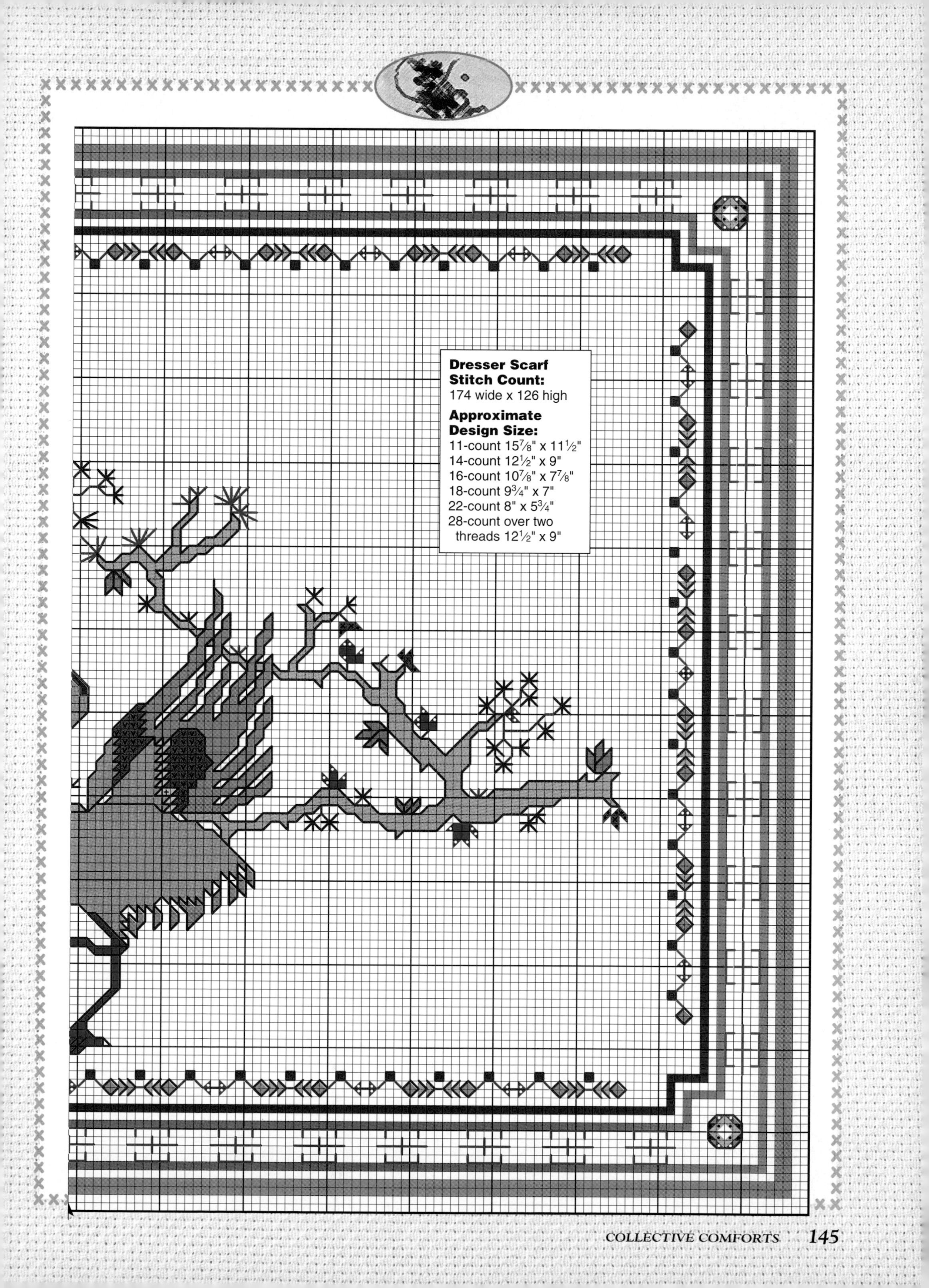

Dresser Scarf
Stitch Count:
174 wide x 126 high
Approximate
Design Size:
11-count 15⅞" x 11½"
14-count 12½" x 9"
16-count 10⅞" x 7⅞"
18-count 9¾" x 7"
22-count 8" x 5¾"
28-count over two threads 12½" x 9"

Zoo Animals

Designed by Kathleen Kennebeck for Zweigart® Design Bank

MATERIALS

44" x 56" piece of rainbow 18-count Baby Snuggle afghan fabric

INSTRUCTIONS

1: Center and stitch designs onto afghan fabric following Stitching Diagram, stitching over two threads and using three strands floss for Cross-Stitch and two strands floss for Backstitch, Smyrna Stitch and French Knot. Use two strands floss of each color indicated for Straight Stitch of pony's mane and tail. Use one strand floss for remaining Straight Stitch.

2: To fringe edges, see Single Fringe Illustration.❦

Seal

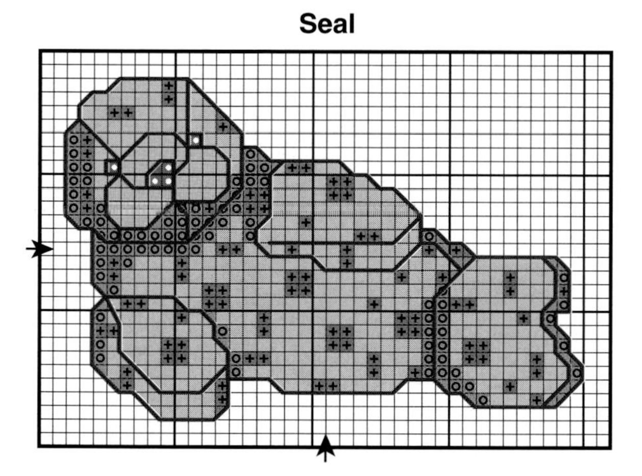

Seal
Stitch Count:
38 wide x 25 high

Approximate Design Size:
11-count 3½" x 2⅜"
14-count 2¾" x 1⅞"
16-count 2⅜" x 1⅝"
18-count 2⅛" x 1⅜"
22-count 1¾" x 1⅛"
18-count over two threads 4¼" x 2⅞"

Seal

X	B'st	¼x	DMC	ANCHOR	J.&P. COATS	COLORS
▪		◪	#310	#403	#8403	Black
✚		◪	#317	#400	#8512	Darkest Silver
▪		◪	#318	#399	#8511	Silver Med.
▫		◪	#712	#926	#1002	Cream Very Pale
▫		◪	#762	#234	#8510	Silver Very Lt.
	⁄		#3799	#236	#8999	Charcoal Dk.

Stitching Diagram

Single Fringe Illustration

Remove selvage edges before beginning. Measure desired fringe length on all outside edges. Mark with water-soluble fabric marker; stay stitch along this line. Unravel all threads from fabric edge to stay-stitching, working each thread separately or the threads will knot. Knot groups of lengthwise threads to form fringe. Trim ends even after knotting is complete.

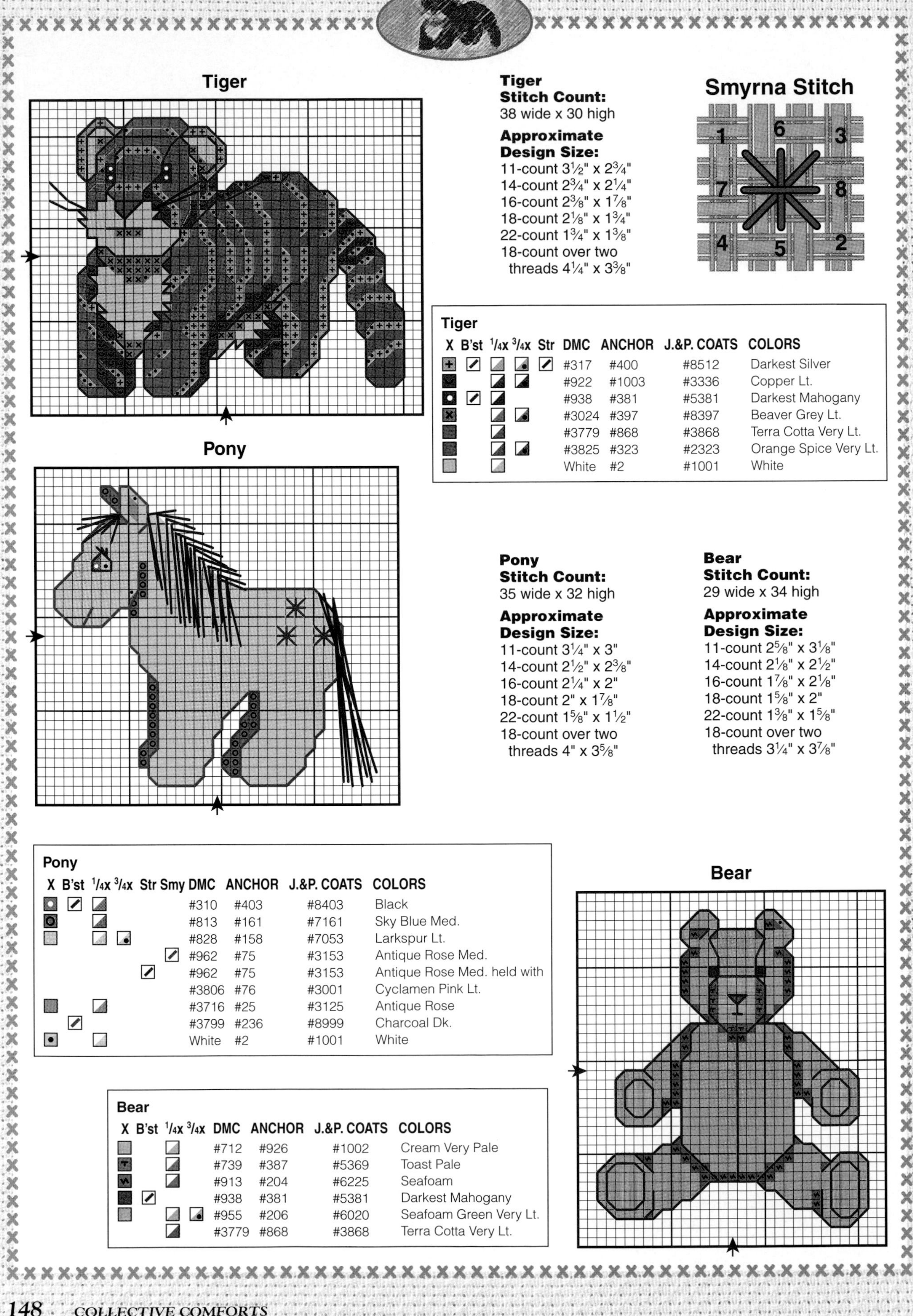

Tiger

Tiger
Stitch Count:
38 wide x 30 high

Approximate Design Size:
11-count 3½" x 2¾"
14-count 2¾" x 2¼"
16-count 2⅜" x 1⅞"
18-count 2⅛" x 1¾"
22-count 1¾" x 1⅜"
18-count over two threads 4¼" x 3⅜"

Smyrna Stitch

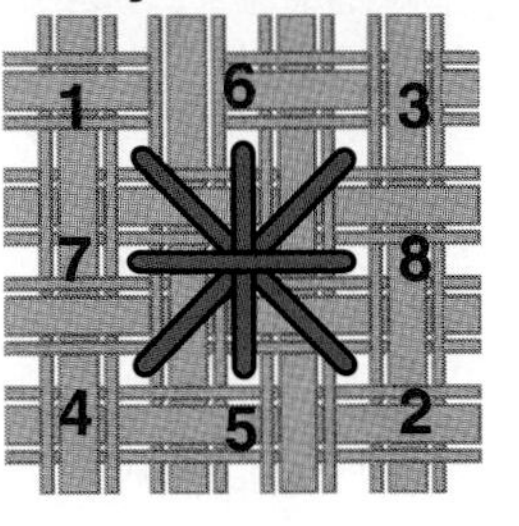

Tiger

X	B'st	¼x	¾x	Str	DMC	ANCHOR	J.&P. COATS	COLORS
■	■	■	■	■	#317	#400	#8512	Darkest Silver
■		■	■		#922	#1003	#3336	Copper Lt.
■	■	■			#938	#381	#5381	Darkest Mahogany
■		■	■		#3024	#397	#8397	Beaver Grey Lt.
■		■			#3779	#868	#3868	Terra Cotta Very Lt.
■		■	■		#3825	#323	#2323	Orange Spice Very Lt.
■		■			White	#2	#1001	White

Pony

Pony
Stitch Count:
35 wide x 32 high

Approximate Design Size:
11-count 3¼" x 3"
14-count 2½" x 2⅜"
16-count 2¼" x 2"
18-count 2" x 1⅞"
22-count 1⅝" x 1½"
18-count over two threads 4" x 3⅝"

Bear
Stitch Count:
29 wide x 34 high

Approximate Design Size:
11-count 2⅝" x 3⅛"
14-count 2⅛" x 2½"
16-count 1⅞" x 2⅛"
18-count 1⅝" x 2"
22-count 1⅜" x 1⅝"
18-count over two threads 3¼" x 3⅞"

Pony

X	B'st	¼x	¾x	Str	Smy	DMC	ANCHOR	J.&P. COATS	COLORS
■	■	■				#310	#403	#8403	Black
■		■				#813	#161	#7161	Sky Blue Med.
■		■	■			#828	#158	#7053	Larkspur Lt.
					■	#962	#75	#3153	Antique Rose Med.
				■		#962	#75	#3153	Antique Rose Med. held with
						#3806	#76	#3001	Cyclamen Pink Lt.
■		■				#3716	#25	#3125	Antique Rose
	■					#3799	#236	#8999	Charcoal Dk.
■		■				White	#2	#1001	White

Bear

Bear

X	B'st	¼x	¾x	DMC	ANCHOR	J.&P. COATS	COLORS
■		■		#712	#926	#1002	Cream Very Pale
■		■		#739	#387	#5369	Toast Pale
■		■		#913	#204	#6225	Seafoam
■	■			#938	#381	#5381	Darkest Mahogany
■		■	■	#955	#206	#6020	Seafoam Green Very Lt.
		■		#3779	#868	#3868	Terra Cotta Very Lt.

Koala							
X	B'st	1/4x	3/4x	Fr	DMC	ANCHOR	J.&P. COATS	COLORS
■	/	■		●	#310	#403	#8403	Black
//		■			#778	#968	#3080	Antique Mauve Very Lt.
■		■			#3024	#397	#8397	Beaver Grey Lt.
■		■			#3042	#870	#4221	Antique Violet Lt.
■		■	■		#3740	#872	#4223	Antique Violet Dk.
V	/	■			#3799	#236	#8999	Charcoal Dk.
•		■			White	#2	#1001	White

Koala

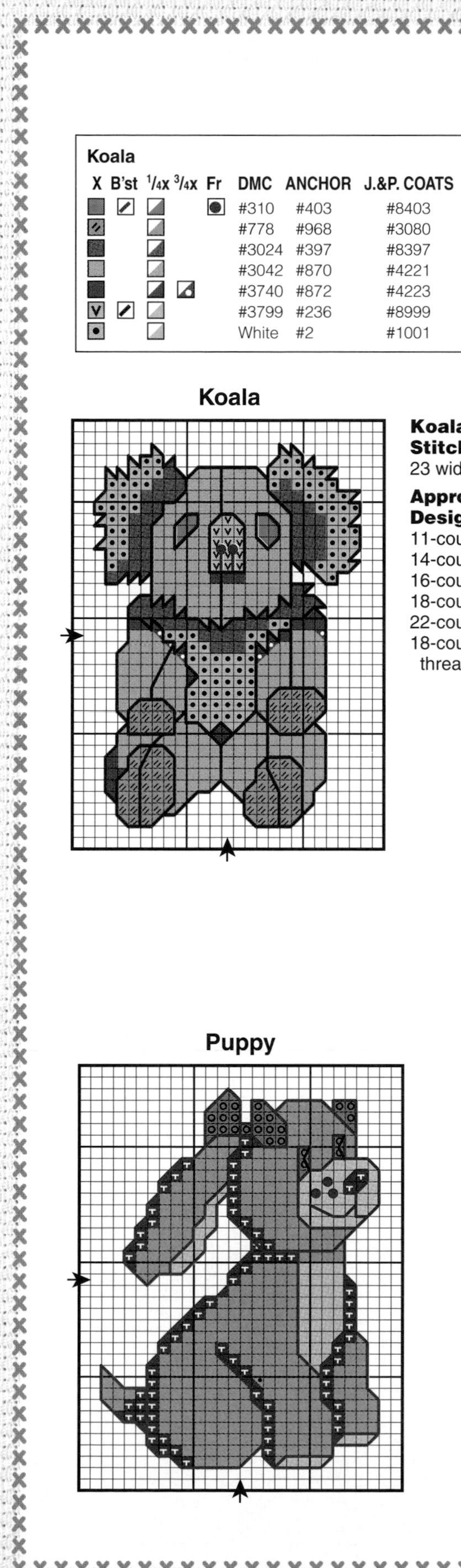

Koala
Stitch Count:
23 wide x 33 high

Approximate Design Size:
11-count 2⅛" x 3"
14-count 1¾" x 2⅜"
16-count 1½" x 2⅛"
18-count 1⅜" x 1⅞"
22-count 1⅛" x 1½"
18-count over two threads 2⅝" x 3¾"

Duck

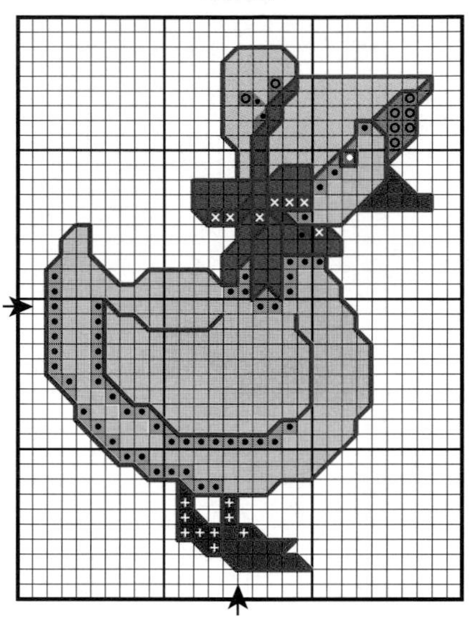

Duck							
X	B'st	1/4x	3/4x	DMC	ANCHOR	J.&P. COATS	COLORS
o				#310	#403	#8403	Black
×		■		#312	#979	#7979	Azure Blue Dk.
+		■		#400	#351	#5349	Mahogany Dk.
•		■		#762	#234	#8510	Silver Very Lt.
■		■	■	#798	#131	#7022	Blueberry Dk.
◎		■	■	#813	#161	#7161	Sky Blue Med.
■		■		#828	#158	#7053	Larkspur Lt.
■		■		#922	#1003	#3336	Copper Lt.
	/			#3799	#236	#8999	Charcoal Dk.
■		■		White	#2	#1001	White

Puppy
Stitch Count:
24 wide x 33 high

Approximate Design Size:
11-count 2¼" x 3"
14-count 1¾" x 2⅜"
16-count 1½" x 2⅛"
18-count 1⅜" x 1⅞"
22-count 1⅛" x 1½"
18-count over two threads 2¾" x 3¾"

Duck
Stitch Count:
26 wide x 35 high

Approximate Design Size:
11-count 2⅜" x 3¼"
14-count 1⅞" x 2½"
16-count 1⅝" x 2¼"
18-count 1½" x 2"
22-count 1¼" x 1⅝"
18-count over two threads 3" x 4"

Puppy

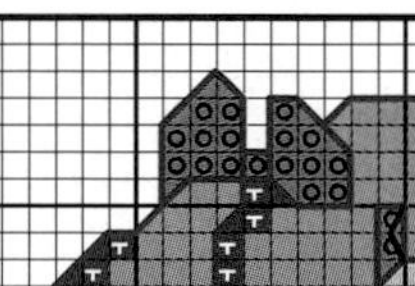

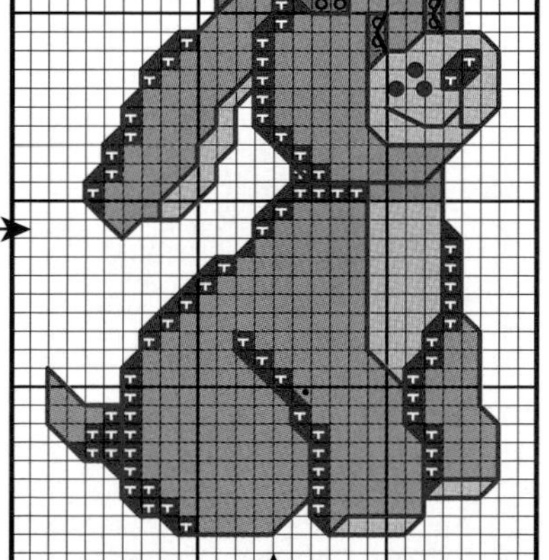

Puppy								
X	B'st	1/4x	3/4x	Fr	DMC	ANCHOR	J.&P. COATS	COLORS
	/				#310	#403	#8403	Black
◎		■			#813	#161	#7161	Sky Blue Med.
■		■			#819	#271	#3280	Antique Rose Pale
	/			●	#938	#381	#5381	Darkest Mahogany
T		■			#962	#75	#3153	Antique Rose Med.
■		■	■		#3716	#25	#3125	Antique Rose

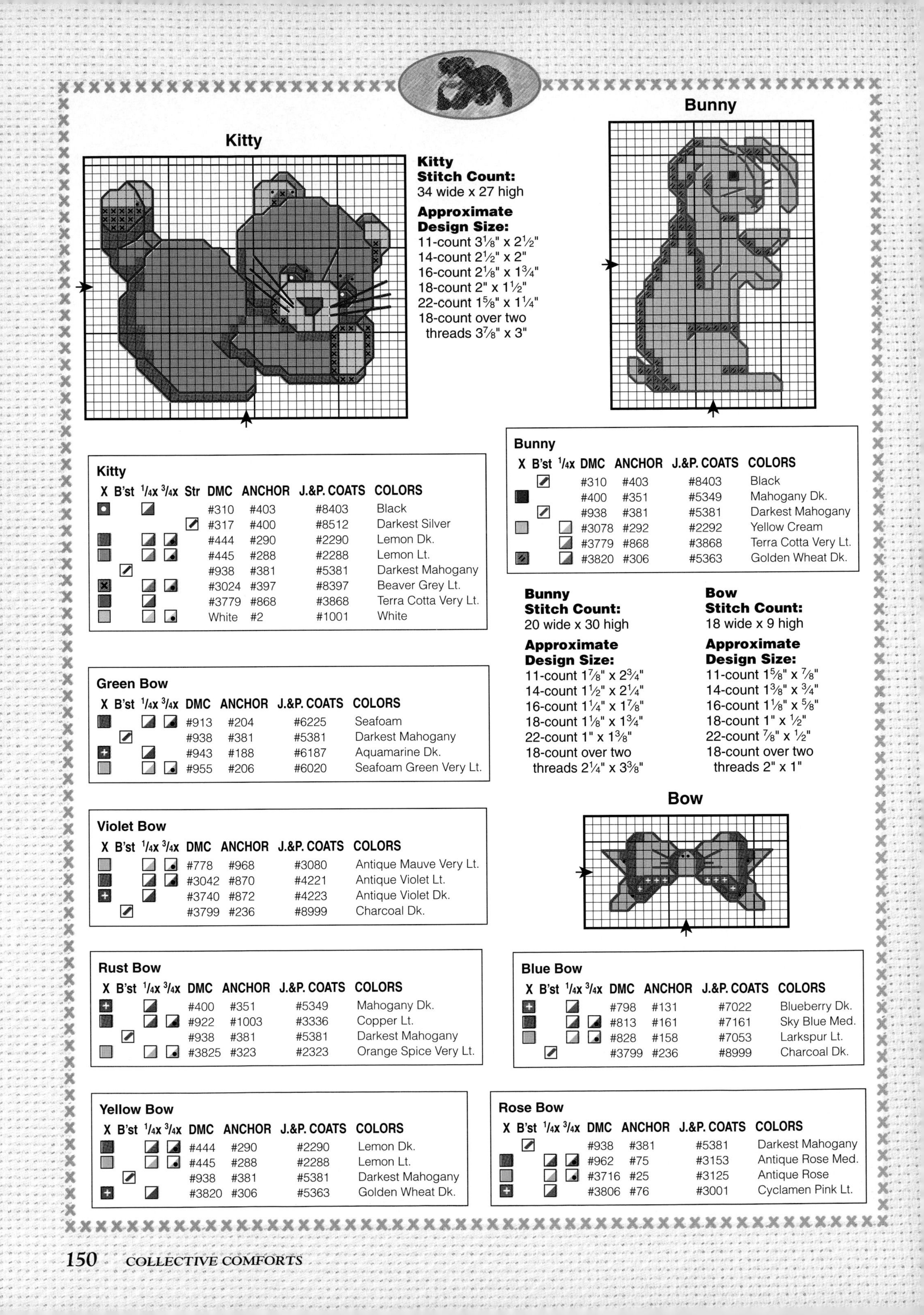

Kitty

Kitty
Stitch Count:
34 wide x 27 high

Approximate
Design Size:
11-count 3⅛" x 2½"
14-count 2½" x 2"
16-count 2⅛" x 1¾"
18-count 2" x 1½"
22-count 1⅝" x 1¼"
18-count over two threads 3⅞" x 3"

Bunny

Kitty

X	B'st	¼x	¾x	Str	DMC	ANCHOR	J.&P. COATS	COLORS
•		■			#310	#403	#8403	Black
				■	#317	#400	#8512	Darkest Silver
■		■	■		#444	#290	#2290	Lemon Dk.
■		■	■		#445	#288	#2288	Lemon Lt.
	■				#938	#381	#5381	Darkest Mahogany
×		■	■		#3024	#397	#8397	Beaver Grey Lt.
■		■			#3779	#868	#3868	Terra Cotta Very Lt.
■		■	■		White	#2	#1001	White

Bunny

X	B'st	¼x	DMC	ANCHOR	J.&P. COATS	COLORS
	■		#310	#403	#8403	Black
■			#400	#351	#5349	Mahogany Dk.
	■		#938	#381	#5381	Darkest Mahogany
■		■	#3078	#292	#2292	Yellow Cream
		■	#3779	#868	#3868	Terra Cotta Very Lt.
■		■	#3820	#306	#5363	Golden Wheat Dk.

Bunny
Stitch Count:
20 wide x 30 high

Approximate
Design Size:
11-count 1⅞" x 2¾"
14-count 1½" x 2¼"
16-count 1¼" x 1⅞"
18-count 1⅛" x 1¾"
22-count 1" x 1⅜"
18-count over two threads 2¼" x 3⅜"

Bow
Stitch Count:
18 wide x 9 high

Approximate
Design Size:
11-count 1⅝" x ⅞"
14-count 1⅜" x ¾"
16-count 1⅛" x ⅝"
18-count 1" x ½"
22-count ⅞" x ½"
18-count over two threads 2" x 1"

Bow

Green Bow

X	B'st	¼x	¾x	DMC	ANCHOR	J.&P. COATS	COLORS
■		■	■	#913	#204	#6225	Seafoam
	■			#938	#381	#5381	Darkest Mahogany
+		■		#943	#188	#6187	Aquamarine Dk.
■		■	■	#955	#206	#6020	Seafoam Green Very Lt.

Violet Bow

X	B'st	¼x	¾x	DMC	ANCHOR	J.&P. COATS	COLORS
■		■	■	#778	#968	#3080	Antique Mauve Very Lt.
■		■	■	#3042	#870	#4221	Antique Violet Lt.
+		■		#3740	#872	#4223	Antique Violet Dk.
	■			#3799	#236	#8999	Charcoal Dk.

Rust Bow

X	B'st	¼x	¾x	DMC	ANCHOR	J.&P. COATS	COLORS
+		■		#400	#351	#5349	Mahogany Dk.
■		■	■	#922	#1003	#3336	Copper Lt.
	■			#938	#381	#5381	Darkest Mahogany
■		■	■	#3825	#323	#2323	Orange Spice Very Lt.

Blue Bow

X	B'st	¼x	¾x	DMC	ANCHOR	J.&P. COATS	COLORS
+		■		#798	#131	#7022	Blueberry Dk.
■		■	■	#813	#161	#7161	Sky Blue Med.
■		■	■	#828	#158	#7053	Larkspur Lt.
	■			#3799	#236	#8999	Charcoal Dk.

Yellow Bow

X	B'st	¼x	¾x	DMC	ANCHOR	J.&P. COATS	COLORS
■		■	■	#444	#290	#2290	Lemon Dk.
■		■	■	#445	#288	#2288	Lemon Lt.
	■			#938	#381	#5381	Darkest Mahogany
+		■		#3820	#306	#5363	Golden Wheat Dk.

Rose Bow

X	B'st	¼x	¾x	DMC	ANCHOR	J.&P. COATS	COLORS
	■			#938	#381	#5381	Darkest Mahogany
■		■	■	#962	#75	#3153	Antique Rose Med.
■		■	■	#3716	#25	#3125	Antique Rose
+		■		#3806	#76	#3001	Cyclamen Pink Lt.

General Instructions

Tools of the Stitcher

Fabrics

Most counted cross-stitch projects are worked on evenweave fabrics made especially for counted thread embroidery. These fabrics have vertical and horizontal threads of uniform thickness and spacing. Aida cloth is a favorite of beginning stitchers because its weave forms distinctive squares in the fabric, which makes placing stitches easy. To determine a fabric's thread count, count the number of threads per inch of fabric.

Linen is made from fibers of the flax plant and is strong and durable. Its lasting quality makes it the perfect choice for heirloom projects. Linen is available in a range of muted colors and stitch counts.

In addition to evenweave fabrics, many stitchers enjoy using waste canvas and perforated paper. Waste canvas is basted to clothing or other fabric, forming a grid for stitching which is later removed. Perforated paper has holes evenly spaced for 14 stitches per inch.

Needles

Cross-stitch needles should have elongated eyes and blunt points. They should slip easily between the threads of the fabric, but should not pierce the fabric. The most common sizes used for cross-stitching are size 24 or 26. The ideal needle size is just small enough to slip easily through your fabric. Some stitchers prefer to use a slightly smaller needle for backstitching. When stitching on waste canvas, use a sharp needle.

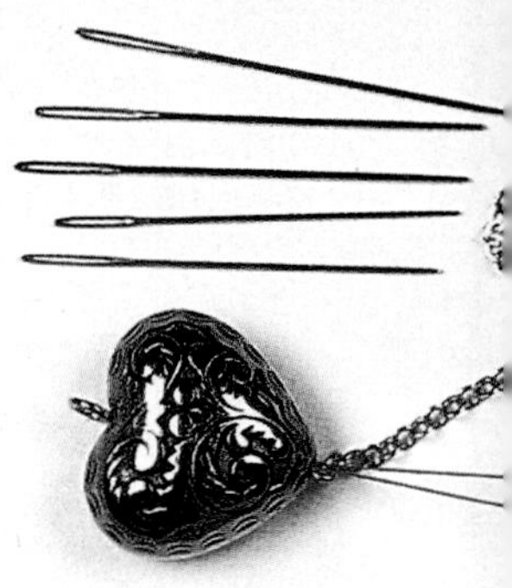

Hoops, Frames & Scissors

Hoops can be round or oval and come in many sizes. The three main types are plastic, spring-tension and wooden. Frames are easier on the fabric than hoops and come in many sizes and shapes. Once fabric is mounted it doesn't have to be removed until stitching is complete, saving fabric from excessive handling.

Small, sharp scissors are essential for cutting floss and removing mistakes. For cutting fabrics, invest in a top-quality pair of medium-sized sewing scissors. To keep them in top form, use these scissors only for cutting fabrics and floss.

Today's cross-stitcher can achieve a vast array of effects in texture, color and shine. In addition to the perennial favorite, six-strand floss, stitchers can choose from sparkling metallics, shiny rayons, silks, narrow ribbon threads and much more.

Six-Strand Floss

Six-strand floss comes in a variety of colors and is available in metallics, silk and rayon as well as cotton. Most projects are worked using two or three strands of floss for cross-stitches and one or two strands for backstitches. For ease of stitching and to prevent wear on fibers, use lengths no longer than 18".

Pearl Cotton

Pearl cotton is available in #3, #5 and #8, with #3 being the thickest. The plies of pearl cotton will not separate, and for most stitching one strand is used. Pearl cotton has a lustrous sheen.

Flower & Ribbon Threads

Flower thread has a tight twist and comes in many soft colors. It is heavier than one ply of six-strand floss – one strand of flower thread equals two strands of floss. Ribbon thread is a narrow ribbon especially created for stitching. It comes in a large number of colors in satin as well as metallic finishes.

Blending Filament & Metallic Braid

Blending filament is a fine, shiny fiber that can be used alone or combined with floss or other thread. Knotting the blending filament on the needle with a slipknot is recommended for control.

Metallic braid is a braided metallic fiber, usually used single-ply. Thread this fiber just as you would any other fiber. Use short lengths, about 15", to keep the fiber from fraying.

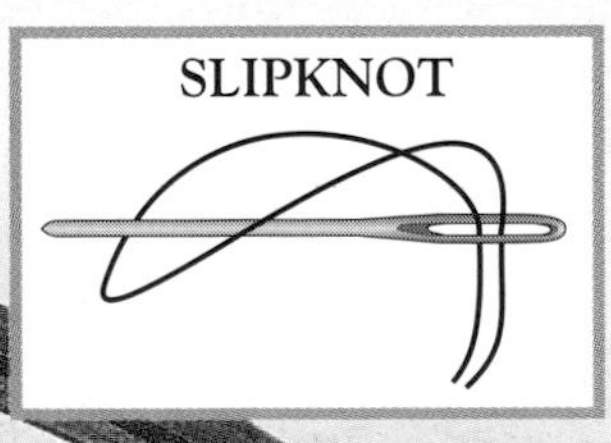

Stitching with Beads

Small seed beads can be added to any cross-stitch design, using one bead per stitch. Knot thread at beginning of beaded section for security, especially if you are adding beads to clothing. The bead should lie in the same direction as the top half of cross-stitches.

Bead Attachment

Use one strand floss to secure beads. Bring beading needle up from back of work, leaving 2" length of thread hanging; do not knot (end will be secured between stitches as you work.) Thread bead on needle; complete stitch.

Do not skip over more than two stitches or spaces without first securing thread, or last bead will be loose. To secure, weave thread into several stitches on back of work. Follow graph to work design, using one bead per stitch.

Assemble fabric, floss, pattern and tools. Familiarize yourself with the graph, color key and instructions before beginning.

Preparing Fabric

Before you stitch, decide how large to cut fabric. If you are making a pillow or other design which requires a large unstitched area, be sure to leave plenty of fabric. If you are making a small project, leave at least 3" around all edges of design. Determine the design area size by using this formula: number of stitches across design area divided by the number of threads per inch of fabric equals size of fabric in inches. Measure fabric, then cut evenly along horizontal and vertical threads.

Press out folds. To prevent raveling, hand overcast or machine zigzag fabric edges. Find center of fabric by folding horizontally and vertically, and mark with a small stitch.

Reading Graphs

Cross-stitch graphs or charts are made up of colors and symbols to tell you the exact color, type and placement of each stitch. Each square represents the area for one complete cross-stitch. Next to each graph, there is a key with information about stitches and floss colors represented by the graph's colors and symbols.

Color keys have abbreviated headings for cross-stitch (x), one-half cross-stitch (½x), quarter cross-stitch (¼x), three-quarter cross-stitch (¾x), backstitch (B'st), French knot (Fr), lazy daisy stitch (LzD) and straight stitch (Str). Some graphs are so large they must be divided for printing.

Preparing Floss

The six strands of floss are easily separated, and the number of strands used is given in instructions. Cut strands in 14"-18" lengths. When separating floss, always separate all six strands, then recombine the number of strands needed. To make floss separating easier, run cut length across a damp sponge. To prevent floss from tangling, run cut length through a fabric-softener dryer sheet before separating and threading needle. To colorfast red floss tones, which sometimes bleed, hold floss under running water until water runs clear. Allow to air dry.

Beginning & Ending a Thread

Try these methods for beginning a thread, then decide which one is best for you.

1: Securing the thread: Start by pulling needle through fabric back to front, leaving about 1" behind fabric. Hold this end with fingers as you begin stitching, and work over end with your first few stitches. After work is in progress, weave end through the back of a few stitches.

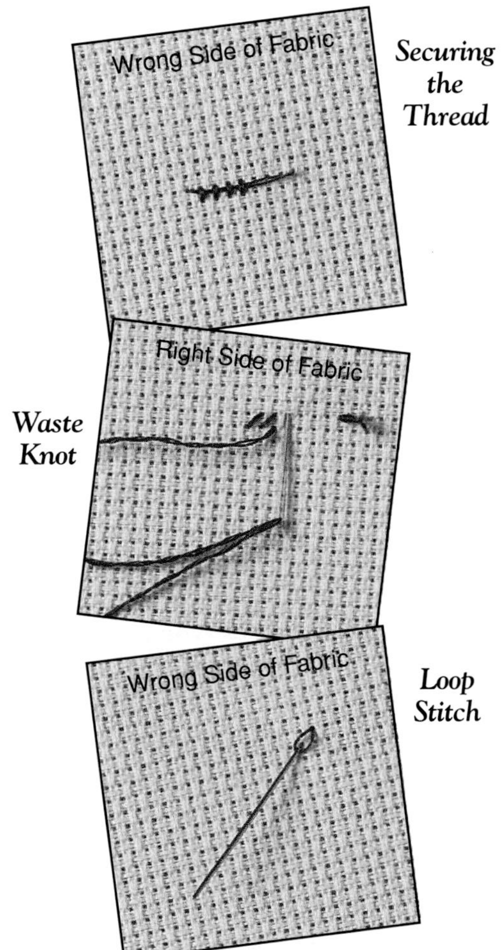

2: Waste knot: Make a knot in end of floss and pull needle through fabric front to back several squares over from where your first cross-stitch will be. Come up at first stitch and stitch first few stitches over floss end. Clip knot.

3: Loop stitch: This method can only be used for even numbers of strands. Cut strands twice the normal length, then take half the number of strands needed and fold in half. Insert loose ends in needle and bring needle up from back at first stitch, leaving loop underneath. Take needle down through fabric and through loop; pull to secure.

For even stitches, keep a consistent tension on your thread, and pull thread and needle completely through fabric with each stab of the needle. Make all the top crosses on your cross-stitches face the same direction. To finish a thread, run the needle under the back side of several stitches and clip. Threads carried across the back of unworked areas may show through to the front, so do not carry threads.

Master Stitchery

Work will be neater if you always try to make each stitch by coming up in an unoccupied hole and going down in an occupied hole.

The sewing method is preferred for stitching on linen and some other evenweaves, but can also be used on Aida. Stitches are made as in hand sewing with needle going from front to back to front of fabric in one motion. All work is done from the front of the fabric. When stitching with the sewing method, it is important not to pull thread too tightly or stitches will become distorted. Stitching on linen is prettiest with the sewing method, using no hoop. If you use a hoop or frame when using the sewing method with Aida, keep in mind that fabric cannot be pulled taut. There must be "give" in the fabric in order for needle to slip in and out easily.

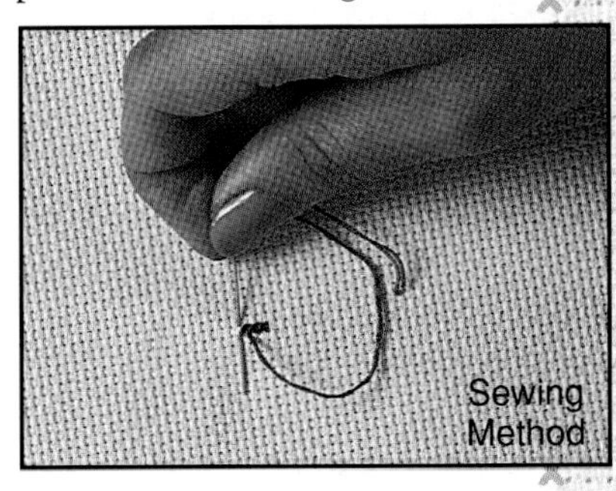

In the stab method, needle and floss are taken completely through fabric twice with each stitch. For the first half of the stitch, bring needle up and pull thread completely through fabric to the front. Then take needle down and reach underneath and pull completely through to bottom.

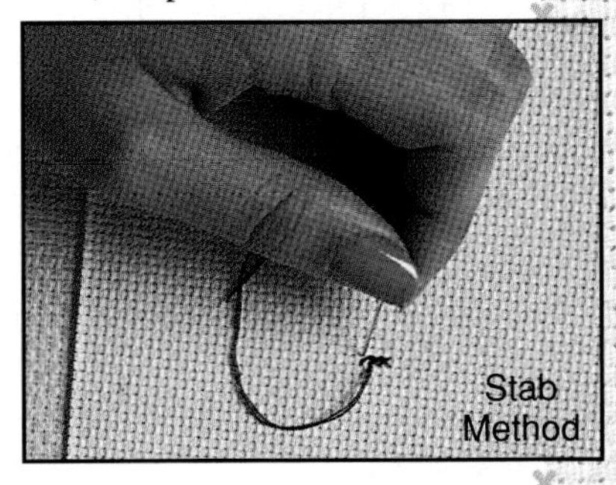

Working on Evenweave

When working on linen or other evenweave fabric, keep needle on right side of fabric, taking needle front to back to front with each stitch. Work over two threads, placing the beginning and end of the bottom half of the first Cross-Stitch where a vertical thread crosses a horizontal thread.

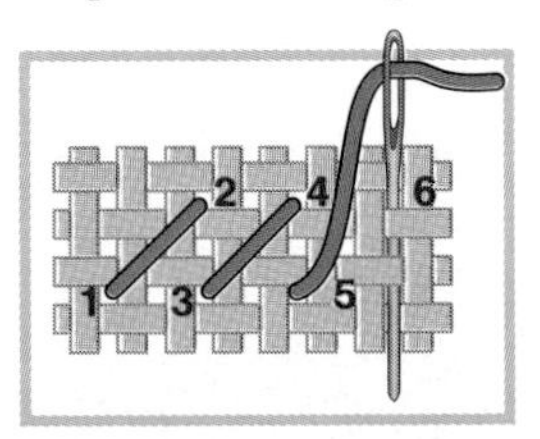

Cleaning Your Needlework

Careful washing, pressing and sometimes blocking help preserve and protect your stitched piece. After stitching is complete, a gentle washing will remove surface dirt, hoop marks and hand oils that have accumulated on your fabric while stitching. Even if a piece looks clean, it's always a good idea to give it a nice cleaning before finishing. Never press your work before cleaning, as this only serves to set those hoop marks and soils that are best removed.

Using a gentle soap such as baby shampoo or gentle white dishwashing liquid and a large, clean bowl, make a solution of cool, sudsy water. If you use a handwash product, make sure the one you choose contains no chlorine bleach. Fill another bowl or sink with plain cool water for rinsing.

Soak your stitched piece in sudsy water for five to ten minutes. Then gently and without rubbing or twisting, squeeze suds through fabric several times. Dip piece several times in fresh cool water until no suds remain.

On rare occasions floss colors will run or fade slightly. When this happens, continue to rinse in cool water until water becomes perfectly clear. Remove fabric from water and lay on a soft, white towel. Never twist or wring your work. Blot excess water away and roll the piece up in the towel, pressing gently.

Never allow a freshly washed piece of embroidery to air dry. Instead, remove the damp piece from the towel and place face down on a fresh, dry white towel. To prevent color stains, it's important to keep the stitched piece flat, not allowing stitched areas to touch each other or other areas of the fabric. Make sure the edges of fabric are in straight lines and even. To be sure fabric edges are straight when pressing dry, use a ruler or T-square to check edges. Wash towel several times before using it to block cross-stitch, and use it only for this purpose.

After edges are aligned and fabric is perfectly smooth, cover the back of the stitched piece with a pressing cloth, cotton diaper or other lightweight white cotton cloth. Press dry with a dry iron set on a high permanent press or cotton setting, depending on fabric content. Allow stitchery to lie in this position several hours. Machine drying is acceptable after use for items like towels and kitchen accessories, but your work will be prettier and smoother if you give these items a careful pressing the first time.

Framing & Mounting

Shopping for Frames

When you shop for a frame, take the stitchery along with you and compare several frame and mat styles. Keep in mind the "feeling" of your stitched piece when choosing a frame. For example, an exquisite damask piece stitched with metallics and silk threads might need an ornate gold frame, while a primitive sampler stitched on dirty linen with flower thread would need a simpler, perhaps wooden frame.

Mounting

Cross-stitch pieces can be mounted on mat board, white cardboard, special padded or unpadded mounting boards designed specifically for needlework, or special acid-free mat board available from art supply stores. Acid-free framing materials are the best choice for projects you wish to keep well-preserved for future generations. If you prefer a padded look, cut quilt batting to fit mounting board.

Center blocked stitchery over mounting board of choice with quilt batting between, if desired. Leaving 1½" to 3" around all edges, trim excess fabric away along straight grain.

Mounting boards made for needlework have self-stick surfaces and require no pins. When using these products, lift and smooth needlework onto board until work is taut and edges are smooth and even. Turn board face down and smooth fabric to back, mitering corners.

Pins are required for other mounting boards. With design face up, keeping fabric straight and taut, insert a pin through fabric and edge of mounting board at the center of each side. Turn piece face down and smooth excess fabric to back, mitering corners.

There are several methods for securing fabric edges. Edges may be glued to mat board with liquid fabric glue or fabric glue stick. If mat board is thick, fabric may be stapled.

Mats & Glass

Pre-cut mats are available in many sizes and colors to fit standard-size frames. Custom mats are available in an even wider variety of colors, textures and materials. Using glass over cross-stitch is a matter of personal preference, but is generally discouraged. Moisture can collect behind glass and rest on fabric, causing mildew stains. A single or double mat will hold glass away from fabric.

BASIC STITCHERY

CROSS-STITCH (x): There are two ways of making a basic Cross-Stitch. The first method is used when working rows of stitches in the same color. The first step makes the bottom half of the stitches across the row, and the second step makes the top half.

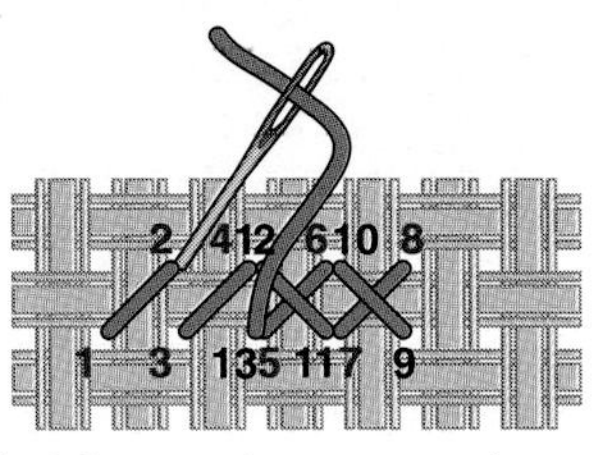

The second method is used when making single stitches. The bottom and top halves of each stitch are worked before starting the next stitch.

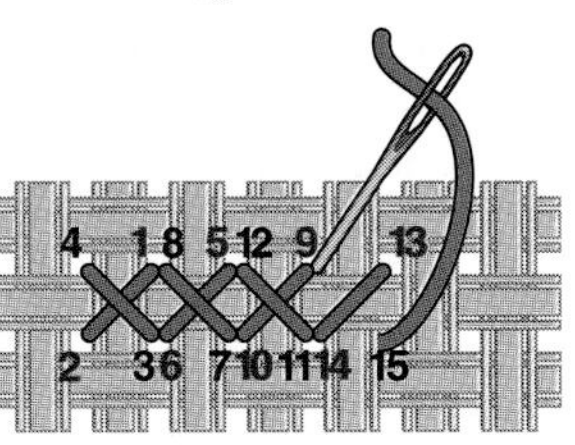

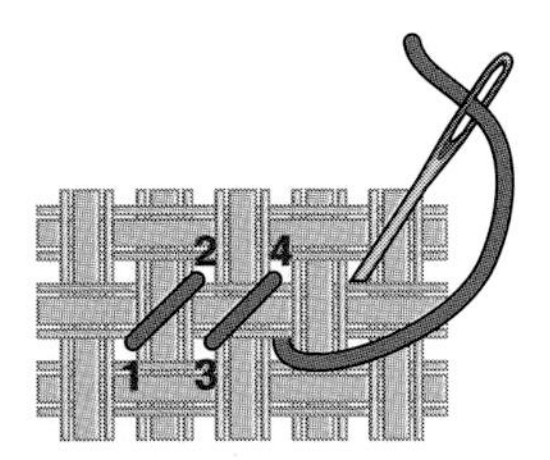

HALF CROSS-STITCH (½x): The first part of a Cross-Stitch. May slant in either direction.

QUARTER CROSS-STITCH (¼x): Stitch may slant in any direction.

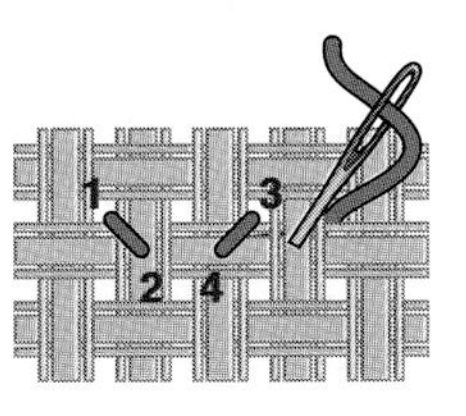

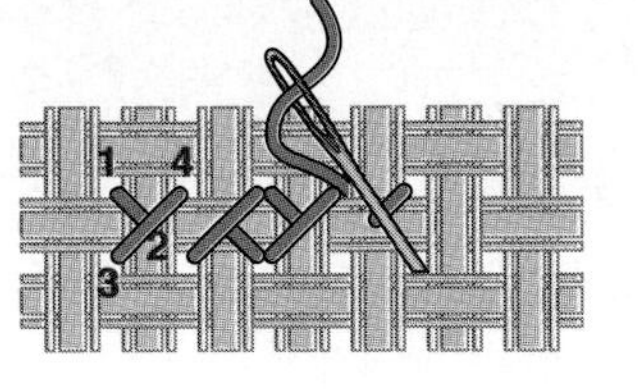

THREE-QUARTER CROSS-STITCH (¾x): A Half Cross-Stitch plus a Quarter Cross-Stitch. May slant in any direction.

HERRINGBONE STITCH

BULLION STITCH

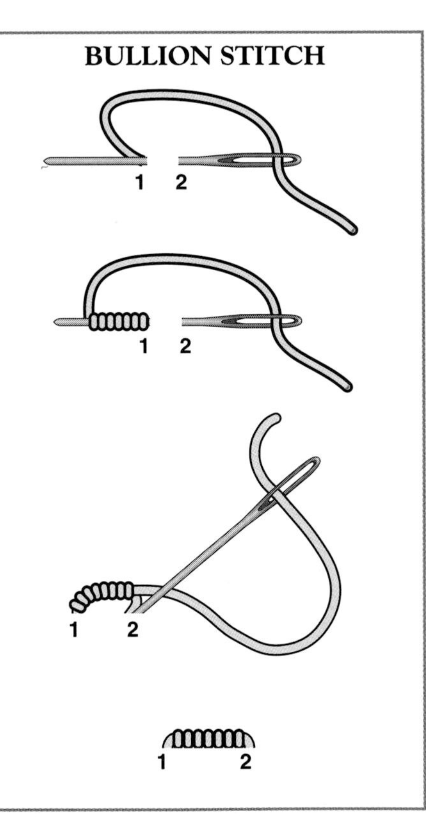

EMBELLISHING WITH EMBROIDERY

EMBROIDERY stitches add detail and dimension to stitching. Unless otherwise noted, work Backstitches first, then other embroidery stitches.

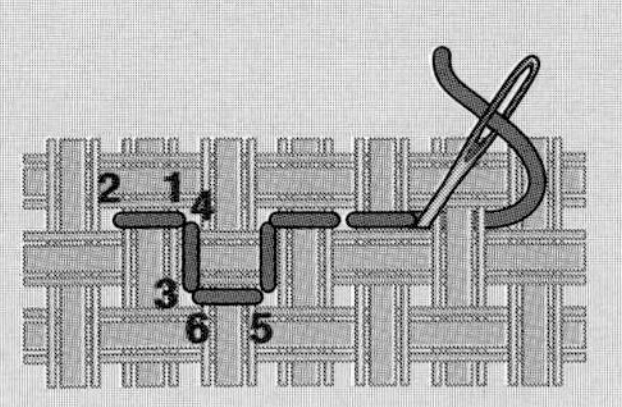

FRENCH KNOT

LAZY DAISY

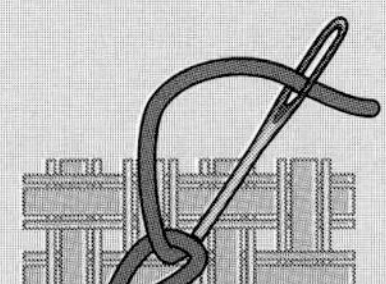

STRAIGHT STITCH

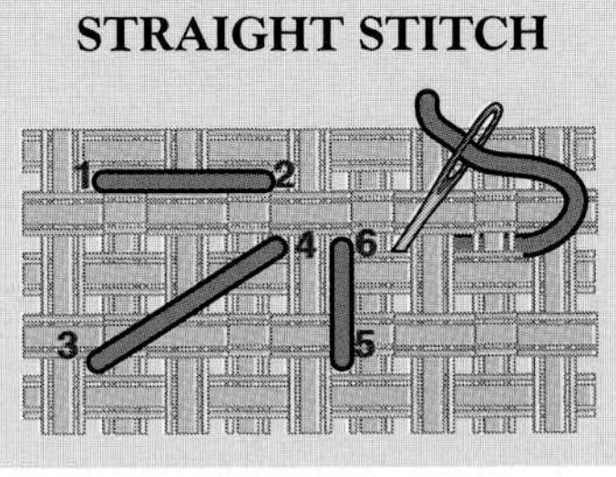

Acknowledgments

We would like to express our appreciation to the many people who helped create this book. Our special thanks go to each of the talented designers who contributed original designs and to our extraordinary models: A.C. & Janice Upright, Bonne & Savannah Reed, Beth Bledsoe, Joni Easley, Jill Waggoner, Jana Robertson, Chelsea Garrett, Fran Rohus, Diana Kordsmeier and Donna Robertson, who patiently posed for each photograph.

The beautiful photography locations in Texas were provided by Harold & Myra Sue Rester, Mt. Pleasant; Billy & Judy Hammonds, Mt. Pleasant; Mataline Broach, Mt. Pleasant; Maurice & Karen Kidwell, The Red Geranium, White Oak; Georgia's Garden Center, White Oak; A.C. & Janice Upright and Susan Conger, Longview; Eddie & Jackie Calicutt, Arp; and Mary Barnett, Arp.

A special thanks to Allens Nursery, Tyler; B&B Antiques, Gladewater; Broadway Florist, Big Sandy; Mike & Gina Joseph, Kilgore; Bill Whitaker, Tyler, for supplying our wonderful photography props and The Frame Up Galley, Tyler, for the beautiful framing.

Our sincerest thanks and appreciation goes to the following manufacturers for generously providing their products for use in the following projects:

CHARLES CRAFT, INC.

Aida — Fairy Footprints, Floral Fairies, Mischievous Mice

Monaco — Peony & Poppy, Spring Flowers, Merry, Merry Christmas, Birds & Buttons

Waste Canvas — Tender Loving Care

COATS & CLARK

Anchor Embroidery Floss — Fairy Footprints, Hebrew Welcome

Anchor Marlitt — Chanukah Prayer

DARICE®

Metallic Cord — Heavenly Angels

DMC®

Embroidery Floss — Peony & Poppy, Floral Hearts Afghan, Seed Packets, Ring of Flowers, Spring Flowers, Victorian Squares, Love is Eternal, Warm Friendships, Where There is No Vision, Honor the Women, Iris Place Mat, Meditation, Antique Auto, Four Churches, Spindrift, Somebunny Special, Good Name, Floral Fairies, Merry, Merry Christmas, Christmas Joy, Home for the Holidays, Little Church in the Winter, Partridge in a Bear Tree, Heavenly Angels, Merry Christmice, Mischievous Mice, Dear Santa, Tender Loving Care, Birds & Buttons, Hebrew Welcome, Musical Duet, Zen Garden, Zoo Animals

#5 Pearl Cotton — Spindrift

FAIRFIELD PROCESSING CORP.

Pillow Form — Peony & Poppy, Fairy Footprints, Mischievous Mice

Batting — Victorian Squares, Home for the Holidays, Little Church in the Winter, Heavenly Angels

KREINIK

Blending Filament — Mischievous Mice, Dear Santa, Hebrew Welcome

Fine (#8) Metallic Braid — Merry, Merry Christmas, Christmas Joy, Heavenly Angels

MILL HILL

Ceramic Buttons — Birds & Buttons

PLAID ENTERPRISES, INC.

Folk Art Paint — Christmas Joy

REED BAXTER WOODCRAFTS, INC.

White Oak Box — Birds & Buttons

SUDBERRY HOUSE

Fancywork Box — Hebrew Welcome

Hand Mirror — Zen Garden

Petite Tray — Where There is No Vision

Round Footstool — Ring of Flowers

TAYLOR'S WORKSHOP

Banner Rack — Countryside Nursery

WICHELT IMPORTS, INC.

Aida — Chanukah Prayer

Angelica — Floral Hearts Afghan

Jobelan® — Ring of Flowers, Love is Eternal

Melinda Cloth — Meditation

Royal Crown Danish Linen — Victorian Squares

WIMPOLE STREET CREATIONS

Apron & Pinafore — Tender Loving Care

WRIGHTS®

Lace — Heavenly Angels, Merry Christmas

Metallic Braid — Dear Santa

Tassels — Victorian Squares

ZWEIGART®

Aida — Seed Packets, Warm Friendships, Honor the Women, Partridge in a Bear Tree, Heavenly Angels, Merry Christmice, Dear Santa

Annabelle® — Four Churches, Musical Duet

Baby Snuggle — Zoo Animals

Jubilee — Zen Garden

Linda® — Merry Christmas

Lugana® — Somebunny Special, Good Name

Meran — Spindrift

Rustico Aida® — Where There is No Vision

Valerie — Christmas Joy

SPECIAL CREDITS

Birds & Buttons — Project stitched by Janet Giese for Janelle Marie Designs

Pattern Index

Designer Index